# WOMEN AT RISK

# WOMEN AT RISK

## Domestic Violence and Women's Health

**Evan Stark, Ph.D., M.S.W.**
**Anne Flitcraft, M.D.**

SAGE Publications
*International Educational and Professional Publisher*
Thousand Oaks   London   New Delhi

*For information address*:

 SAGE Publications, Inc.
2455 Teller Road
Thousand Oaks, California 91320
E-mail: order@sagepub.com

SAGE Publications Ltd.
6 Bonhill Street
London EC2A 4PU
United Kingdom

SAGE Publications India Pvt. Ltd.
M-32 Market
Greater Kailash I
New Delhi 110 048 India

Printed in the United States of America

**Library of Congress Cataloging-in-Publication Data**

Stark, Evan.
 Women at risk: Domestic violence and women's health / authors, Evan Stark, Anne Flitcraft.
   p.  cm.
 Includes bibliographical references and index.
   ISBN 0-8039-7040-4 (acid-free paper). —  ISBN 0-8039-7041-2 (pbk.: acid-free paper).
   1. Wife abuse—United States.  2. Family violence—United States.
 3. Abused wives—Medical care—United States.  4. Abused women—Medical care—United States.  5. Patriarchy—United States.
   I. Flitcraft, Anne, 1948-  .  II. Title.
HV6626.2.T72   1996
362.82'92'0973—dc20                                     95-50153

This book is printed on acid-free paper.

 97  98  99  10  9  8  7  6  5  4  3  2

Sage Production Editor: Tricia K. Bennett

# Contents

# Acknowledgments

The articles and chapters adapted for this book reflect the support of two decades of coworkers and friends.

The idea of analyzing the medical dimensions of woman battering was conceived while we were participants in two lively group efforts, the East Coast Health Discussion Group (ECHDG), a radical collaboration to revise theories of health and medical care, and the New Haven Project for Battered Women (NHPBW), one of the early shelters for battered women in the United States. ECHDG participants Sally Guttmacher and her husband, the late Eric Holtzman, Joann Lakumnick, Meredith Turshen, Alonzo Plough Jr., and Janette Valentine became our intellectual mentors as well as lifelong friends. Vicente Navarro added a key element to friendship and intellectual guidance by opening the pages of the International Journal of Health Services to our work at a time when feminist, radical, and more conventional academic publications showed little interest in the problem. From the original NHPBW, the friendships of Sophie Turner, Patricia Dillon, and Patricia Weel have been particularly important.

The research reported in Chapter 1 was supervised by Dr. William Frazier, then a young specialist in plastic surgery and director of the emergency department at Yale. In addition to providing research staff and computer support, Frazier introduced us to Steve Record, a methodologist who grasped the challenge of identifying domestic violence in a system that routinely looked past its evidence. The larger trauma study at Yale—the basis for Chapters 3 and 4—was supported by research grants from NIMH (MH 30868) and overseen by Tom Lalley, Director of the Crime and Antisocial Behavior Division. As a consistent advocate for research on women, he helped focus our concerns, demanded the highest level of rigor, and assisted with advice at key stages in the work. Early and ongoing support for our work also came from Mark Rosenberg at the Centers for Disease Control and the Office of Domestic Violence under President Carter. Charles Lindblom and Ted Marmour provided a home for the work at the Institution for Social and Policy Studies, and Gary Tischler supported Anne with an NIMH postdoctoral fellowship. Sociologist Terence Hopkins honed the theoretical framework of our work as supervisor of Evan's Ph.D. dissertation at SUNY-Binghamton. Chapter 2 was written while Evan was on a Fulbright at the University of Essex where the intellectual companionship of Nikki Hart, Mick Mann, Karl Figlio, Paul Thompson, and Peter Townsend helped us through a difficult period.

Reconstructing the experience of battered women from the evidence in medical records was akin to an archaeological dig. Records were handwritten, filed in vast shelves beneath the hospital, and accessed only through manual requests. We owe an enormous debt to our core research staff of Anne Grey and Judy Robison (later joined by Karen Barr and Dr. Marty Roper). For 4 years, they retrieved, deciphered, and coded thousands of women's medical histories, maintaining their capacity for humor and objectivity in the face of work that was as exhausting emotionally as it was physically. All the while Corky Simoes remained unflappable, extending her numerous duties as administrative secretary to counseling (albeit without license) friends, staff, and wayfarers. The success of our team also depended on a vast army at Yale-New Haven Hospital and Yale Medical School's Department of Surgery, including staff of the medical records department, data entry clerks, social work staff, and nurses in the emergency room.

The chapters in Parts II and III reflect our efforts over the past decade to bring violence prevention and intervention into contemporary clinical practice. A Henry Rutgers Fellowship, a sabbatical, and support from Ray Caprio, Marcia Wicker, and other Public Administration colleagues have allowed Evan to maintain an agenda that includes training, clinical work, and advocacy alongside traditional scholarship. One result is the growing interest in child protection, mental health, psychiatry, and social work reflected in Chapters 3, 4, and 6. Whatever insight these chapters offer into mothers of abused children, women who attempt suicide, or battered women in the mental health setting is due, in no small part, to the mentoring (and friendship) of Laurie Harkness, Joyce and Rudy Duncan, Jack Sternbach, Jean Hay, Enid Peterson, and Susan Schechter, social workers all.

The support and enthusiasm—and flexibility—of colleagues at the University of Connecticut's Outpatient Services at the Burgdorf Health Center have enabled Anne to expand her efforts in clinical violence prevention while maintaining her inner-city practice and teaching in general internal medicine. We are profoundly grateful for the help of Marie Begley, R.N., and Drs. Aida Vega, Harry Katz-Pollack, Ellen Nestler, Bruce Gould, Ken Abriola, and Claudia McClintock.

Chapters 7, 8, and 9 have their genealogy in the work of the Domestic Violence Training Project (DVTP), which we codirect. Identified as the main provider of health training in Connecticut, the program has been running since its inception by Kate Paranteau, a lifelong advocate for women whose wisdom, tenacity, and professional skill have earned her—and DVTP—a national reputation. But it is for Kate's friendship—along with the support from fellow DVTP staff Carol Marci and Robyn Tousey-Ayers—that we are most thankful. Grants from Connecticut's Department of Health and the Commonwealth Foundation have allowed us to practice what we preach, that is, system change through professional education, training, and advocacy.

It would be disingenuous not to acknowledge that our critical stance on policy and practice—including the practice of the battered women's movement with which we strongly identify—has created special problems in legitimacy. If we stand up to be counted in this climate, it is because of the courage we have witnessed in the hundreds of battered women with whom we have worked and because of the support we received from our parents and from Heidi Hartmann, Sharon Vaughan, Elaine (Carmen) Hilberman, Eve Buzawa, Barbara Hart, Lucy Freidman, Ken Fox, Carla DeGerolomo, and so many others whose commitment to women's liberation is matched by a stubborn unwillingness to be politically correct.

Owing so much to so many, it is finally to one another and to our children, Aaron, Sam, Daniel, and Rachel, that we owe the most important debt.

EVAN STARK
ANNE FLITCRAFT

# Introduction

In 1975, en route from California to New Haven, we stopped in St. Paul to see an old friend, Sharon Vaughan. Several days of searching produced a work address at a large Victorian house in a not yet gentrified section of the city. We knocked and a woman opened, then quickly closed the door. A second knock—this time with Evan holding our young son—got us admitted.

Women were everywhere: answering phones in a small office; meeting in huddled groups behind half-closed sliding doors; preparing lunch in the kitchen; and moving, with children in tow, up and down the stairs and in and out the back door. In an alcove at the top of the first landing, two women were sitting, their heads hung on one another's shoulders, their arms loosely draped around each other, audibly sobbing.

After several minutes, Sharon descended the stairs and buoyantly announced she had just completed her first grant proposal. Then, with all the grace of Kathryn Hepburn, she waved her hand in a gallant sweep and introduced Women's Advocates, the first American shelter for battered women. "What do you think?" she asked, breaking into a broad smile.

Answering Sharon's question occupied a good portion of the next two
decades. The chapters collected in this volume are products of this work.

*    *    *    *    *

A year after the visit to St. Paul, we were living in New Haven, housing
women on the run and working with a small group to plan a 24-hour
hotline and shelter. We both had been exposed to violence in the
community during the 1960s—Anne as a VISTA volunteer in Cleveland
and Evan as a community organizer in Minneapolis. But the levels of
coercion these women described were beyond anything we had seen or
read about. The physical results of dozens, sometimes hundreds, of
assaultive episodes were appalling. The women who used our home as
a safe house were as likely to be middle class as poor, as likely to be
white as black or Hispanic. Regardless of race or background, the
women had all gone to tremendous lengths simply to survive. There was
one more thing. They recounted long and complicated histories of
frustrated help seeking. The medical, criminal justice, and social service
professionals, it seemed, had either ignored their plight or done things
that actually made it worse.

During the summer of 1976, a grant to visit shelters in Europe brought
us to the Chiswick section of London. We walked past a stone wall with
the words "A HOUSE FOR WOMEN" scrawled in large letters and
knocked at the door of Chiswick Women's Aid, the best known battered
women's refuge in the world. Erin Pizzey answered. Without hesitation,
the founder of Women's Aid waved us into an extraordinary scene of
noise and chaos. There were 90 women and children staying in the
six-bedroom house. "If they can manage this," Pizzey quipped, "they
can handle anything."

That night, led by a Jamaican lawyer who had just escaped from her
abuser, a group of us took rolls of wallpaper and a portable toilet,
crossed town in an old bus that belonged to the shelter, and "seized" an
abandoned railroad hotel. Twenty-four hours later, the hotel was ready
to host its first battered women.

## The Research Base

These images of women doing for themselves framed our thinking
when, in 1977, Anne asked Dr. William Frazier, director of the emer-

gency room at Yale-New Haven Hospital, if she could do her medical school thesis on battered women who used the surgical emergency service.

"What's a battered woman?" Dr. Frazier asked.

Dr. Frazier was only the first of several skeptics who listened to us patiently and then gave us unselfish support. At the time, there was no evidence that domestic violence was a common health problem. What we had to offer, besides the partnership between a physician and a sociologist, was experience with shelters and hotlines that demonstrated that male violence against partners was epidemic. It seemed inconceivable that this epidemic could have bypassed the medical gaze.

So began our 20-year collaboration to identify the medical dimensions and health consequences of domestic violence.

In taking up this work, we faced two methodological challenges. When we began the research, there were few services or protections for battered women. It was commonly believed that asking patients directly about violence might expose them to further danger, and therefore, interview studies were ethically suspect. The next best source of information were women's medical histories. But using these records posed the problem Kempe, Silverman, Steele, Droegemueller, and Silver (1962) had faced in attempting to document child abuse in the early 1960s. The phenomena we wanted to study were officially invisible. Like Kempe et al., we needed an *index of suspicion* to uncover cases of domestic violence that had not been designated as such. We addressed this problem by postulating that, like child abuse cases, the injury patterns and context of battering could be used to distinguish domestic violence from accidental injury.

Starting with a sample of 520 records of women's visits to the surgical emergency service (the basis for Chapter 1), our research eventually encompassed the clinical histories of 4,500 women who used the hospital in the late 1970s and early 1980s, including more than 1,000 battered women, emergency room patients, mothers of abused children, women who attempted suicide, rape victims, psychiatric emergency patients, and women using the hospital's obstetrical service. Our initial goal was simply to document the extent of domestic violence and its significance for women's health. Only gradually, as we analyzed the notes, diagnoses, treatment strategies, and referrals compiled over the years by hundreds of physicians, nurses, social workers, and psychiatrists, did a third goal emerge: to evaluate the appropriateness of the clinical response and suggest ways to improve it.

Originally published between 1978 and 1995, the papers collected here report the major findings of these studies.

The chapters in Part I review the empirical findings from the early research, show how domestic violence and the medical response converge in the evolution of a battering syndrome, and link this process to larger social and historical currents. The theoretical framework developed in these chapters draws on feminism and Marxism as well as on more conventional sociological and psychiatric paradigms. We situate woman battering in the struggles that surround sexual inequality, emphasizing the social (rather than the psychological or interpersonal) dimensions of male domination and female subordination. Women are battered in this schema not because individual men use violence or other inappropriate means to stifle their subjectivity but because male resistance to women's personal and political liberation is reinforced by the very systems to which women turn for help, including organized medicine. This part also emphasizes how the key dimensions of battering—from its prevalence and dynamics in a given population to the paradigms used to explain domestic violence in different societies—take shape amidst class, race, and sexual struggles for the most fundamental material, social, and psychic resources.

Part II views the overall significance of domestic violence for women's health through the prism of child abuse, female suicidality, and homicide, three of its most extreme outcomes. The chapter on mental health that introduces the part on clinical interventions (Part III) reframes prevailing models of treatment in terms of recent knowledge regarding the coercive elements in battering. Part III also traces the implications of the theory and data for improved practice in medicine, social work, and community health.

*     *     *     *     *

For 5 years, our small research staff diligently abstracted millions of bits of information on women and their health problems from records that ranged in size from a few pages to several volumes. In addition to the usual information on complaints, examination results, diagnoses, prescriptions, and referrals, the charts often included extensive commentary as clinicians struggled to explain why a population of previously normal women developed a complex psychosocial and medical history subsequent to a series of "accidents."

The initial conclusion of our research was that more women sought medical treatment for injuries resulting from domestic violence than for any other cause. This finding was used to support political initiatives on behalf of battered women, including the controversial Violence Against Women portion of President Bill Clinton's 1994 Crime Bill. Conservative writers and syndicated journalists critiqued our "gender feminist" orientation and dubbed our conclusions "guesstimates" and "noble lies" (Sommers, 1994, p. 202). Meanwhile, in the wake of expanded services and the commitment of medical resources, direct interview and questionnaire studies continued to document substantially the same or higher figures than we uncovered. For example, a recent survey of 648 randomly sampled women who sought treatment at four emergency departments in Denver found that more than half (54.2%) had been threatened or physically injured by a husband or boyfriend at some time in their lives (Abbott, Johnson, Koziol-McLain, & Lowenstein, 1995). This is about 250% higher than our estimate that one female injury victim in five had a history of domestic violence.

Our empirical claims about the importance of domestic violence as a source of female injury are supported by data presented in Chapter 1 as well as in Chapters 3, 4, and 5. Although it has momentous implications for women's health as well as for the allocation of resources, the conclusion should not surprise persons familiar with domestic violence or its effects on systems other than medicine. When we began our work, Parnas (1967) had already reported that police received more calls regarding "domestics" than murder, aggravated assault, battering, and all other serious crimes combined. The key factor here—often missed by our critics—is the historical nature of battering relationships, the extent to which the perpetrator's continued access to his victim creates a cumulative burden of injury on the community that is unique in our society. Some sense of this burden can be garnered from a recent London survey (Mooney, 1993) that reveals that victims of domestic violence had suffered an average of 7.1 assaults during the previous 12 months, resulting in an average of 4.3 injuries and an annual assault incidence rate of 85 per 100. Although further historical and cross-sectional data may negate these findings, it is hard to imagine a source of female injury, accidental or otherwise, that is more common. To appreciate our more limited claim about medically relevant injury, readers need only compare the fact that, whereas nonbattered adults may make one injury visit to an emergency service in their lifetime, battered women average more than one such visit each year.

A second important finding of our work involved the links of domestic violence to a range of family and women's health problems, including child abuse, homicide, alcohol and drug abuse, rape, poor pregnancy outcomes, and female suicide attempts. Battered women (or their children) suffer a disproportionate risk of these problems only after the onset of domestic violence. The composite picture that emerges is of a *battering syndrome* that, if not curtailed through early intervention, evolves through predictable stages into a pattern of entrapment that is as devastating as the trauma of physical assault.

Equally important, as the chapters in Part II document, domestic violence is a major cause of these problems, accounting for half of all child abuse, for instance, a third of female suicide attempts (and half of those by black women), 40% of primary homicides, and equally significant proportions of rape, female alcoholism, drug use, and depressive illness. In the world of social and medical science, evidence that problems are statistically correlated often has little practical importance or else is neglected because it implies that sacred academic or professional boundaries should be bridged. We have known for a decade that deliberate childhood injury and fatality commonly result when a batterer extends his violence to the child. But the child protection establishment has only recently opened a dialogue with the battered women's community. Even fewer inroads have been made into psychiatry or substance abuse treatment.

A third major conclusion of this work is that the medical response to abuse directly contributes to the isolation and entrapment that are hallmarks of the battering syndrome. Although the chapters in Part I provide an elaborate theoretical explanation for this seeming paradox at the micro- and macrolevels, each part of the volume considers how current ways of understanding and treating domestic violence contribute to its perpetuation. So significant are the effects of medical neglect, minimization, labeling, and victim blaming that, in Chapter 6, we conceptualize battering as a dual trauma constituted from parallel strains of male coercion and clinical mistreatment.

Recent support for communitywide violence prevention by federal health and justice agencies and professional medical associations are important steps in remedying the dual trauma of interpersonal violence. Coupled with these efforts, the massive use of health services by battered women offers clinicians a window of opportunity for early intervention and prevention. The chapters in Parts II and III provide the information needed to take advantage of this opportunity by routinely identifying, assessing, and referring domestic violence victims at all health care sites, psychiatric and medical, primary as well as emergent.

*        *        *        *        *

Major changes in the status of domestic violence have occurred since we began our work. An enormous body of specialized literature on the problem has appeared and the response to battered women has burgeoned into an international network of services that extends from Boston to Cape Town and includes an extensive state-run regulatory apparatus in addition to thousands of community-based programs. Virtually invisible to medicine two decades ago, today domestic violence is recognized as a major problem by virtually every medical, nursing, and public health organization in the United States.

The chapters in this volume have been substantially revised and updated to reflect these developments, including our own growing commitment to professional education and to make the theoretical argument and presentation of data more accessible to the large number of students and general readers interested in the problem. It would have taken a completely different book, however, to integrate fully the vast specialized literature or to revise our theoretical conceptions to account for all the current political changes, including the new commitment by medicine. Indeed, by conserving many of the original references in the early essays, we hope to acknowledge important early work and emphasize its relevance to current concerns.

We are cautiously optimistic about recent developments in the domestic violence field. At the same time, the critical tone of the early essays resonates with our deep concern that the most vital political elements in the movement by and for battered women will be compromised if state protection and the provision of service to victims are overemphasized.

The clinical issues domestic violence presents are similar to those presented by a range of other social ills. Nevertheless, the scope and political context of domestic violence require a broad reframing of women's health, as well as the changes in medical response outlined in Parts II and III.

In our view, male violence against partners in contemporary society is a defensive response to women's progressive liberation from maternity and domestic servitude, a liberation that is as inevitable in an expanding capitalist economy as it is inconceivable apart from women's self-activity across a broad terrain. That women will be "free" yet must always free themselves is no less true in individual relationships than in society as a whole, and this paradox is the immediate source of the suffering that concerns us here.

We have chosen health as the focus of inquiry because that is where we work, because it is in the medical system that the most physical and behavioral consequences of assault are seen most vividly, and because we believe that viewing domestic violence through the prism of women's health throws new light on medical practice, not only on domestic violence. If we criticize medical practice (and say little about the negative effects of legal, criminal justice, or social work intervention), this is because, more than the other services, medicine's identification with science and healing symbolizes its central role as an interpreter of the human condition.

The most dramatic evidence in these chapters concerns the physical injury and death women and children suffer as the direct result of male violence. This reflects our initial belief that horrendous criminal acts of violence lay at the heart of woman battering. It was this belief that led us to emphasize shelter for women, that brought us to the emergency room as the site of research, and that is reflected in our early emphasis on injury. What we have learned since—in no small part from the hundreds of battered women with whom we have worked—is that our initial belief was wrong. In fact, the clinical dimensions of battering— from repeated injury to addiction, suicidality, child abuse, severe mental illness, and homicide—are best understood less as the product of male violence than as the cumulative result of women's entrapment by an extreme (though common) form of male domination. Violence is a necessary condition in trapping women in battering relationships. But it is rarely sufficient to explain the level of harm, degradation, or pathology that follows domestic violence. The medical, psychiatric, and behavioral problems presented by battered women arise because male strategies of coercion, isolation, and control converge with discriminatory structures and institutional practices to make it extremely difficult, sometimes impossible, for women to escape from abusive relationships when they most want or need to.

The distinction between violence and coercion may seem too subtle to have practical implications. On the contrary, however, shifting the emphasis from violent acts to the ways in which male control converges with larger processes of discrimination has enormous importance in identifying who is being victimized, which strategies we define as criminal, where and how we intervene, and how we balance advocacy for women's liberation with the important emphasis on personal safety through police protection and shelter. It is impossible to study the health of battered women without discerning their desire to share in power, not simply to be protected from its excesses. Nor is this a concern only for health providers. Keeping our "mind on freedom," as the old civil rights song put it, remains the greatest challenge as the battered women's movement seeks to protect women from individual injury by forging working alliances with the very political, legal, economic, and service systems once believed to be the primary source of women's social injury.

# Part I

## Theoretical Perspectives

# 1

# Medicine and Patriarchal Violence

By conservative estimate, 3 to 4 million women are assaulted by male partners each year in the United States and at least four times this number, between 12 and 15 million women, have been assaulted by their male partners in the past (Flynn, 1977; Straus, 1977-1978). In approximately 10% of these cases, the assault is speedily followed by effective protection or permanent estrangement from the aggressor. But there is mounting evidence that the vast majority of these beatings are part of an identifiable pattern of ongoing, systematic, and escalating abuse that often extends over a lifetime (Dobash & Dobash, 1977-1978; Flitcraft, 1977; Gelles, 1974; Pizzey, 1974). We refer to this pattern as *woman battering.*

In the late 1960s, Parnas (1967) reported that the police received more calls concerning "domestics" than concerning murder, aggravated assault and battering, and all other serious crimes combined. The repeat nature of these calls was illustrated by reports from Kansas City that 80% of the domestic homicides there were preceded by one or more complaints of assault to the police and 50% were preceded by five or

AUTHORS' NOTE: This chapter is adapted from Stark, Flitcraft, and Frazier (1979). Reprinted with permission of the *International Journal of Health Services.*

3

more calls (cited in Lachman, 1978). Despite little documentation, victims of domestic violence describe attempting to access other service systems as well. Why then are millions of women trapped in abusive relationships?

A common answer is that little can be done to prevent abuse because it is a "private" event caused by a combination of psychopathology, behavior learned in childhood, a culture that endorses violence as a means for resolving conflicts, and stresses peculiar to family life (Hanks & Rosenbaum, 1977; Renvoize, 1978; Rounsaville, 1977; Snell, Rosenwald, & Robey, 1964; Walker, 1979; Whitehurst, 1971). If women and children are the most obvious victims, the argument goes, this is because they are physically vulnerable and dependent. According to a current psychological theory, the duration of female abuse is explained by *learned helplessness,* a depressive syndrome evoked by severe and repeated assault and characterized by a reluctance to seek help (Walker, 1979). The paucity of institutional data supports the belief that victims fail to report domestic violence.

Personal problems can obviously motivate any assault. What distinguishes partner violence against women is that immediate stimuli converge in a singular consequence—female subordination. Regardless of whether a man beats his wife when he is drunk, stalks his girlfriend out of jealousy, or sets fire to his partner's house when he is depressed, the selection of women as objects of coercion and control gives these events a single social meaning. Mediated through structures of inequality and read back into the proximate causes and diverse means employed in domestic violence, this meaning shapes the event into patterned behavior and gives it dimension, prevalence, and a history. The seeming paradox—that behavior violating basic canons of law, liberty, and decency remains widespread despite the presentation of its consequences to the systems charged with health and protection—marks the event as purposeful social behavior that can be explained (or resolved) only in the social realm (Schechter, 1978).

This chapter looks at battering through the prism of women's encounters with the medical system, an important and unexamined realm of their help seeking. Three issues guide our inquiry. The first involves an empirical challenge to estimate the prevalence of domestic violence in the medical complex and distinguish its clinical sequelae. The second is to explain the emergence of the identified clinical profile, what we call the *battering syndrome.* A correlative task entails analyzing the contribution of the medical response (and, by extension, the other "helping" services) to this syndrome. The third issue is to explain why a population of otherwise normal women develop the profile of battering after they are assaulted. This entails showing how the implicit support medical intervention gives violent men plays into the overall constitution of patriarchal authority. At each step, we try to decipher the political in the personal, that is, to show how women's struggle to affirm and men's struggle to deny their liberty become embedded, through battering, in their personal problems.

Part I reviews the complete medical histories of women who sought assistance with injury from an urban emergency service. Using an index of suspicion, we determined how many women are at risk for abuse in the emergency population and compared this to the number actually recognized as such. The remarkable number of injuries attributable to domestic violence and the distinctive pattern of medical and psychosocial problems that accompany the adult trauma history reflect the diminishing realm of options available to women as they become entrapped in battering relationships. Our research tool tells us little about why physicians misread so many cases or why, despite this misreading, they respond in ways that actually aggravate the predicament of the (largely unidentified) population of battered women.

Cicourel (1964) argues that to understand official data fully, one must gauge its meaning to its recorders and to the system that generates it. Part II reviews women's medical charts archaeologically, as social products that can tell us about how medical culture depicts the universe. This examination reveals how the medical system's need to manage a persistent patient population fosters an implicit alliance with violent men. Ironically, the medical system thrives as numerous acts of failed treatment reproduce, and even strengthen, the invidious sexual contradictions that ensure a constant flow of female problems. Regardless of why a given clinician grasps for pseudopsychiatric labels when he or she confronts a clinical profile that defies classification within the individualist model of pathophysiology, this response increases the vulnerability of patients whose minority status makes them already vulnerable (Blum, 1978; Kelman, 1975). Critics have attributed medical insensitivity to women to the "commodification of health care" or, alternately, to dominance by an elite of male doctors (Berliner, 1975; Ehrenreich & English, 1979; Health Policy Advisory Center, 1970; Waitzkin & Waterman, 1974). In contrast, our focus is on how medicine as medicine— as a process of presumably scientific diagnosis, referral, and treatment—codetermines traditional sex hierarchies and contributes, even when individual health providers intend otherwise, to the suppression of struggles to overcome these hierarchies.

Part III critically reviews current theoretical perspectives on battering and proposes an alternative conceptualization. The review uncovers a host of contradictory findings and theories, both within disciplines and depending on whether analyses target psychological, interpersonal, cultural, or economic dimensions of the problem. Despite their differences, most researchers share the premises that domestic violence reveals male power, that violent families constitute a deviant subtype, and that battered women generally fail to act on their own behalf. In contrast, we argue that woman battering reflects the erosion of male authority, that domestic violence stands on a continuum with normative forms of male domination, and that woman battering grows out of women's struggles to overcome their contradictory status, not from their compliance with or dependence on men. For instance, we interpret the oft-rejected survey reports that women use physical violence in conflict situations as often as men (Straus, 1977-1978) to argue that battered women are aggressive rather than helpless, passive, masochistic, or otherwise "sick." The seeming paradox remains: Only women who are assaulted by partners suffer the battering syndrome. This, we believe, is because partner violence by men (but not by women) is socially reinforced at every level of women's experience.

In the concluding sections, we analyze the contribution of the helping services to woman battering in terms of their historical role in mediating larger conflicts between a capitalist economy (which seeks to level all invidious distinctions) and the patriarchy (which seeks to maintain sexual hierarchy). Again in contrast to current thinking, we argue that the emergence of woman battering as a major expression of male control signals the nadir rather than zenith of male power. The erosion of male authority in the home is reflected empirically in the declining importance of the father-husband in working- and middle-class families, the relative decline in male-run family businesses, the socialization of domestic work in public and private services, and the increasing share of total income commanded by women. It is this decline, we believe, that explains why male power in the home must now be sustained by chronic—and increasingly explicit—outside intervention along a broad social front. The very transparency of such support and the desperate nature of violence and coercion in millions of relationships suggest that the larger contradictions excited by changes in the sexual status quo cannot be suppressed for long.

Women's economic contribution has always been a key focus of male control. Even so, and regardless of how unfairly this work is distributed, the family's major responsibilities, the early socialization of children and the formation of personality, are labors of love and never reducible to economic principles. Indeed, several historians have argued that the distortion of role assignments in the 19th century stimulated an autonomous "women's sphere," an extended community of intimates in marked contrast to the emerging capitalist world, where social connectedness among men appeared mainly in fetishistic forms (Cott, 1977; Sklar, 1976; Smith-Rosenberg, 1975). In demanding that women's domestic work be socialized in a range of public services to which women flocked for employment, this community tore the veil from the imagery that linked women's biological and cultural identities and made it possible to reconceptualize the family as a space free of exploitation, part of an extended community of love between equal subjects, the ideal to which many abused women cling. It is against this unfolding possibility that the use of violence and coercion to defend traditional hierarchies must be understood.

The disappearance of the family's traditional economic and social roles—the decline of the patriarchy as a specific familial form—contrasts markedly with the subjective and objective extension of male domination throughout every aspect of life in the United States. Thus, although the classic patriarchy is dead, we argue that the social services, broadly construed to include education, religion, and recreation as well as medicine, law, criminal justice, and welfare, function today as a reconstituted or extended patriarchy, reinforcing female subordination by any means necessary, including violence.

Neither privacy nor personal life nor social connectedness remain in the millions of homes in which women are repeatedly beaten. For this reason, the violent family provides a point of departure, what might be termed a *boundary case,* to see how the male-dominated family is reproduced in the final instance, when one adult member tries to escape.

## The Study: Abuse in a Medical Setting

Emergency medical services in the United States are oriented toward high-technology interventions in extreme trauma and illness. To the poor, minorities, and large segments of the white working class, however, emergency medical services are the only available source of basic medical care (Skinner & German, 1978). This conflict in how scarce health resources should be used is reflected in the tendency for emergency physicians to view minor, chronic, or social ills as inappropriate causes for them to intervene and to fragment complex social ailments diagnostically into isolated and relatively treatable symptoms. This pattern is disclosed in Kempe et al.'s (1962) work on child abuse. Rather than acknowledge familial assault as the etiology of children's medical problems, physicians perform extensive medical workups in search of obscure blood and metabolic disorders that explain an accumulating history of multiple bruises and fractures.

Abused women who hesitate to call police or social workers for help will use medical services when they are injured (Schulman, 1979). Our study was designed to provide a preliminary estimate of the prevalence and dimensions of domestic violence in a medical population among whom the problem was considered trivial or nonexistent. An additional goal was to evaluate medicine's response to these women. Because domestic violence was not a diagnostic category when the research began and because of dramatic findings resulting from Kempe et al.'s (1962) skeptical reading of medical data on children's injuries, we developed an index of suspicion to identify abuse retrospectively from women's adult trauma histories. Designated instances of domestic violence were obviously counted. In addition, we hypothesized that assaults or injuries with no known cause might result from abuse (probables). So might incidents where the recorded etiology contrasted markedly with the injury pattern described (e.g., bilateral facial contusions from "walking into a door"), that is, suggestives.[1] The use of the index to identify at-risk women based on probable and suggestive injuries as well as positive episodes was validated by identifying similarly suspicious injury episodes among positive women, by finding that the frequency and pattern of injury among positives, probables, and suggestives was markedly different than the pattern among those classified as nonbattered (negatives), and by differentiating the clinical profile of battered from nonbattered women.

## METHODS

The study population consisted of 520 women who sought aid for injuries at a major urban emergency room during 1 month. The full medical records were successfully retrieved for 481 of these women (92.5%), and previous emergency visits, hospitalizations, clinic records,

**TABLE 1.1** Description of Battering Risk Groups (BRG)

| BRG | Percentage of Women, by Sample Visit (N = 481) | Percentage of Women, by Trauma History (N = 481) | Percentage of Injuries per BRG (N = 1,419) | Injuries per Woman | Injuries per Year per Woman |
|---|---|---|---|---|---|
| Positive | 2.8 | 9.6 | 22.5 | 6.35 | .973 |
| Probable | 5.2 | 4.8 | 10.7 | 6.26 | 1.127 |
| Suggestive | 9.8 | 10.6 | 13.6 | 3.08 | .822 |
| Negative | 82.2 | 75.0 | 53.2 | 1.83 | .346 |

and social and psychiatric service notes were analyzed. Each episode of injury was examined—some 1,419 trauma events ranging in frequency from 1 to more than 20 per patient—and the women were subsequently classified according to the following criteria:

- Positive: At least one injury was recorded as inflicted by a husband, boyfriend, or other male intimate.
- Probable: At least one injury resulted from a "punch," "hit," "kick," "shot," or similar action and deliberate assault by another person, but the relationship of assailant to victim was not recorded.
- Suggestive: At least one injury was inadequately explained by the recorded medical history.
- Reasonable negative: Each injury in the medical record was adequately explained by the recorded etiology, including those recorded as sustained in "muggings" or "anonymous assaults."

## SUMMARY OF FINDINGS

### Prevalence and Frequency

During the sample month, physicians identified 14 battered women (2.8%), although an additional 72 women (15%) had injuries we classified as probable or suggestive. Based on full trauma histories, however, 9.6% of the 481 women were positively identified as having been assaulted by a partner at least once and an additional 15.4% had trauma histories strongly indicative of abuse (Table 1.1, columns 1 and 2). Thus, based on trauma histories, one woman in four in this emergency population could be identified as battered, roughly nine times the number identified based on current visit reports.

The geographic location of the emergency service in a low-income and largely minority community skews outpatient use, making any generalizations about race, income, and domestic violence suspect (Zonana & Henisz, 1973). It is noteworthy, however, that white and minority women and welfare and medically insured women were significantly represented in the battered subset of this sample.

Of the more than 1,400 injuries these women had ever brought to this hospital, 75 (5%) were positively identified as abusive incidents based on physician records of a partner assault. An additional 340 (24%) fell into the probable or suggestive categories of this methodology. Thus, 30% of injuries presented by this cohort appeared to be directly associated with abuse. Importantly, almost half of the probable and a quarter of the suggestive incidents occurred to women who also evidenced positive abusive episodes, strongly supporting the methodology and indicating that only a tendency to disaggregate social ailments into discrete episodes prevented the appearance of battering as an ongoing process of repeated assault. Of all injuries ever presented by the 481 women to the hospital, almost half (46.8%) were presented by victims of domestic violence (Table 1.1, column 3).

The finding that women in the positive battering risk group had three times as many injury visits as nonbattered women (6.35 injury visits as compared with 1.83 injury visits) supports the hypothesis that injury is an ongoing fact of life for abused women. Women in the probable risk group had almost identical trauma histories as women in the positive risk group, again validating the identification method. Women in the suggestive risk group were injured at the same rate as positives and probables (.82 compared with 1.127 and .97 incidents per year) but had accumulated only half as many injury episodes (Table 1.1, columns 4 and 5), suggesting their abuse was of more recent onset.

Whereas physicians saw 1 of 35 of their patients as battered, a more accurate approximation is 1 in 4; whereas they traced 1 presenting injury in 20 to partner assault, the actual figure approached 1 in 3 (30%). Injury is an extreme consequence of assault and is reported infrequently. Thus, its institutional prevalence comprises only a small proportion of the true prevalence of domestic violence in the patient population. What clinicians officially portrayed as a rare occurrence was, in all likelihood, the single major cause of women's injuries.

## Duration

The duration of women's abuse was determined by comparing the women who had ever been abused (25% of the sample) with those presenting at-risk injuries during the study month (18%). This showed that 72% of the abused women must still be considered at risk. A higher estimate is probably more accurate. Comparing the overall prevalence (25%) with the incidence of at-risk episodes during the past 5 years (23%) suggests that domestic violence ended in just 8% of the cases. As many as 92% of the women who have ever been in an abusive relationship in this population are still at risk, though it is impossible to tell whether the perpetrator is the same.

## Sex-Specific Character of Abuse

The deliberate, sexual, and familial dimensions of abuse are reflected in the predominance of central injuries to the body, the chest, the breast, and the abdomen and by the high rate of violence during pregnancy. Battered women were three times more likely than nonbattered women to be pregnant when injured. Consequently, these women evidenced a significantly greater number of miscarriages. Once the child was born, the battered mothers were 10 times more likely than nonbattered women to report child abuse or to fear it. Importantly, 50% of all rapes among the population studied involved women at risk for battering. In a follow-up study, Roper, Flitcraft, and Frazier (1979) found that of the 174 rape victims who came to the emergency room during the previous 2 years, almost a third had documented histories of battering. In fact, of rape victims over 30, 58% were battered women.

## Self-Destructive Behavior and Associated Problems

Anecdotal reports and convenience samples suggest that domestic violence victims experience a range of psychiatric and psychosocial problems in addition to physical injury (Gayford, 1975a, 1975b; Hilberman & Munson, 1977-1978; Nichols, 1976; Walker, 1979). An outstanding question is whether these problems precede domestic violence or emerge as a result of the stress and entrapment associated with battering.

The psychosocial profiles of battered and nonbattered women were compared prior to the first reported episode of at-risk injury. With the exception of alcohol abuse, battered women were no more likely than nonbattered women to present with psychosocial problems, drug abuse, or psychiatric disorders; to attempt suicide; to use mental health services; or to acquire psychosocial labels (Table 1.2).

**TABLE 1.2**  Problem Incidence and Referrals of Nonbattered Women and Battered Women Prior to First Recorded Assault (per 100 women)

| Problem/Referral | Nonbattered Women | Battered Women Before Assault |
|---|---|---|
| Suicide attempt | 3 | 6 |
| Drug abuse | 1 | 2 |
| Alcohol abuse | 1 | 7[a] |
| Psychiatric emergency service | 7 | 9 |
| Community mental health center | 3.6 | 4 |
| State mental hospital | 1 | 2 |
| Psychosocial labels | 2 | 4 |

a. $\chi^2$ significant at < .001.

**TABLE 1.3**  Overall Problem Incidence and Referrals of Nonbattered and Battered Women (per 100 women)

| Problem/Referral | Nonbattered Women | Battered Women |
|---|---|---|
| Suicide attempt | 3 | 26[a] |
| Drug abuse | 1 | 7[a] |
| Alcohol abuse | 1 | 16[a] |
| Psychiatric emergency service | 7 | 37[a] |
| Community mental health center | 3.6 | 26[a] |
| State mental hospital | 1 | 15[a] |
| Psychosocial labels | 2 | 22[a] |

a. $\chi^2$ significant at < .001.

If the risk of various problems is initially similar, following a reported episode of domestic violence, battered women reveal a complex profile of psychosocial problems. If rates of various problems among nonbattered women are taken as the norm, battered women had a relative risk of attempting suicide that was 8 times as great as normal, a risk of drug abuse that was 6 times greater, a rate of alcohol abuse that was 15 times as great, and a rate of hospitalization in the state mental health facility that was 14 times as great. The absolute numbers summarized in Table 1.3 are equally significant: 1 in every 4 battered women attempted suicide at least once; 1 in 7 of the battered women abused alcohol; 1 in 10 abused drugs; and more than 1 in 3 were referred to emergency psychiatric services and the community mental health center, whereas

1 in 7 was eventually institutionalized at the state mental hospital. In sum, the battered women were an otherwise normal population who developed a complex profile of psychosocial problems subsequent to the presentation of an initial episode of domestic violence at the hospital.

## Patterns of Medical Response

Medical responses to battering take two forms in the emergency room. On the one hand, nearly 1 in 4 (24%) of the battered women received minor tranquilizers or pain medications, whereas fewer than 1 in 10 (9%) nonbattered women received such prescriptions. This response is not simply a poor therapeutic choice given evidence that domestic violence is ongoing. It is also dangerous given the record of attempted suicides by victims of battering. On the other hand, medicine disposes of battering by characterizing it as a psychiatric problem for the victim. Psychiatric referrals followed nonbattering injuries only 4% of the time, whereas the largely unidentified victims of battering were referred 15% of the time to emergency psychiatric facilities, clinics, local community mental health centers, or the state mental hospital.

The medical records of battered women were replete with pseudo-psychiatric labels, such as "patient with multiple vague medical complaints" or "multiple symptomatology with psychosomatic overlay." This highlights the tension between patient demand for help and medicine's frustration in the absence of overt physiological disorder. The use of such phrases to characterize patients makes it extremely difficult for them to get sympathetic, quality treatment.

From the standpoint of the emergency service, battering appears as a widespread and ongoing pattern that includes, in addition to repeated assaults, a host of derivative psychosocial problems as well as repeated acts of physical injury and self-destructive behavior. Although the pattern is seemingly invisible to medicine, the clinical response to abused women differs markedly from the response to other injury patients. Moreover, the clinical syndrome emerges only after the first abuse-related injury is presented to the hospital, although it is unlikely that this visit marks the actual onset of abuse. At best, medical interventions are ineffective; at worst, they contribute to the victim's diminishing options. It is imperative, therefore, to consider how the clinical syndrome of battering and the medical encounter are linked.

## Medicine Constructs the Battering Syndrome

Jacoby (1975) argues that the search for a palatable model of therapeutic cure after World War I led the neo-Freudians to forget the radical
insights of their master, particularly his volatile notion of sexuality. In
the late 19th century, a similar social amnesia prompted medical care to
replace ideas positing social reform as the source of population health
with a politically safe, individually oriented, physiology-based therapeutics that imagined the healthy body as an efficient machine perform-
ing its assigned tasks in functional isolation from a determinant social
universe (Turshen, 1977). The germ theory advanced by Koch and
Pasteur won out over the radical and environmental theories of Chadwick, Engels, Virchow, Snow, and others as part of a general conservative reaction to working-class and socialist movements (Ackerknecht,
1953; Berliner, 1975; Stark, 1977). In fact, medicine's conquest of
infectious and communicable diseases at an individual level occurred
long after the dramatic decline in tuberculosis and other serious conditions in society as a whole due to improvements in diet and general living
standards, improvements that resulted from massive social struggles
(McKeown, 1977; Stark, 1977). Despite this obvious interdependence
between improved health and improved social conditions, the singular
mandate of "allopathic medicine" rested on its unidimensional claim
that all disease had biological origins and should be treated through
manipulation in individual pathophysiology. References to poverty or
the environment notwithstanding, modern therapeutics remain deaf to
the complex social etiology of most health conditions.

The aim of medical diagnosis is to aggregate immediate symptoms
with the history of the symptoms and relevant physiological data (lab
tests, X rays, and physical findings) into preexisting scientific disease
categories. These, in turn, suggest a particular therapeutic response in
accord with recognized precepts of medical practice. The response
typically completes a single process, particularly in the emergency
service where any follow-up care is rare, and legitimates the symptom
or disease entity as the appropriate object and the individual as the
appropriate limit of "the medical gaze" (Foucault, 1973).

Within the medical paradigm, the aggregation of symptoms at any
given presentation constitutes a medical event and the aggregation of
isolated events makes up the medical history. In this framework, the
symptoms are not read to illuminate a person's history, but the reverse.
The social dimensions of the patient's experience, her history as she has

lived it in the presence of the medical system, disappear behind a developing catalogue of prior symptoms and medical events that are continually reorganized in the doctor's mind, ostensibly to illuminate a discrete pathophysiological moment. The fact that the physician-patient contact is fraught with political meaning remains concealed in the ideological content of seemingly objective conclusions and referrals.

Only when the normal processes of observation and interpretation break down does medical diagnosis move from specific symptoms or disease entities toward its outer boundary, a focus on the individual. The persistence of particular patients, the failure of well-tested therapies to control a given set of symptoms, the epidemic prevalence of particular symptoms in a given population, or the incongruity of symptoms and available physiological explanations all create a "crisis of the cure" that forces medicine to the limits of its perception. But even here the medical object is conceived abstractly, more closely resembling the fictional individualist of 19th-century liberalism than a socially mediated being whose options are constrained by pressing realities (Crawford, 1977; Turshen, 1977). Instead of critically reappraising the biological origins of the patient's condition, the physician holds the victim of domestic violence accountable for unresponsiveness to therapy.

Ironically, conventional medicine has gained legitimacy as the major causes of mortality and morbidity have shifted to problems whose etiology is either largely social (as with violence, addiction, or infant mortality) or a mix of social and biological factors (as with heart disease, cancer, or hypertension). By attributing medicine's relative ineffectiveness against these ailments to limited knowledge or technique rather than the inherent limits of its approach, medical "failures" actually prompt massive investments in research and technology as well, of course, as a continual flow of patients.

Thus, the dilemmas medicine confronts in domestic violence—and its response—are similar in many respects to those posed by a range of other health problems whose etiology is social. Victims of domestic violence are persistent in their help seeking and appear in large numbers at the emergency service. Yet no apparent physiological (or individual) event links one injury to another or one presentation to the next. At first, single episodes of injury are seen as legitimate medical problems. But as it becomes clear that neither the women presenting with these injuries nor the injuries, on an aggregate, are responding to treatment, these women's problems are reinterpreted as symptoms of particular social or psychopathologies, for example, alcoholism or depression. Because it is now the women who are seen as owning the problems, they (e.g., rather than their assailants) become the object of medical management.

Whatever their clinical origin, psychosocial diagnoses of battered women are commonly used to suppress rather than address the problems they pose to the medical system and paradigm. Diagnoses such as well-known alcoholic, drug abuser, hysteric, hypochondriac, or depressive are typically applied to battered women without any stated therapeutic intent, indeed often without eliciting any treatment or referral of any kind (Mollica & Redlich, 1978). In shifting the focus from the woman's condition to the woman herself, these labels explain her continued suffering in a way that leaves the medical paradigm intact. The process is by no means benign. Even as they salve medicine's wounds, labels isolate women from further care and so help to transform them into apparently helpless objects available to be subordinated by particular men.

Medical support for battering cannot be ascribed to the malfeasance of sexist physicians. The fact that clinicians as a group respond in a distinctive (and punitive) way to battered women (as an aggregate), even though they fail to recognize the problem as individuals, signals the presence of systemic processes operating behind their backs to constrain medical practice as a whole and legitimate this peculiar brand of interpreting events. Because the results include women's entrapment in abusive relationships, the process effectively aligns the structure, pro-cedures, and ideology of medical practice with parallel systems of authority, including the system of male domination. Through this align-ment process, the relatively fragile power of the perpetrator and the even less coherent authority employed by clinicians are fused into a single tyranny whose evolution one can observe in the medical histories of battered women.

The following discussion describes woman battering as a staged process of progressive entrapment. Although the entrapment process appears to reflect changes in the level of violence or coercion at home, these are shaped by predictable shifts in the medical response. At each point in this process, the interpretations and interventions behind which physicians seek refuge put the safety of their patients in jeopardy.

STAGE 1: THE INJURY APPEARS

When the battered woman first appears at the emergency service, her discrete injury is defined as the only object for medical care. That the injury was caused by a punch is no more significant than that it resulted from a fall and, if the cause is recorded, there is no comment. The woman's history is considered only to resolve an apparent diagnostic dilemma. For instance, a physician confused by the coexistence of abdominal pain and a broken arm may ask, "Did he also hit you in the abdomen?" But if the physical evidence leaves no incongruities, no questions are asked. Thus, the fact that domestic violence is noted on the records of one battered woman in nine has less to do with the severity of injury or whether women are forthright than with the number of pragmatic problems partner violence poses to physicians constrained to analyze discrete, individual symptoms.

The limited repertoire of interventions at the physician's disposal bounds his perception of what has happened to the woman. These strategic limits are imposed through a medical definition of the situation that displaces any alternative interpretations women offer and protects the physician from pollution by a complex social etiology that might take the interview far afield. Lacking a coherent physiological explanation for the injury event, unaware of the woman's future risk due to partner violence, and wary of the complex of needs that may emerge if he probes more deeply, he attributes the early consequences of abuse to an accident. From the first encounter with the patient, under seemingly "normal" conditions, the reconstruction of her situation begins.

Even a limited focus on injuries could reveal the sexual origins of physical abuse and its link to male coercion. These accident victims are more likely to have facial injuries and 13 times more likely than other victims of accidents who come to the emergency service to have been injured in the breast, chest, or abdomen (Flitcraft, 1977). The sex-familial specificity of battering is revealed even more clearly by the shocking frequency of abuse-related accidents during pregnancy, a finding that supports descriptive reports that 25% to 50% of abuse victims are assaulted during pregnancy (Gelles, 1975; Rounsaville & Weissman, 1977-1978).

Even within the conventional framework, the perpetrators of domestic violence could be identified using the same methods employed to detect a hazardous consumer product or the carrier of a sexually transmitted disease. Among positive women, 88% are beaten either by husbands (54%) or boyfriends (34%) and the remainder by sons or relatives. Access through marriage remains a clinically significant source of injury even after relationships are legally dissolved. Divorced or separated women faced the same risk of battering as married women. Indeed, once married, the risk of abuse falls significantly only for the widowed (Flitcraft, 1977; Flynn, 1977). In an independent sample of battered women in the same emergency population, two thirds of the victims were divorced or separated (Rounsaville & Weissman, 1977-1978).

A national health campaign followed a single death from swine flu. The typhus victim and carrier were quickly identified. But the source of what may be the single major cause of women's injuries remains invisible, though the source's identity could easily be gleaned from medical charts, even without taking a history of adult trauma.

Just when the batterer might emerge as the source of multiplying and discrete accidents, something else enters the medical stage instead.

## STAGE 2: FROM INJURY TO ISOLATION

We reported that domestic violence is followed by a sharp increase in women's risk of addiction, attempted suicide, and a range of other health and mental health problems. Medicine, however, inverts this etiological sequence by interpreting addictive or self-destructive behaviors as the source of women's troubles, including any abuse. This reading makes it unnecessary to ask why a population of otherwise normal women develops this extraordinary clinical profile. The reorganization of women's problems in medicine's eyes shapes how women define their situation, limits their access to resources needed for safety, and so helps determine the overall progression of their "disease."

Treating domestic violence injuries as isolated episodes of trauma does nothing to prevent subsequent injury. Past interventions were probably more effective. From 1900 through the 1920s, major cities employed women police officers with social work training to help find emergency housing for battered women (Roberts, 1976). In the 1950s, before the widespread prescription of antidepressants, medical records show that domestic violence victims were more likely than they are now to be referred to social work. At present, battered women return repeatedly to the emergency service. At first, these visits are noted simply by recording repeated trauma. Gradually, however, the accumulation of injuries is supplemented by physician notes about vague medical complaints. Finally, a complex of problems is recognized, including trouble with neighbors, alcoholism, drug abuse, attempted suicide, depression, fear of child abuse, and a variety of alleged mental illnesses.

By recording the woman's secondary problems, medicine acknowledges what the patient's repeated visits have signified from the start, that therapy designed only to provide symptomatic relief to emergency complaints cannot relieve her condition. Until now, the woman has suffered the burden of symptomatic treatment in isolation. Her persistence, reflected on the medical record by the aggregation of incongruous injuries presented to the emergency service, pressures the medical system to assume the failure of the cure and to recognize that the collection of trauma has been borne by a particular woman.

To the individual physician, patient persistence presents a problem in cooperation, not simply in diagnosis and response. To the medical system, persistence means a flow of third-party payment. But it also raises the specter of uncontrolled or inappropriate demand. Physician and hospital interests now converge: From the relative standpoints of the medical paradigm and the hospital's flow charts, the solution to the problems the patient has suddenly appears to lie in the problem the patient is. The secondary problems the abused woman has developed in the course of her treatment provide medicine with labels to use to organize a history of otherwise unrelated accidents. The woman is, after all, a drug abuser or an alcoholic or she is suffering from one of a myriad of such female disorders as depression, hysteria, or hypochondriasis. Both the designation of a psychosocial problem and the use of a pseudo-psychiatric label explain not only why the woman has had so many injuries but also why she often has fights or why she has such a poor self-image. In other words, she is hurt because this is what happens when persons abuse drugs or alcohol or are emotionally unstable. The key attraction of these designations to medicine is that, by subjecting the patient to hospital control within the classic categorical limits of the medical paradigm, it solves two problems at once. The actual source of the patient's repeated injuries may now be noted, but her frequent fights or trouble at home are dismissed as a tragic but inevitable consequence of her more basic problem with drugs or emotional disorder. The dynamics of this process require further elaboration.

Ironically, even as the medical system recognizes the battered woman as a unique individual, it uses her volitional capacity to control rather than help her. To paraphrase Esterson and Laing (1970), the process by which the woman was injured is situated within a field over which she is presumed to have decision-making responsibility, as if it resulted from her deliberate praxis. In the same moment, her praxis is defined as pathological, as a weakness that must be exorcised. Her abuser too tells her she is both responsible and crazy. Her persistence leads clinicians to construct a distinct persona from the complex of incongruous symptoms they have seen up to now. But her personhood is defined as symptomatic of a more profound disorder.

At this stage in the evolution of battering, it is difficult to distinguish the natural etiology of the problems that accompany physical abuse from etiological factors associated with institutional neglect and inappropriate interventions. Shortly after her initial report of abuse, the patient develops other problems linked to the experience of the battering relationship but separable from it, from the standpoint of the medical system at least, in both time and space. These problems may evolve from prior medical attempts to control the woman's complaints with classic psychiatric methods (e.g., she may abuse her antidepressants); they may involve headaches or other suffering directly attendant on repeated beatings or the stress of living with the threat of assault; they may reflect the use of drugs or alcohol to self-medicate the pain others have refused to acknowledge; or they may reflect the isolation from help and support that leads victims to turn anger that might otherwise be directed at assailants and helpers against themselves. Whatever the source or actual time sequence, the appearance of self-destructive behavior alongside the emotional and physical effects of abuse permits the physician to integrate the woman's demand to be seen as a whole person with his or her own desire to reestablish clinical control within an individualistic framework. For the woman, her psychosocial problems signal entrapment within a predictable syndrome associated with battering; for the physician, they offer a solution, a cognitive and therapeutic strategy for encompassing otherwise unintelligible experiences.

The medical contribution to these secondary disorders is not minimal. Despite failing to recognize domestic violence, physicians respond differently to the victims of physical abuse than to other accident victims. For instance, victims of abuse are significantly more likely to leave the emergency service with a prescription for pain medication or minor tranquilizers despite the fact that such medication may be contraindicated by the head and abdominal injuries prevalent among these patients. Only 1 in 10 nonbattered accident victims receive these prescriptions, but 1 in 4 of the women we identified as battered did. In a British sample of 100 battered women, 71 received antidepressant medication (Gayford, 1975b). Psychiatric researchers recommend such medication for 80% of abused women (Rounsaville & Weissman, 1977-1978). In addition, despite the central injuries battered women suffer, physicians are less likely to follow them clinically than they are nonbattered women. In short, even where battering is not officially recognized, physicians make a collective (if implicit) diagnosis that selects abused women from the general population of injured patients and treats them in predictable ways that differ from the standard pattern of good medical practice.

The tendency toward control implicit in the shift of diagnostic focus from the symptom to the individual's sociopathology is actualized through patterns of labeling and psychiatric referral. As the depth of the family crisis generates accidents at rates that overwhelm the piecemeal therapeutic response, physicians draw labels from their cultural arsenal that frame the victim of abuse as a stereotypic female. At the time of injury, abused women are referred to psychiatric staff five times more frequently than victims of accidental trauma. These women, who present with frequent headaches, bowel disorders, painful intercourse, and muscle pains but whose X rays and lab tests are normal, are labeled "neurotic," "hysteric," "hypochondriac," or "a well-known patient with multiple vague complaints." One nonbattered woman in 50 leaves with such a label; 1 battered woman in 4 does and is given tranquilizers, sleeping medication, or further psychiatric care as a result (Flitcraft, 1977). The accumulation of these labels is reflected in the medical and psychiatric epidemiology of "female disorders," whose prevalence helps justify expanded funding for the medical system that does the labeling.

STAGE 3: FROM ISOLATION TO ENTRAPMENT

Whatever physicians intend these responses to accomplish, the general consequence is to isolate abused women from resources and to reduce their capacity to understand, adequately respond to, or resolve their crisis by leaving the violent home or struggling through to autonomy against the hurt inflicted by a malevolent other. Medical isolation converges with the partner's attempts to isolate the battered woman from family and friends. The woman's entire world can now be contained by her assailant's definition of reality: She is what he tells her she is and this is the person seen by her treaters. If the woman's repeated efforts to get help or, failing that, to escape from the most painful aspects of her situation through self-destructive behavior are defined as her primary problem, the cure typically involves the reimposition of traditional female role behavior and, more often than not, within the same male-supremacist context in which she is being beaten.

Among the primarily female patients with whom the woman is now categorized, the price of cure is an admission of dependence. Even as medication helps the woman "forget" her abuse as a political-ethical issue, it reminds her daily that she cannot survive on her own. From a legal standpoint, being labeled mentally ill or alcoholic also ensures that the woman must depend on the goodwill of her caretakers in such future attempts at independence as working outside the home or gaining custody of children. Isolation in the treatment context may aggravate the desperation that drove her to self-destructive behavior in the first place, evoking the very symptoms alleged by her label. The abused woman continues to talk to herself. Only now, she believes that what she is saying is foolish.

From the medical records, it is impossible to discover the exact interaction between medical labeling and the high incidence of drug abuse, suicide, rape, child abuse, or actual mental breakdown among abused women. Clearly, however, the isolating effects of labeling and the referrals it prompts both give the woman an added incentive to escape from her situation (including now her relation to the medical system) and reduce her capacity to do so realistically. The abused woman is often labeled at the height of her vulnerability, during a particularly severe crisis, for instance, when the signs of her outward collapse readily suggest the inner illogic or pathological determinacy implied by the label. Because of this, what could be dismissed as a transparent misrepresentation of her existential condition is often internalized as an alternative interpretation of her entire experience as a woman. Now, like her physician, she may perceive her life with an abusive male as symptomatic of an underlying pathology, dependency, and helplessness. This interpretation completely discredits the courage she mustered to survive her beatings in the past, as well as the integrity she salvaged by trying to make a bad relationship work or to save the man she once loved. Her partner's message, that she is sick for resisting his will, is now reinforced by her physicians. She may even require her partner's help. In this light, the suicide attempts of nearly one battered woman in three, often with the antidepressants they have been given to help them cope, can be read as acts of autonomy, as expressions of what Marcuse (1958) calls "the great refusal" to choose between equally pathological alternatives, objectification at the hands of a violent other or self-alienation within an allegedly benign medical definition. A desperate act of existential responsibility, a refusal to pretend one can remain sane in the face of an intolerable tyranny, is interpreted as confirmation of pathology that justifies subjecting the woman to even further control.

In addition to replicating the means and determinants of isolation and self-destructive behavior clinically, medicine now recognizes a history of assault as part of a syndrome to which it gives a distinct materialist content and social form. If medical ideology helps elicit symptoms of sociopathology, medicine's response to these symptoms, its cure, is to reimpose "women's work" by reconstituting the family around the abused woman as the setting in which she must be treated.

When they receive referrals, battered women are typically sent to detox programs, drug dependence units, mental health clinics, or mental hospitals and to a variety of counseling agencies, all of which approach the primary problem (e.g., alcoholism or depression) as a disease and any secondary problems (such as frequent fights) as arising from a failure to adjust to conventional familial or sex role expectations. Recovery is similarly defined along two tracks: cessation of the disease (e.g., the addiction) and reintegration into "normal" (i.e., sex stereo-typed) familial relationships.

The focus on gender roles is not entirely misplaced because domestic violence frequently occurs in disputes about child care, sex, housework, and money (Dobash & Dobash, 1977). In these situations, violence may put an end to verbal conflict, there may be mutual fighting, or, most often, violence may simply exact obedience even without conflict. Here again, institutional intervention converges with subjugation at home. At the state mental hospital to which one battered woman in eight is eventually committed, female stereotypes are enforced with a ven-geance. Release is often conditional on a willingness to perform routine housework and to look pretty (Chessler, 1971). The main problem is not the stereotyped expectation, but the fusion of two power centers— the mental hospital and the abusive partner—to constrain women's options. However important it may be to help some female patients adapt to gendered norms, pressures on battered women to adjust occasion an overwhelming sense of powerlessness against which they rebel, appearing crazy. When she returns home, the woman retains the negative experience of institutionalization in her memory as the alter-native to making things work.

Less dramatic referrals for case management or family services can be equally destructive. Social service agencies rarely select abuse as the focus of intervention, even when batterers seek help along with their victims (Nichols, 1976). Instead, from behind the morass of personal and interpersonal disorders described by a client, the social worker discovers what he or she has been trained to expect from the beginning, the multiproblem family. Spawned in such a milieu, the woman has brought her baggage to her present home. Not only is she beaten because she drinks but both her alcoholism and the violence are inextricable parts of the peculiar family constellation that reproduces itself across the generations, particularly in low-income or minority communities (Hanks & Rosenbaum, 1977; Wolfgang & Ferracuti, 1967). The family is not the battered woman's problem. She is a problem for it to manage.

Whether a woman is referred to individual counseling or to family support services, the challenge assumed by the helping system is the same: to preserve the multiproblem family by ministering to its many needs. At least since the 1920s, when social work replaced its earlier interest in family violence with euphemisms such as "marital discord," reformers have preferred family reconciliation to making women and children wards of the state (Davis, 1967; Platt, 1969; Pleck, 1977). Of course, when social services reinforce families where ongoing abuse occurs, women and children become permanent customers.

The cycle is now complete. Each new incident of violence points the helper to the unresolved secondary problem and elicits a reinvigorated effort to stabilize families that would otherwise collapse under the weight of their internal contradictions. As agency and family become inextricably joined, a new constellation emerges, the violent family, an oxymoron that appears as a tragic but inevitable side effect of working things out. Police, physicians, child protective workers, alcohol counselors, therapists, and a range of aides learn to accept the tragedy as routine. The woman learns to measure time from one beating to the next and this is also how her chronology is organized by medicine. Meanwhile, interventions geared toward stabilization teach all family members, including the victim(s) of abuse, to accept this rhythm as "just life." A subtle change remains unnoticed. Entrapped in the violent family, the woman's subjectivity becomes flattened. She is no longer hurt during periodic struggles. Rather, her abuse takes on a ritualistic and disembodied character. Like the notes in the medical record of "hit by ashtray" or "kicked by foot," it seems to lack agency.

Physicians rarely note any differences between victims of domestic violence and patients injured during a fall. Yet in each encounter, over a lifetime and on an aggregate basis, abused women are treated differently. To respond to the clinical dilemmas abuse poses to medical management, individual physicians draw on diagnostic, referral, and treatment strategies that extend a woman's suffering and mystify its cause. Neither the substance nor the consequences of the medical response, however, are fully explained by the need to manage persistent patients and otherwise incomprehensible injuries.

## Toward a Theory of Social Causation

### CURRENT THEORETICAL APPROACHES

Drawn largely along the lines of academic disciplines, current theoretical approaches trace domestic violence to proximate causes such as personality problems and interpersonal family dynamics; structural variables, such as poverty and economic stress; or cultural norms that support violence or sexism. Scant attention has been paid to the interplay of macroevents (such as sexual inequality) and the microdynamics of male domination. In part, the failure to offer a comprehensive theory reflects confusion (which derives from political differences) about whether what is to be explained is a private event, as the terms *domestic* or *family* violence imply; it is a transhistorical phenomenon "violence against women"; or it is a historically specific constellation of structural, cultural, and psychodynamic forces identified here as woman battering.

The term *syndrome* refers to a cluster of clinical events with no obvious biological, psychiatric, or psychosocial explanation (Selye, 1956). Even from an enlightened medical purview, a great mystery surrounds the fact that a subgroup of otherwise normal injury patients exhibits a clinical profile that includes multiple episodes of trauma, as well as medical and psychosocial problems. To solve the mystery of the battered woman, to decipher what lies behind the appearance of the violent family as a relatively stable historical phenomenon, one needs to identify the social logic that guides a complex interplay between women's development, the response by violent men, the helping response, and larger economic forces. This logic lies beyond the grasp of the medical paradigm and so operates behind the backs of individual physicians to shape their otherwise illogical case-by-case responses to physical abuse. The absence of clinical reflexivity helps explain why battering appears as a syndrome rather than as the distinct result of women's entrapment in battering relationships. From the initial confusion about abusive injuries through the reconstitution of a family from which the abused woman is trying to escape, the woman experiences a transformation into a "battered woman" who is chronically dependent on a variety of "helpers," including her partner. Although a patriarchal specter haunts the battered woman's first medical visit, the structural alignment of medicine and the patriarchy is actualized through thousands of encounters over an extended time.

Despite medicine's role in woman battering, none of the immediate actors we have discussed controls the resources required to organize so widely destructive an event. This is why, however useful descriptively, theories that aggregate personality characteristics or interpersonal dynamics into profiles of typical victim-participants or abusive situations are ultimately unrewarding as explanations of battering. Psychologists studying volunteer or clinical samples report battered women suffer learned helplessness, are ineffectual or masochistic (Hanks & Rosenbaum, 1977; Hendrix, LaGodna, & Bohen, 1978; Pfouts, 1978; Snell et al., 1964; Walker, 1979), and fail to distinguish the causes from the consequences of entrapment or to capture the psychological variety associated with differences in race or class. The typical batterer is described as an inarticulate, emotionally limited, frustrated man; unhappy with his work; economically insecure; obsessed with loyalty; and quickly angered, who resents his children, abuses alcohol, and was severely disciplined as a child (Gayford, 1975a; Gove & Grimm, 1973; Martin, 1977; Renvoize, 1978). This portrait is a parody of the peculiar combination of depersonalization and pathetic, if deeply felt, needfulness and frustration that typifies the American male in a variety of settings. Indeed, aside from selection bias and other methodological problems that make attempts to generalize from discrete data suspect, the incredibly high prevalence of domestic violence and associated problems, such as divorce, jealousy, controlling behavior, alcoholism, drug use, depression, and so forth, suggests that what researchers have dubbed "the violent family" is less an aberrant subtype than a variant of the American family, an example of what we term *normal pathology.*

Battering can no more be explained by proximate causes or characteristics of participants than can lynching be explained by the characteristics of the lynch mob or its victims. Contrasting the dynamics in violent and nonviolent partner relationships can be useful, as the research reported here suggests. But the ultimate significance of this exercise lies in what it reveals about the overall construction of male domination and female subordination. When rates of various problems identified through cross-sectional or descriptive studies are shaped into images of violence-prone or multiproblem families, the traditional (presumably noncoercive) family is evoked as a normative counterpart. This dichotomy discounts the links between violent and nonviolent forms of sex-specific domination or between forms of dominance within the family and without and legitimates the stabilization strategies identified above.

Alternately incorporated into kitsch melodrama or news reporting by the media, the statistical artifacts of abused women as powerless victims and of batterers as multiproblem deviants elicit a sense of estrangement. Victim and batterer see themselves in the projected imagery, but as isolates and grotesques, not as persons for whom recognition is a step toward understanding or change. Meanwhile, the "calculus of harms" by which family violence is distinguished throws the lives of those who suffer from domination-as-usual into a mystifying relief.

The confusion occasioned when the dynamics of domination are reduced to empirical sound bytes is illustrated by debate about whether family violence is sexually symmetrical. Surveys indicating that women hit or kill their partners almost as often as they are hit or killed (Lundsgaarde, 1977; Straus, 1977-1978; Wolfgang, 1956) have been interpreted by some to mean there is a hidden population of battered men (Steinmetz, 1977-1978), though no such population has surfaced in police reports, medical records, or clinical samples (Dobash & Dobash, 1977-1978). Others explain female violence as only defensive. Behind this disagreement are political differences about whether to equate all forms of family violence (and seek to manage female as well as male aggression) or to distinguish woman battering, a social event that reflects the confluence of structural, institutional, and private factors. These differences have profound clinical implications. The consequences when a man assaults a stranger (male or female) or when a woman assaults her partner or a stranger or is assaulted by a stranger are a function of the assailant's intent and the means employed. Only women attacked by their partners exhibit the syndrome of multiple injuries, medical problems, isolation, psychosocial problems, and almost paralyzing terror we identify with battering (Hilberman & Munson, 1977-1978).

Battering is not about fighting, even when its consequences are severe. Fighting occurs in many cultures, communities, families, and relationships without jeopardizing the liberty of those involved and may even strengthen group life by resolving unspoken tensions, ending conflict, or establishing rights. In contrast, battering occurs when persons have been forcibly isolated from potentially supportive kin and peer relations and become locked, like hostages, into situations in which objectification, subordination, and continued punishment are inevitable. Physical fighting presents a moral concern; battering presents a political reality. Unlike the battered husband, the abused woman cannot escape even if she wants to because her situation is mediated by the reproduction and enforcement of her dependent status through all society. Thus, even if an abused woman "wins" a particular fight, she, not the man with whom she is fighting, ends up as battered.

Recognizing the limits of a microdynamic approach, some researchers have traced abuse to broad social factors, such as class, income, and race, suggesting there are higher rates of domestic violence among working-class, poor, or black Americans (Chester & Streather, 1972; Lystad, 1975; Steinmetz, 1974). There is evidence, however, that as much abuse is reported in wealthy as in poor communities (Connecticut Task Force on Abused Women, 1978), that batterers are frequently middle-class and professional men (Marsden, 1978; Walker, 1979), that there is little difference in the use of force among working- and middle-class parents (Straus, 1971), and that racial differences disappear when other variables are controlled (Centerwall, 1984).

If social class appears to have little aggregate significance for domestic violence, economic privilege undoubtedly contributes to male power in intimate relationships. Goode (1971) argues that men convert the superior economic resources they command outside the home into the privilege of beating their wives to resolve domestic disputes. Lachman (1978) identifies a peak in domestic violence when economic and family pressures peak in the life cycle, after the birth of a second child for instance. These resource theories fail to explain why sex, rather than ability, is a key to economic power, what men "win" when they beat their wives, or why women appear to become entrapped after they are hit. In addition, domestic violence has become a public issue when men's relative economic advantage over women is declining, not growing, a fact that highlights the defensive nature of male violence as other sources of male power erode. Furthermore, the risk of abuse appears to increase with status discrepancies, for example, when a man's status is lower as well as higher than his partner's (Hornung, McCullough, & Sugimoto, 1981).

Cultural explanations of domestic violence emphasize the hierarchical implications of traditional sex roles, the unique emphasis low-income cultures place on violence, and the extent to which the media positively sanction violence as a solution to a range of problems, including interpersonal conflicts.

Sex roles are an important source of expectations and behavior. The rage men discharge in violence against men and women arises, in part, from the gulf between the ideals of manhood transmitted through cultural stereotypes and the felt ineffectualness men suffer on or off the job (Sennett & Cobb, 1973). Fulfilling these stereotypes is identified with acquiring status through consumer goods, among which women are often counted, and men scapegoat women when the projected ideals prove unsatisfying and beyond reach. The morbid jealousy that precipitates numerous assaults on wives often contains a fetishistic dimension: Medical records reveal victims who have been kicked repeatedly like a broken TV, a commodity in which a large emotional investment has been made but that now symbolizes the world of false promises (Aronowitz, 1973). When men assault women for failing to restore the subjectivity and self-esteem appropriated at work, we can associate battering with yet another dimension of the mysterious process that Marx (1967) calls "the fetishism of commodities."

A culture of poverty emphasizing immediate gratification has been used to explain why low-income groups quickly resort to violence when they face frustration (Lewis, 1965). Some researchers argue that for poor and working Americans, a marriage license is a hitting license and domestic violence is simply a normative means of settling disputes (Steinmetz & Straus, 1973). Apart from the questionable empirical basis for these claims, Flitcraft (1977) found that battered women self-medicated with drugs and alcohol only after violence began and as a function of their isolation from (not their involvement with) supportive peer and kin networks. As Fanon (1978) argues, many other so-called deviant behaviors are ways of resisting poverty, not its result.

The most popular cultural explanation is that violence is as "American as apple pie." Not only does the argument miss the key fact about violence in modern societies, that it is punished under some conditions and positively sanctioned, even organized, under others, but it conceals both the varied political substance of violence—for example, the sex-specific dynamic of battering—and the different uses to which it is put in different historical periods. In encounters with battered women, medicine reinforces not violence as such but obedience to the hierarchical authority of men. Although obedience is a cultural value, it is most economically achieved without violence because the actor's authority is seen as legitimate, usually as a result of material circumstances. In traditional patriarchal societies, the male's right to appropriate women's labor, that is, housework, sexuality, child care, and the like, is rooted in his command over family property generally. A potential in all hierarchical relationships, violence has become a key to male authority today because its cultural legitimacy and material basis in family property have eroded.

In the early 1970s, feminist critics called attention to rape and sexual abuse as examples of the misogyny inherent in a sexist culture. In this view, the sexual divisions of labor and opportunity, like women's subordination at home, are objectifications of a male chauvinism that is sometimes learned, sometimes innate. Physically more powerful than women, men are allegedly trained to solve their problems forcibly, whereas female socialization emphasizes passivity and dependence. From this vantage, battering is the domestic counterpart to rape, a reminder of the privileges seemingly bestowed on violent men by nature (Brownmiller, 1975; Martin, 1977; Straus, 1976).

Unquestionably, male culture has always romanticized violence, and, as surely, women have struggled to resist, survive, and avoid male violence directed at them. Though force may always have been used to guarantee female dependence, particularly in the home, to avoid what Juliett Mitchell calls " 'simplistic materialism' " (quoted in Zaretsky, 1973, p. 75), this truth must be specified historically in ways that permit one to chart its changing meaning under different conditions and to identify different strategies of resistance. Contrasts like the one drawn by 19th-century feminist Frances Power Cobbe (1878) between "the kicking districts" of working-class Liverpool and the relatively "mild" beatings administered to London women suggest that complex social factors may determine whether and in what combination physical, ideological, political, or economic force is used to control women and to what particular end. Because the forcefulness of the sexist critique derives from reducing the range of variation within and between societies to universalize the importance of gender as a source of identity, it obscures this complex determination, including the determinants of sexism itself. One result is the portrayal of sexism as an immutable part of the social fabric, too deeply embedded in character and culture to respond to more than personal or temporary remedies. Beyond this, the feminist characterization of society as a whole as a patriarchy conceals often decisive contradictions between specific patriarchal forms and the political economy, contradictions that women exploit to gain their independence. Conversely, by equating female oppression with men and focusing exclusively on the cultural and interpersonal dimensions of male power (e.g., the consciousness-raising phase of the women's movement), Brownmiller (1975) and other feminist writers conceal the new configurations assumed by male domination (and its convergence with class and race-based discrimination) as women have been liberated from their traditional family roles to enter the wage market.

In contrast to these explanations, battering is best understood by delineating the historically specific tensions (as well as the supportive linkages) between patriarchal structures and the larger economy and pursuing these tensions and linkages through the microdynamics of heterosexual struggle. Our thesis is deceptively simple, that battering reflects a defense of patriarchal authority as its material and cultural supports are subverted by women's liberation and the rationalizing influence of the market. In the household, domestic violence often begins not because women are submissive, but in response to conflicts over women's work, cooking, child care, sex, or money (Dobash & Dobash, 1977; Schechter, 1978). As intensely personal as these struggles seem, they are infused at every point with notions of female possibility and male power that are socially derived from a broad array of experiences in the community, economy, and wider society. Historically, battering became a public issue during periods when women's economic opportunities converged with widespread challenges to traditional family roles (Gove & Grimm, 1973). In each of these periods—during the 1830s and 1840s, in the late 19th century, and in the 1960s and 1970s—women took advantage of an expanding economy to enter the job market and give political expression to their awakening consciousness (Cott, 1977; Farrager & Stansell, 1975; Gilman, 1935; Sklar, 1976). Men responded defensively to these changes in women's independence at both the macrolevel—witness the rise in rape and assault by younger males in the 1970s (Silberman, 1978)—and in thousands of individual relationships.

## PATRIARCHY VERSUS CAPITALISM

Thus far, our analysis of woman battering has focused on two layers of social construction, the clinician-patient encounter and the encounter between the medical system and the violent family. The inappropriate medical response is "driven" by women's persistent presentation of a range of problems whose explanation is beyond the grasp of the medical paradigm. As a result, clinical strategies are used to manage victims of domestic violence—from labeling through family stabilization—that reduce women's options and reconstitute fragments of their life history into portraits of individual or family pathology that appear to have a private source. The medical interpretation of domestic violence as a private event takes shape from, reinforces, and shapes the dynamic of coercion at home, until the two sources of authority fuse through predictable stages into a battering syndrome. A social reality—male domination—appears as a private hell borne by a new psychological type—the battered woman—and carried into the world by the violent family.

After close examination, most current accounts of domestic violence are little more than attempts to aggregate some combination of these private fragments into a coherent social picture, reproducing the essentialist illusion that misogynist violence is intrinsic to men ("When men discovered they could rape," writes Brownmiller, 1975, p. 14, "they proceeded to do it") or derives from certain personality, genetic, or family constellations. In part, the contradictory findings reported in these accounts reflect the methodological problems confronting a social science establishment with little experience in interdisciplinary theory building. But the persistence of ambiguity when battering is studied in a cultural or economic milieu suggests an important truth about the reality itself, namely that battering is a multidimensional phenomenon that can be traced to diverse, perhaps even contradictory, impulses and dynamics. Battering takes on a unitary appearance only insofar as the various layers at which it is constructed are themselves organized around a common interest with respect to particular individuals. The widespread appearance of otherwise normal women who stay in violent relationships and families defined by violent behavior reflects the fact that the helping services, unwittingly or otherwise, have assumed the task of organizing and stabilizing contradictory realities. In so doing, however, they are mediating larger social tensions between patriarchal and economic structures on which we have only touched.

Virtually every aspect of abusive relationships—from the parts of the body targeted in assaults through the occasions on which coercion is exercised to the areas of female resistance—involve women's "work," that is, activities for which women are assumed to be responsible (or from which they are prohibited) because of their sex. And it is over women's work that capitalism and the patriarchy clash most directly. Struggles around women's appropriate domestic responsibilities are age-old. In contrast with previous economic systems, however, capitalist expansion requires that ever new sources of labor, including women, be drawn into paid employment. This displaces household production, preferentially rewards female labor that seeks its future outside the home, and challenges all forms of authority, including male dominance, that prevent women or other groups from freely developing and alienating their capacities (Benjamin, 1978; Hartmann, 1976; Lasch, 1977; Mead, 1953; Zaretsky, 1973). As Hartmann (1976) puts it,

> The emergence of capitalism in the fifteenth to eighteenth centuries threatened patriarchal control based on institutional authority as it destroyed many old institutions and created new ones, such as a "free" market in labor. It threatened to bring all women and children into the labor force and hence to destroy the family and the basis of the power of men over women (i.e., the control over their labor power in the family). (p. 139)

As an ally of women's liberation, the capitalist economy is hardly unequivocal. The freedom to be exploited that capitalism offers women is achieved by removing obstacles to economic rationality that comprise essential social supports as well as those that obstruct human development. One result is that outside the upper classes the survival of the male-headed family is linked to women's paid work. Even as it economically savages family life, capitalism employs wage and job discrimination by sex in ways that drive women to marry and apply their undervalued labor to housework and keeps women dependent on men generally, if not on specific males. Understood as a circuit of value realization that includes the sale of goods and the reproduction of the workforce as well as goods production, capitalism benefits from a host of biosocial, psychosocial, and sociopolitical functions the family performs (Ewen, 1976; Hartmann, 1976). Not least important, the family provides an individuated outlet for male aggression that might otherwise overflow in social protest.

This contradictory context defines the opposing social purposes to which domestic violence is put. In its most severe forms, violence and coercion directly threaten women's productive capacities, devaluing women's labor and directly obstructing overall social development. At the same time, by sustaining female subordination and forcing women to continue their domestic duties despite the new opportunities for independence capitalism affords, abuse negatively embodies the age-old ideal of a world apart from the cash nexus, a world for which the entrepreneur longs no less than his employees. Even as women's new power to escape domestic violence is inconceivable apart from the broad material basis capitalism provides for women's independence, in its dynamics, family violence also reflects the degradation of individual subjectivity. Women's medical records are replete with instances of men who covet their wives at one moment as if they were unique and irreplaceable then beat them the next as if they were disposable (and replaceable) objects.

If violence could suppress the economic disruption of the traditional family, medicine's role in its reconstruction would be irrelevant. In fact, as many perpetrators themselves claim, violence against intimates is less a solution to the erosion of patriarchal authority and the corresponding political organization of women than a cry for help, a cry to which the services respond.

Since the dawn of industrial production, despite major ideological currents to the contrary, both the father's power to command and the family's power to constitute the reality of its members have been repeatedly compromised by the dissolution of household production (the material basis for patriarchal command and family autonomy), the socialization of the family's (i.e., women's) private functions, and the reconstitution of the family's internal life as a function of the marketing and reproductive needs of business (Ewen, 1976; Horkheimer, 1972). The consequences of these changes included rising divorce and desertion rates (Krishnan & Kavani, 1974), declines in births and family size (Glick, 1975; Sweet, 1974), a shift from work for a master to nurturance and consumption as a social obligation (Horkheimer, 1972), and the emergence of a "woman's sphere" in the late 19th century (Cott, 1977; Smith-Rosenberg, 1975) that shaped the current situation at least as significantly as more formal movements for women's liberation. Exploiting the opportunities for leisure among the new middle classes, women forged broad homosocial networks of friendship and political reform that helped to socialize domesticity by forcing the state and the market to assume the private family functions of education, health care, family planning, child support, and the like (Cott, 1977). In its goals, the process Jane Addams called social mothering was paternalistic, even eugenic, seeking to restore traditional family relations among the lower classes through birth control, case management support for parenting, or with a wage for mothering (such as Aid to Families With Dependent Children [AFDC]) that made it unnecessary for young women to work. In practice, however, the new spheres of social activity stimulated women's liberation by allowing women to extend their domestic skills into paid employment and encouraging them to replace their loyalty to traditional values and relations, including loyalty to men, with a strategic sense of personal development linked to the market. Meanwhile, mass advertising reinforced feminist analyses of women's subjugation by urging that traditional family roles and loyalties be replaced by independent lifestyles based on consumer goods (Ewen, 1976).

Most histories of the helping professions are self-serving stories written for internal consumption that neglect their common functions as well as the larger social or economic influences that shaped the formation of the service sector as a whole. Today's huge edifice of helping services was made possible by the capacity of market capitalism to free an ever larger segment of the workforce from industrial employment. Conversely, the edifice is unthinkable apart from its overall mission, namely to contain the multiple crises in private (i.e., family) life occasioned by capitalism's success. From the 1920s on, with varying degrees of self-consciousness, fee-for-service medicine, social work, psychiatry, and other mental health professions and social services confronted family breakdown primarily as a failure by women to manage their gendered responsibilities for parenting, spousal support, and home maintenance. To this extent, the services functioned as part of an extended patriarchy to stabilize the diminishing sphere of private life and patriarchal privilege and supplement the market's uneven regulation of female labor. To be sure, the principles of the social services, their specific substance (health, education, and welfare), and their predominantly female labor force reflected the socialization of nurturance. The ideals of professionalism preserved the family emphasis on selfless aid free of the cash nexus. At the same time, the services inherited the generalized authoritarian character of the patriarchal family and so often undermined in practice the ideals they were theoretically established to socialize. As illustrated by medicine's role in battering, the services approached the private sphere less as a space where women could prepare for and enjoy the new opportunities than a place where they could be satisfied despite these opportunities. To this extent, instead of liberating women from domesticity, the services reproduced patriarchal relations on an extended scale.

## THE RECONSTITUTED PATRIARCHY

Sociologically speaking, patriarchy is a system of household authority in which loyalty to the master is based on his power to dispose of property, including women, and is embedded in "a community of fate" in which these personal relations of dependence are conceived as natural, as "just life" (Weber, 1968, pp. 1006-1007). Besides personal loyalty, patriarchy depends on piety toward tradition; this latter force, represented historically through institutions such as the chivaree, provides the only constraints on a system of male domination with few legal limits.

Nothing could differ more fundamentally from this situation than the contractual relations voluntarily established in the capitalist labor market between parties who are formally equal or between patients and physicians whose authority extends only as far as specialized professional knowledge permits. The question remains whether the authority medicine employs to stabilize violent relationships is less patriarchal because the bonds that link physicians to batterers are not personal or based in household production. In fact, the alignment of medicine with male violence resembles the traditional patriarchy in its reliance on a male-bonded network, its implicit acknowledgment that the master can do as he wishes to his property, the reading of resistance to domination as sick, its substantive emphasis on women's domestic work, and in its consequences, the entrapment of women in dependent relations on men that appear to be "just life." Indeed, the fact that at least half of the women who are battered are single, separated, or divorced suggests a broader "property right" than was afforded in traditional societies based on blood or kin.

Despite a certain formal continuity in patriarchal authority, however, its interdependence on more advanced forms of economic and social organization symbolizes a decisive shift in the substantive meaning, determination, and ultimate viability of male domination in private life.

The medical and social services gained their widespread legitimacy from their juridical appearance as part of a public sector, a world apart from commodity circulation and profit making organized to serve and protect the private spheres of family and community life. Although they may use fees for service, be an immediate source of profit taking for certain sectors of business, and provide real (if exaggerated) benefits for general health and welfare, the major function of the services is to mediate antagonisms between the social wealth society could produce if its potential were fully exploited and the limits placed on this potential by the system of private ownership. The services do this, in part, by tracing the social crises resulting from the underdevelopment and maldistribution of resources to individual and interpersonal failures. To reiterate, the medical response to domestic violence is not unique in this respect. Numerous health problems, from infant mortality through AIDS, are also disaggregated at a host of medical and service sites into so many personal problems allegedly brought on by bad habits, psychiatric disease, or the environment (Crawford, 1977; Stark, 1977).

Because of its varied roots in different classes and cultures, sexism cannot be reduced to economic principles. At the same time, capitalist social relations infuse every moment of private life, shaping which events will be considered private and which public, defining the relative value of domestic work, and severely limiting the institutional expression of traditional principles—including the professional autonomy of physicians and male dominance at home—opposed to the logic of accumulation.

Thus, capitalism's need for "a world apart" encouraged the patriarchy's survival into the present as a system of authority over private life. In contrast to paid employment, where employees voluntarily exchange a quantity of time for a wage, the material basis of the patriarchal family is the use of loyalty and obedience to appropriate female labor (or its value in wages) directly to support dominant males. To resolve private problems without disrupting this framework, medicine and other services were forced to accommodate loyalty, dependence, and, in lieu of these, coercion, a political compromise that grew more transparent as the inherent legitimacy and rationality of male dominance dissolved. Recognizing this process allows us to follow "the male principle" in its historical flight from the home and into the public sphere, where it embedded itself in the ideology and substantive practices of the services and professions and helped women channel resistance to male authority into so many forms of adaptation to domesticity (Ehrenreich & English, 1979).

The accommodation was mutual. As the economy of mass production and consumption recruited women to paid employment and explicitly targeted the values (such as loyalty and parsimony) that had allowed women to sustain families on a meager "male wage," entrepreneurial culture abandoned all pretense of moral support for the traditional family system. Instead, it turned to the sexual hierarchy as a means to sustain the sex-segregated division of labor, to pacify tendencies toward antisocial behavior by youngsters, and to organize household consumption (Ewen, 1976). Particularly as women extended domestic resistance to the shop floor, pressure increased for the services to assign women responsibility for various family problems, including violence, and to identify the range of work-related ailments with troubles at home. In sum, the sexist practice of medicine, psychiatry, and social work derives largely from the historical development of the helping services as means to reconcile the contradictory pressures of patriarchal and capitalist authority. Physicians do not endorse violence as a means of establishing women's subordination. They merely learn to accept it as a tragic but inevitable by-product of "making things work."

## Conclusion

At the dawn of capitalism, the personal power of men was invested with the added authority of the master of the economic unit. As long as household production prevailed, the authority of male-bonded political institutions (such as the church, the nobility, and the army) appeared as a natural extension of family relations whose patriarchal character was "just life." Family stability was synonymous with social well-being. Apart from the weak constraints imposed by traditions of interpersonal obligation and the greater importance of women in certain forms of household production than in others (Muller, 1977; Rubin, 1975), the economic independence of patriarchal units permitted wife beating to arise in one family for reasons that might have little to do with its emergence in others, according to the whims and habits of individual males. Society took little active interest in female resistance.

In contrast to all previous social orders, the survival of capitalism required that laborers be emancipated from traditional bonds. The captains of industrial production welcomed political and moral support from the church, the army, the professions, or other male-bonded networks. But to reproduce itself on an expanded scale, capitalism had to continually revolutionize the social relations within these networks as well as within families, divesting patriarchal power of both its economic legitimacy and its base in traditional loyalty structures. The "natural" link between male domination and social well-being was permanently broken.

The male-dominated family did not disappear, of course. But outside the upper classes and certain ethnic enclaves, it survived mainly as a residual institution, alternately serving as a repository or an escape from social ills depending on fluctuations in economic development. As wages became the universal medium of exchange, family dynamics were reconstituted as a function of the relative shares of income household members commanded on the market. Periodic boom and bust cycles in industrial production routinely destabilized these dynamics by alternately drawing women and children into the labor force and then driving men out, exposing the contingent nature of male authority in the home and eliciting a range of defensive countermaneuvers, including violence against the increasing autonomy of women and children.

If family power was shaped by an unpredictable economic calculus indifferent to traditional values, capitalism also stimulated a dramatic expansion of social wealth that facilitated an overall increase in the time devoted to personal development and relationships (the so-called cultural revolution) relative to the time spent in productive employment, a tendency Marx terms *disaccumulation* (Sklar, 1969). Research showing that women's employment facilitates escape from domestic violence signals the link to independence. Indeed, both the emergence of the women's sphere discussed earlier and the emergence of a huge edifice devoted to personal support and caretaking are inconceivable apart from the capacity to meet material needs (with improved technology) with ever fewer industrial and support workers. The full development and deployment of women's productive capacities will hasten the day when private life is not bound by the reproductive needs of the economy, diminishing the dependence of one man's leisure on another's exploitation. In grasping this moment of autonomy, women's liberation confronts the patriarch with a tragic choice: Either yield to equal oppression (women into factories and offices, men into nurseries and kitchens) or seek external assistance to hold back the future.

If men have responded defensively to the progressive destablization of traditional sex hierarchy, woman battering developed primarily as a response to the current dilemma, when the survival of patriarchy simultaneously requires women to seek paid employment (providing a material base for women's independence) and to submit at home to an authority with no rational basis whatsoever in social development. Chronic external support is needed to maintain family stability against the tendency to subordinate primary relations to the laws of love and partnership.

Victorian ideology portrayed the family as a haven from an anarchic market and a dehumanizing workplace (Ewen, 1976; Lasch, 1977). But to women, whose unpaid labor has always been the basis for male leisure, this claim was transparent. As capitalist expansion drew women to wage work, they too aspired to enjoy a world apart. But the opposing tendencies of capitalist and patriarchal authority were quickly reconciled in an antagonistic unity that appropriated the new possibilities for female autonomy as so many forms of female dependence on men.

Medicine's contribution to woman battering and the violent family illustrates the role of the services in constructing this unity as well as its consequence. Far from being a cultural aberration, the violent family stands on a continuum with the patriarchal family, a world apart that must assume the costs of progressive irrationality as its private burden. By socializing heretofore private functions of health, child protection, welfare, and the like, the services ostensibly fulfilled traditional feminist demands to socialize domesticity as well as technology's age-old promise that ever greater portions of social labor could be employed to support personal well-being. But for the millions of battered women who reach out for support, this benign face masks pressure for them to resume business as usual.

No amount of investment in the services is likely to ameliorate a situation that originates in the progressive erosion and destablization of patriarchal authority. It would be equally misleading, however, to propose the maxim that for women, at least, "everything changes so that things can remain the same." If the services are less than they claim, the patriarch who arrogantly insists "I can do what I want with my woman" is a mere specter of his precapitalist self, temporarily inflated by the support he receives in reducing his partner to an object.

In sum, battering arises today as services attempt to reprivatize women's work in a context of patriarchal domination against counter-tendencies to socialize the labor of love. This negative role of social services helps explain why the contemporary battered women's movement is the first women's liberation movement rooted in the delivery of an alternative service. Battered woman's shelters must be considered not simply a means to an end but as part of a process that embodies the reality that must eventually be universalized, the abolition of patriarchy, the reconstitution of the family as an extended network of loving equals, the provision of service as a means of empowerment, and the cooperative organization of child care and women's other traditional household chores.

The success of this liberation process depends on whether it continues to draw its momentum from women in the community, expanding its links to the urban-based networks of female resistance that persist among blacks, Puerto Ricans, ethnics, Chicanos, and working-class whites (Caulfield, 1974). Besides providing the base for explicitly political demands for housing, welfare rights, educational reform, health care, and child care, these networks challenge the ideological hegemony of medicine and other services by offering women a strategic repertoire of collective self-help based on inherited principles of female prowess. The most tragic consequence of battering is that it isolates women from these networks, cutting them off from any chance to forge their subjectivity with collective support. When she is isolated, the abused woman seems like a helpless victim.

Apart from a strategy that strengthens these indigenous networks of resistance, an appeal for greater sensitivity among physicians and other helpers seems shallow. Such an approach misses the main conclusion of this research, that because the services are themselves socially constructed to preserve (a male-governed) stability in the private sphere, their reform and the alteration of their logic require a far more fundamental challenge than is possible through professional education, training, or individual advocacy alone.

But a strategy that relies exclusively on providing battered women with shelter must also be critically weighed. However crucial it is to solidify networks of resistance against the fracturing of women's communities by domestic violence and the social services, enormous hazards lie ahead if shelter is promoted as a concealed refuge from the horrors of male-dominated family life, shelter occupants are defined as victims rather than as survivors, safety is emphasized over liberation, and a simulation of community is offered in lieu of direct challenges to existing community power structures. If shelters remain an alternative service, they will eventually ape other treatment programs for the "disadvantaged": A few successful women will get jobs and may even join shelter staff, but the vast majority will find they lack the political skills to extend the momentary solidarity with women in crisis into a permanent freedom movement.

Balancing the organization of indigenous networks of resistance with the provision of individually based emergency service requires that shelter for women be conceived less in terms of specific facilities— though these are crucial—than as the political space opened within families, neighborhoods, and cities, starting with liberated churches, hospitals, or a protective ring within a kin or friendship network, a space where male coercion is not tolerated. In this case, rather than expect the battered woman to leave or denigrate those who stay, we will embrace the romantic ideal, held by so many battered women even in the face of physical crises unimaginable to most persons, that things can be made to work if obsolete fantasies of domination are driven from the scene.

## Note

1. Requiring at least one reported at-risk injury was expected to yield an extremely conservative estimate of prevalence in the emergency room because it excluded (a) victims whose injuries were fully accounted for in some other way, (b) victims who used the service for problems other than injury, and (c) victims who were prevented by assailants from accessing emergency medical services when they were injured but who used other medical services for problems related to domestic violence. In any case, these data cannot be generalized to the population at large.

# Imagining Woman Battering

*Social Knowledge, Social Therapy,*
*and Patriarchal Benevolence*

## Frances Cobbe's Dilemma—Circa 1870

In 1878, the *Contemporary Review* published a startling exposé by British journalist Frances Power Cobbe. Working its way from historical evidence to current court data and the latest headlines, mixing feminist polemic with a subtle analysis of the economic roots of woman battering, "Wife Torture in England" is as comprehensive and profound as anything published since.

Cobbe (1878) follows wife beating from the "blow or two" delivered occasionally in the gentleman's drawing room through "thrashings" with a fist in London to its "climax" in the overcrowded centers of manufacturing, trade, and mining in the north, where tramplings and "purrings" with hobnail boots were common. It is here, among the artisan and laboring classes, among "colliers, puddlers, weavers,

AUTHORS' NOTE: This chapter is adapted from Stark and Flitcraft (1983).

shoemakers, stonemasons, butchers, smiths, tailors" and especially among itinerant Irish laborers, that "the political disabilities under which the whole sex still labors" (p. 58) press down most heavily.

Cobbe touches on the proximate causes of the problem, linking wife beating to alcohol, jealousy, job frustration, poverty, and even to the aggressiveness of certain "hateful viragos" whose husbands live in terror of their wives and must be drunk before attacking them. But she is less interested in why particular men are violent than in the "fatal root" of the problem. Though the most brutal violence occurred among the poorest social strata, the mystery was why the "persistent torture of women" in the laboring classes was so widely tolerated. The answer, she felt, lay in

> the notion that a man's wife is his PROPERTY, in the sense in which a horse is his property (descended to us rather through the Roman law than through the customs of our Teuton ancestors). . . . Every brutal-minded man, and many a man who in other relations of life is not brutal, entertains more or less vaguely the notion that his wife is his *thing,* and is ready to ask with indignation (as we read again and again in the police reports), of any one who interferes with his treatment of her, "May I not do what I will with my own?" (p. 62)[1]

No matter what its immediate cause is in a given home, because domestic torture is rooted in the subordination of women, nothing short of full political and economic equality can bring it to an end.

Frances Power Cobbe entered political life in the 1850s as the leading spirit behind the Society for the Prevention of Cruelty to Animals. The society's strategy was straightforward: Gather and publicize "social facts"; then join with friends in Parliament to propose appropriate legislative reforms. The Cruelty to Animals Act condemned violators to 3 months imprisonment, with or without hard labor. Next, the society took on the evils of orphanages, child exploitation, and child abuse, with similar success. The defense of helpless animals and children provided women with a forum to attack masculine domination publicly (Kate, 1994). Liberals such as John Stuart Mill shared Cobbe's belief that the superior endowment of the "respectable" classes obligated them to protect the less fortunate from moral degeneracy, ignorance, sickness, and physical harm.

But when Cobbe and her friends shifted from poodles, donkeys, and children to women who were victims of male violence, the strategy became problematic. On this issue, it seemed, their erstwhile allies—the "good men" from the "respectable classes" could not be completely trusted. Cruelty to animals and even to children originates in the idiosyncratic moral degeneracy of particular individuals. Expose these horrors and the leaders of respectable society will act on the victim's behalf. In contrast, Cobbe (1878) insists, wife torture is widely tolerated because "good" men derive real benefits from the sexual inequality it supports. Although its forms may vary, sexual subordination is a unifying fact of political life.

Believing that "wife-beating properly so-called" deserved a distinct response, Cobbe campaigned for reforms ranging from a 6-month prison term for assailants to state-guaranteed alimony while the batterer was in jail. One product of this campaign was the Wife Beaters Act of 1882, allowing courts to confine wife or child beaters in the pillory for up to 4 hours and permitting long prison sentences and whipping for a second offense.

Cobbe worried that existing laws might go unenforced. But she harbored even graver fears of the effects on women when the law was enforced. Given the political benefits of wife beating to the middle classes, patriarchal benevolence might prove a mixed blessing. By punishing only the worst incidents of wife torture, Cobbe predicted, court intervention would implicitly set a standard of toleration for "normal" wife beating, thereby actually increasing the average level of women's misery that was to be officially permitted, particularly in those classes where intimidation rather than persistent brutality was the primary means of control. Through its actions, the court was defining wife beating solely in terms of severe assault, again rationalizing rather than challenging (nonviolent) male domination in the middle classes. To this extent, the law managed the problem of wife beating by giving it official notice and definition, but it did not resolve it.

Though Frances Power Cobbe was a working journalist, her critique of protectionist policies for women derived from an important theoretical insight. Observing how particular material circumstances shaped the expression of violence in each class, Cobbe (1878) argued that state intervention is best understood as a way of integrating, rationalizing, and regulating these different responses into an overall pattern of male dominance. In other words, in imagining woman battering, in projecting various images and practices of how male violence should be controlled, state policies were framing and reforming the subordination of women, not bringing it to an end.

This sets the theme of this chapter, that behind official concern with abuse one must always suspect an ideological affinity among those who document the evils at the heart of family life, those who treat these evils, and those who would enact policies to reshape patriarchal authority whatever the personal costs for women and children. The dilemma Cobbe framed—that regulating women's treatment can extend inequality—has enormous practical importance for proponents of women's rights. Because female inequality is the basis for wife beating in the first place, the long-run consequences of protectionist policies to stop male violence may outweigh short-run gains.

## The Evolution of Benevolence: 1870-1970

Cobbe's fear that wife beating would persist in the face of state intervention now seems prophetic. Although all other types of violent crimes, including assaults, had declined in England and the United States by the end of the 19th century, the proportion of husbands involved in wife beating remained constant (Ross, 1993, p. 84). This was in spite of the widespread criminalization of wife beating in the latter half of the 19th century.

Virtually every 20 years after Cobbe (1878) wrote, the popular press joined women's groups and charitable organizations to denounce family violence in the strongest terms. After reaching a peak, however, public interest quickly receded, leaving only the most modest reforms in its wake. Although wife-beating laws remained on the books, by the 1920s the focus of state management had shifted from "brutal men" to "neglectful moms" and delinquent teens (Gordon, 1988). Concern with women's safety in the home resurfaced in the 1930s and the 1950s. In the meantime, women won most of the political rights Cobbe advocated to end male tyranny. In the 1970s, optimism about family violence was quickly shown to be premature by survey data indicating that between 12 and 15 million women in the United States were in abusive relationships (Straus, Gelles, & Steinmetz, 1980).

Cobbe (1878) made two related claims. When it came to state intervention in domestic violence, she believed, the defense of male privilege would outweigh progressive ideals. As important, when the state did intervene, she predicted, even as it regulated certain aspects of wife torture, its actions would extend and rationalize the other aspects of inequality to which wife battering was linked.

The role of benevolence is a good deal more complex today than in 1878. Victorian reforms were the work of political amateurs and a relatively small segment of the upper middle class. Cobbe and her American counterparts were "muckrakers"; research and practice were grist for publicity and reform. Today, the protection and care of the downtrodden belongs to a mass of professionals in health, psychology, social work, philanthropy, and the like. Problems are still treated at an individual level. But interventions are devised for broad categories of social suffering and embedded in normative practices in which these professionals are licensed by the state, meriting the term *social therapy*.

Victorian benevolence derived its authority from its connection to wealth and the paternalistic moralism of the upper classes. In contrast, regardless of their employment, today's professionals occupy a nether-world that is of neither class nor party. More important for our pur-poses, they construct their worldview from a massive body of images and facts produced by yet other, equally large, groups of professional scientists, social scientists, journalists, and the like whose proficiency at framing problems makes Victorian efforts look primitive. No contem-porary altruist would dare address a problem without the official sanction of this body of social knowledge.

The coexistence of edifices devoted to the production of knowledge about social problems and to their treatment is perhaps the greatest change since Cobbe's day. From the urban hospital to the shelter for homeless families, these two worlds are integrated in a vast institutional network to which people come in droves, seeking help for every form of suffering imaginable. Officially, these institutions merely provide a roof beneath which practitioners of therapy ply their trade. In reality, the sheer size, economic weight, and ideological importance of this network give it a central (though by no means homogeneous) role in defining who we are and in shaping the presentation of myriad personal troubles into the public issues about which we insist something be done.

If the accumulation of knowledge and practice around a given social problem helps set the policy agenda, it is also true that official attention— particularly as it constrains the flow of resources, people, and ideas within and between service networks—shapes which public issues will be experienced and treated as personal problems. Indeed, if one under-stands public policy to encompass all the official and quasi-official initiatives that bear on an issue, from research and education through policing and taxation, it is apparent that the what, where, when, who, and why of a given social problem are set as much by where official attention is focused as by research or clinical experience. How a public problem such as wife beating is defined determines how one imagines those who commit and suffer it, what motives are ascribed to their behavior, how they think about themselves, and, ultimately, their future prospects. Policy deploys social knowledge and social therapy, exercising its power less by directly oppressing us, less as a power over or external to us, than by circumscribing our field of belief and action. Like a microwave oven, the discourse of benevolence through which an issue such as battering is projected operates from the inside out, teaching us to reflect on the problem, to be reflexive, to take the point of view of the practitioner toward ourselves, examining, diagnosing (literally "seeing through"), and producing truths about who we are that move us into experience in certain ways. As in the microwave, so in the world of benevolence, the heat only appears to come from the light. In reality, as in Cobbe's day, we frame our experience with the categories acquired in the emergency room, classroom, and courtroom because this is where our lives acquire their social materiality, the stuff of health, learning, justice, domesticity, and the rest without which civil society is unimaginable.

Has the assignment of benevolence to specialists in research, therapy, and policy making eliminated its problematic character when it comes to wife beating? To answer this question, we analyze how partner violence against women was imagined in Great Britain and the United States at the moment when the modern battered women's movement was born. Two elements are added to Cobbe's (1878) postulates. Cobbe clearly articulated the roots of woman battering in sexual inequality as well as the limits maintaining this inequality placed on overall social development. But she failed to see how preserving male privilege mollified discontents rooted in economic or racial injustice or how, conversely, the state's response to sexual inequality mediated convergent inequalities in race and class. Cobbe's picture of injustice against women clearly highlighted the civil liberties dimension of the problem. But she had little to say about how the forces for positive change, of which she herself was a part, helped set the public agenda.

## COBBE'S DILEMMA—CIRCA 1990

At first glance, Cobbe's (1878) argument feels as outdated as the magazine in which it appeared. Nothing seems more marked about the current response to wife battering than its deep penetration of every layer of society.

In contrast to previous cycles of concern, when wife beating quickly disappeared from view, in the mid-1990s, 20 years after the first shelters for battered women opened in England and the United States, support is growing, not diminishing. Four differences are marked. First, although feminist reformers such as Cobbe in Britain and Elizabeth Cady Stanton in the United States played an important role in publicizing wife beating, the primary pressure for reform in the past came from moral puritans and law and order advocates (Pleck, 1987). The driving force today is the women's movement. Second, although community-based programs for victims were attempted in the 19th century, today's movement is rooted in a new, woman-based institution that provides safety and advocacy for victims in thousands of communities in the United States and Great Britain and throughout most of the developed world— the battered woman's shelter. Third, federal, state, and local governments have injected millions of dollars into community-based programs, creating a freestanding political interest in sustaining woman battering as a focus of concern.

Perhaps the most important difference today is the interest shown in wife torture by the infrastructure of social knowledge and social therapy. Although some sectors of this system have responded sluggishly, by the early 1990s, policing, medicine, psychiatry, education, the courts, and the child protection system had implemented procedural reforms to stop wife beating. Meanwhile, since the first scholarly pieces on wife battering were published in the 1970s, more than 2,000 articles and dozens of doctoral dissertations and books on the problem have appeared. A new social knowledge of family life has documented the physical abuse of millions of women and children in their homes on a regular basis by adult males with whom they are presumed to be intimate.

In sum, many of those about whom Cobbe (1878) was most skeptical are at the forefront in denouncing family violence. So successful is this movement, so prevalent are working relationships between the opponents of violence against women and the forces of regulation (police, courts), healing, and research, that it seems churlish to suggest of the current alliance what Cobbe observed about the old, that it may actually help evoke the very social reality it claims to oppose. Or has benevolence really discarded its patriarchal cloak?

Recent accounts of domestic violence in the United States and Britain signal a major shift away from the romantic images that dominated discussions about the family and privacy since at least the 17th century. In the past, wife beating was occasionally defended as a male preroga-

tive, albeit against an ideal of domesticity that was set against the
capitalist marketplace, that "jungle filled with wilde beasties." In contrast, the new imagery pictures family violence as tragic but as a
somehow inevitable by-product of culture, personal history, or even
family life itself, a chronic situation requiring what the French sociologist
Jacques Donzelot (1977) terms *permanent policing*. If, as family researchers Suzanne Steinmetz and Murray Straus (1973) insist, the family
is the cradle of violence, how are we to prevent it? Because "abolishing
the family" is not a popular alternative, the implication is that we should
invest heavily in its public scrutiny and restraint.

Here then is Cobbe's (1878) dilemma in a new guise. For if violence
is intrinsic to how we imagine families, certain groups, or cultures, the
risk is great that management strategies may go far beyond what women's
advocates intend. Cobbe warned against moving so zealously ahead that
we inadvertently recruit the benevolent patriarchs to a disciplinary
project that reverberates against ourselves. Indeed, sympathetic critics
have already observed the conversion of the battered women's movement into a service that constrains and disciplines the women it is
supposed to protect (Loseke, 1992).

The literature on battering is silent about the potential dilemmas that
arise from relying on patriarchal benevolence for protection from male
violence (cf. Walker, 1990), let alone about the larger sociopolitical and
economic context in which the regulation of domestic violence is played
out (cf. Pleck, 1987). The social knowledge of battering is presented to
social therapy and the state de nouveau, as a discovery of a heretofore
hidden reality, and all parties to the policy debate accede in this illusion.
This is true even of otherwise excellent histories of the battered women's
movement by Schechter (1982) and Dobash and Dobash (1992). As
knowledge marches on, there is no sense that the new images projected
about women and families may lean as heavily on political ideology as
the old romantic images of domestic bliss.

One way to address this conceit is to compare the same ostensible
phenomenon—what we call the imagining of woman battering—in
different historical and political settings. Very different constellations
of knowledge, therapy, and policy formed around partner violence
in Britain and the United States. Similarly, these constellations were
deployed in very different ways to solve specific problems of regulation.

In Britain, battering was initially traced to the cycle of deprivation
whereby the poverty and attendant immaturity of one generation presumably evoked this behavior in the next. In the United States, despite

a wider variety of approaches, most assumed that persons who hit or are hit as adults learned this behavior from their parents or culture (Straus, 1977-1978; Walker, 1979). In this account, the battered woman is pictured as a pathetic victim of circumstances, a pattern we term *social genetics* because it implies that one set of social tragedies leads automatically to another.

## England: Mugging, Battering, and the Cycle of Deprivation

In August 1972, the British media borrowed the term *mugging* from America and began applying it regularly to robberies committed by young adults where force was threatened or used. The phenomenon was neither new nor rising. But its public redefinition and the importation of the label from America elicited and legitimated a specific intellectual and political response. The label moved speedily through what Hall, Critcher, Jefferson, Clarke, and Roberts (1979) call its *career,* changing from an image in American media to an image of America in Britain to a widely accepted image—and forecast—of British society. The context imported with the label recast council estates as slums and ghettos where lawlessness created a need for law and order. As sociologists studied the "minority problem" and government statisticians divided crime figures by race for the first time, the notorious SUS laws were introduced and used to stop and search young blacks in Brixton and elsewhere. In the midst of sharply rising unemployment, the image of the mugger provided a ready scapegoat for fear and anger. By recasting its future in racial images adapted from the American media, Britain justified expanding political control over black immigrants, school leavers, and other riotous segments of the working class.

Neither the career nor the political role of domestic violence in Britain is as clear. Hall et al. (1979) think the media's inherent interest in violence made mugging an excellent source of legitimation for expanded state repression. But a distinct absence of public attention has always legitimated violence against women. The mugger, rapist, and child beater were held in contempt. But not the wife beater. Despite highly romanticized reports of its regulation in feudal Europe, wife beating until very recently ranked with banditry as a widely accepted social crime, that is, as an individual act serving a larger—and positively sanctioned—social purpose. If its meaning has changed, it is because the balance of power has shifted between the victims of violence and those who benefit from it, a shift reflected at the center of knowledge and service.

Whatever the differences between the phenomena, the discovery of domestic violence has elicited images that are in every way as mystifying as those elicited by mugging. Thus, whereas 19th-century references to wife beating suggest its legitimate use to discipline lower-class "viragos," the current discussion of battering simultaneously recognizes the seriousness of the act and transforms it into an anonymous, almost irrational process with no clear social location, an act requiring professional interpretation and management, not simply punishment. Muggers are no more recognizable than hired assassins. But the newspapers picture them nevertheless, head lowered, young, black, and handcuffed, their particularity a caricature of the fear of attack rooted deep in the collective unconscious. By contrast, the batterer is known, both by his victim and those to whom she turns for help. He is accessible and within limits, completely predictable. Yet unless a homicide results, the batterer is never pictured as such. His remains a crime apparently without authorship. Nor is he given official recognition by the services. The state invests the mugger with interest, using his crime and punishment to link fear for personal safety to the protection of private property. But the state attends to battering only reflexively, because its victims demand attention and it is their story that makes news.

As the terms *wife torture* or *battering* suggest, victims of partner violence are not just hit. Neither temporary protection nor shelter will suffice to protect the battered woman. Indeed, the damage to women's selves that researchers have uncovered is so fundamental that some form of basic reconstruction is called for. The issue, of course, is whether the victim, the perpetrator, or some other constellation should be targeted.

Mugging is publicized in ways that conceal the normative violence of the status quo, racial discrimination or malnutrition for example, behind isolated acts of estranged aggression that call forth precisely that extension of state intervention that underlies normative violence. To this degree, the images of mugging and rape are analogous. Both instill a sense of vulnerability in the public and a corresponding dependence on police authority in the case of mugging and a "strong man" in the case of rape (Marcus, 1992).

In contrast, the image of battering is constructed to do two things. First, by portraying family problems apart from their political context, the new imagery ideologically separates the subordination of particular homemakers to "bad" husbands from welfare state policies that reinforce female subordination along a broad front. Even as families become the stage where failings of state benevolence are expressed in escalating fights, the conceptualization of this hostility is designed to evoke ever higher levels of state protectionism. From the standpoint of working-class women, domestic battering, mugging, rape, and the omnipresent dependence structured by welfare policies often feel like mere variations on a unitary theme of estrangement in a world "haunted by men" (Gordon & Riger, 1991).

Second, in Britain in particular, the social knowledge of battering works to separate poor or immigrant women from so-called normal others. It also separates the family as the good and proper source of personal discipline in the community and political solidarity in the state from pathological households apparently incapable of sustaining appropriate domestic standards. The genealogy of abuse is held to lie deep within the body or personality of its participants or in their culture, and there is no suggestion at all (as there is in the American image of abuse) that violence results from the politics of family life as such.

The evolution of the British image began with the story of Erin Pizzey, the courageous founder of Chiswick House, the first battered woman's shelter in the current period. Pizzey (1974) describes how the house she opened as a meeting place for neighborhood women was immediately filled by victims of abuse. By now it seems so natural to identify abuse as the distinguishing characteristic of these women that we forget the political context in which the demand for emergency shelter arose or its early and continued links to the expanded intervention of the welfare bureaucracy in the lives of the poor.

In fact, women initially gathered around Chiswick to demand economic justice, oppose racial discrimination, and, most important of all, secure housing. The demand for shelter is incomprehensible apart from the chronic housing shortage in postwar London, the marginal status of immigrant families thrown aside by massive disinvestment in jobs, and the subjective expression of these conditions, the fact that more than 100,000 persons were already squatting in London when Chiswick opened. What was new was not the "solution" (free housing for poor families) but the emergence within the free housing movement of female resistance to male domination. What was also new was the identification of male power with physical abuse.

The public definition of Chiswick as *the* battered woman's shelter par excellence evolved as part of a broad political dialogue about how to define the problem of the poor as well as women's problems. At issue was whether the new militancy in immigrant communities was best managed through repression (the position of the Tories), through structural change (the position of the Labour left), or by rationalizing the welfare state (the moderate position among Labour and the Liberals).

Pizzey (1974) fails to explain the importance of the fact that Chiswick was initially funded by Bovis, the building conglomerate owned by Sir Keith Joseph, then conservative secretary of state for social services (Marsden, 1978). More than any other figure, Joseph was identified with the view that "inadequate people tend to be inadequate parents and that inadequate parents tend to rear inadequate children" (Townsend, 1975, p. 12). This proposition exemplifies social genetics because it is constructed as if one social affliction leads inevitably, almost organically, to another presumably less primary affliction, and in a virtually unmediated way.

More than 100 refuges were founded in Britain after Chiswick opened, primarily by Women's Aid, a feminist coalition that consistently advocated a political solution to battering to supplement the provision of emergency shelter. But Pizzey's (1974) account of abuse remained the source of "authentic" knowledge in the British media. Like her sponsor, Pizzey argued that domestic violence was transmitted intergenerationally and that battered women had an abnormal need for violence (Pizzey & Shapiro, 1981). Because of this, psychiatry was the appropriate means to address abuse, not law or politics, as Women's Aid contended. Stories of Pizzey's clients typically accompanied her argument.

Pizzey's rise to media mogul was quickly followed by scholarly support for the cultural stereotypes she evoked. Invited by Pizzey to interview Chiswick residents, psychiatrist J. J. Gayford presented residents with a catalogue of problems that included divorce, teen marriage and pregnancy, drug abuse, alcoholism, illegitimacy, and child abuse. Gayford lacked a control group or any other comparative source of information about the prevalence of these problems in the general population. As a result, regardless of which problems women identified or in what number, he was able to present the results in the form of "rates" of social pathology that seemed to stand on their own. Because these rates were produced by women who were battered, he concluded there was a causal chain validating the psychiatric hypothesis.

Battered women, Gayford (1975a, 1975b) concludes, are pathetic, almost childlike individuals on whom social inheritance has imposed tragic, yet somehow inevitable, choices. Gayford (1976) says, " 'Such women need protection against their own stimulus-seeking activities.

Though they flinch from violence like other people, they have the ability to seek violent men or by their behavior provoke attack from the opposite sex' " (Parliament, 1974-1975, p. 37). Gayford's ambiguous reference to "other people" evokes an image of supposedly normal persons who presumably can control their stimulus-seeking activities and who lack "the ability" to provoke attack.

Thus, a policy imperative (framed by Sir Keith Joseph) led to support for a particular intervention (the Chiswick refuge) and analysis (Pizzey, 1974), and this, in turn, generated a social knowledge of pathology to support it (Gayford, 1975a, 1975b). The circle was completed when, in 1975, the Select Committee on Violence in Marriage concluded open hearings by citing Gayford's data as the source of its image of the battered woman as someone who had "been inadequately prepared for adult life" (Wilson, 1976, 1983). The committee believed that upbringing in violent or disordered homes (i.e., the homes of the poor) disposed battered women to violence in adult life. Policymakers concurred that battering signified deprivation. At the same time, deprivation was reduced to a multiplicity of inevitable pathologies among which battering was prominent.

As important as this imagery was in framing woman battering, tracing poverty to a self-perpetuating cycle of deprivation also gave the Thatcher government a handle on rising militancy, particularly among urban immigrants, as well as left-wing demands for structural reform. Constrained by this context, what began as a militant initiative to create a range of services sensitive to the specific justice needs of women was quickly transformed into the "battered woman's refuge," a form of social therapy premised on a number of negative stereotypes of poor immigrant women. Although borrowing heavily from previous theories of poverty, the social knowledge of battering emerging from the Chiswick refuge offered new and seemingly independent proof that poverty and pathology lay behind violence, not sexual or class inequality. In the end, the Joseph-Pizzey-Gayford image of the battered woman provided support for Joseph's strategy, stepped-up intervention in the daily lives of the poor by caseworkers, home visitors, and the like.

## America: The Social Construction of the Violent Family

The economic crisis in Britain evoked a political response that targeted militancy among the working poor, employed social knowledge—

including knowledge about interpersonal violence—that blamed the poor for their own victimization, and emphasized crisis management and individual casework. Policymakers in the United States also were concerned about the poor as well as the cultural recomposition of the workforce and the resulting challenges posed to traditional forms of authority by women, immigrants, blacks, and youth. But their main focus was on the family as such, an arena where they believed there was a consensus among professors, professionals, and policymakers. President George Bush (1992) summed up two decades of discussion about drugs, crime, poverty, welfare, violence, and education when he concluded, "the major cause of the problems . . . is the dissolution of the family" (p. 9). Thus, the social knowledge of wife abuse in the United States has been framed by and has helped to frame the larger problem of managing the "crisis in the family."

The fact that U.S. policy addresses partner violence across social classes reflects the relatively greater influence of feminists in the United States than in Britain, their greater importance in the labor market, and, in local communities at least, their political independence. These same factors, however, also contributed to the family crisis that policy set out to address. Although it gives perfunctory acknowledgment to sexual inequality, the scholarly work most often cited in the U.S. debate portrays wife battering as one instance of a pattern of family violence (including child abuse, peer violence, and elder abuse) to which families are predisposed by their peculiar history, dynamic, or culture, what sociologists Straus et al. (1980) call *social heredity*.

The postwar American family was a composite of conflicting forces. Following Henry Ford's understanding of market dynamics, postwar Keynesianism saw the family-to-factory-to-Ford connection as the key to economic growth. The governing assumption was that, with prosperity returned, children would follow their fathers to the factory and then, like their fathers, employ rising wages for family consumption, thereby stimulating industrial growth and reducing social expenditures. The formula depended on postwar contracts that tied higher wages to increased productivity and the willingness of women to abandon the labor market and resume their domestic work of balancing the demand for consumer durables with other facets of family management. Two events undermined the theory. Demands for higher wages ran far ahead of productivity, leading to an unprecedented wave of bread-and-butter strikes and the displacement of significant portions of the wage package into future "benefits" with no immediate economic effect. As important, millions of women remained in the labor market though they shunned the factory, using their new independence to take their children and abandon the traditional family, both physically and spiritually. One result was that instead of displacing depression-level state expenditures for family support, prosperity increasingly relied on state subsidies for families and on an expanding service sector that supported these families and provided employment for female heads of households.

These and related changes put the family sciences in a quandary. The field's livelihood rested on the belief that the family was a world apart, a distinct institution with a distinct moral economy that required a distinctive body of expertise. At the same time, scholars were pressed to explain why family life for an increasing proportion of Americans had become inconceivable without state subsidies for basic necessities such as housing, food, medical care, clothes, education, child care, mental health, and old age benefits. The family was structurally and spiritually vulnerable as well. Not only the poor but millions of middle-class Americans now turned for routine family maintenance to a range of health, mental health, and social service professionals.

Family violence theory addressed this dilemma by projecting an image in which the distinctiveness of the family lay not in the nurturance it gave to moral, emotional, and private life—as the Victorians had believed—but rather in the peculiar forms of pathology to which it was susceptible. To illustrate this, researchers presented rates of various forms of violence contained in family life, contending that these, in turn, generated other forms of pathology, including criminal violence and war. In this schema, the previous concern for the sanctity of the home was reframed as a form of resistance, an elaborate artifice designed to shut out the gaze of researchers, treaters, and other specialists. Far from intruding in private matters, the intervention of social knowledge and social therapy behind closed doors was essential to the protection of those for whom the family was supposed to care most: children, women, and the elderly. Moreover, because family violence arose from the very nature of family life—from its emotional intensity, for example, or from power inequalities intrinsic to family roles—chronic scrutiny and social management were indispensable to its survival. This claim challenged the moral dichotomy between the state and private life so dear to conservatives. But in its emphasis on the state's role as protector of the innocent, this claim also reframed patriarchal benevolence in a way that seemed consistent with women's desire to "get out from under."

## FROM FAMILY HARMONY TO FAMILY CONFLICT

The model of family violence evolved gradually from the earlier emphasis on family conflict. Until the 1950s, family sociologists in the United States argued that family harmony was an essential component and reflection of family stability (Safilios-Rothschild, 1970). Women's distinctive role in achieving harmony was to manage the family's economic and psychic resources in peaceful competition with other families. By urging women to interpolate the "real needs" of their husbands and children through the medium of consumer durables, sociology joined mass advertising and economic theory in reconstituting the home as a fetish toward which family relations were now mere means. Family sociology gave product loyalty a moral reading and translated family dynamics into economic terms by accumulating data on attachments, emotional investments, exchange, and values.

Even before the Great Depression, women's assignment as managers of consumption conflicted with their responsibility for domestic bliss. As Ewen (1976) argues, a continuing theme since the 1920s was the alliance of modern advertising with housewives in defining the virtues of traditional domesticity as so many obstacles to the free alienation of their capacity for consumption and wage work. Craig's wife (Kelly, 1926) is portrayed as crazy in the 1920s play of the same name because she puts family success before personal virtue. The women and children in *Middletown* look almost hedonistic in their willing exchange of basic family supports for the Ford and other consumer delights (Lynd & Lynd, 1929). Much has been made of the resurgence of domestic imagery after World War II, presumably designed to rationalize women's exodus from wartime employment. In fact, however, despite the best efforts of Dr. Spock, Doris Day, Debbie Reynolds, and the rest to give the aura of domestic purpose to the new consumer fortresses constructed in the suburbs, women's labor market participation continued to climb after the war with barely a ripple. Films like *Diary of a Mad Housewife* (1970) echoed a theme popularized in David Reisman's (1953) *The Lonely Crowd* and William Whyte's (1956) *Organization Man* that overconformity with traditional mores was explicitly pathological.

Although millions of women used their rising wages and job opportunities to escape from conventional households, the vast majority employed consumerism to constitute their individuality through, as well as against, traditional family roles. The challenge to Keynesian demand theory was clear: Women's responsibility for consumption and a second wage instilled an aggressive individuality that threatened the familial basis for labor discipline and social demand. This was the problem taken up by the family sociology of the 1950s, namely how to interpolate women's new aggressiveness through conventional family arrangements. The consensus was that women should reconcile new responsibilities with old roles in the same ways that staff-line differences in the firm were resolved, through efficient task allocation, leadership, time management, and shared decision making. These were technical skills. Political skills were also needed, however, because women's relative share of power inside the home was changing as well, though this received less notice. Men were invisible in this analysis. No one asked who in the family decided what. What seems obvious in retrospect was that women were being asked to mind a store whose boss was no longer showing up for work.

Even as women's family roles were being redefined to contain their new aggressiveness, a subversive egalitarianism seethed below the surface. Adapting sociologist Talcott Parsons's ideas of family dynamics, functionalists in the social sciences remained optimistic about this process, explaining that family tensions were prerequisites for a higher equilibrium. But by the early 1960s, social critics such as Betty Freidan (1963) in the United States and R. D. Laing (1959) and his colleagues in Britain were observing that conflicts between individual assertiveness and family order were unlikely to resolve this simply. Realizing that newly discovered capabilities were incompatible with one's gender role could take a profound psychological toll (Laing & Esterson, 1980).

Alongside the technical work of time management and resource allocation, women now found they had the distinctly political assignment of keeping the lid on at home. Feminist writers emphasized that de facto discrimination prevailed in the marketplace despite women's formal equality—lower wages and job segregation reinforcing their dependence on husbands, for example (Hartmann, 1976). Within the household, however, the opposite trend was equally potent, namely that women (and youth as well) found themselves substantively equal (with access to money, mobility, and the like) but formally bound by the quaint conventions of patriarchy. The situation was not merely tense, it was inherently unstable, with a shift in one arena—an increase in divorce or the expansion of the service sector, for instance—reverberating in challenges to power relations in the other. A range of therapies prospered off the heady belief that families could confront these contradictions without being blown asunder. In the functionalist mainstream, meanwhile, power struggles were anesthetized by studies declaring that marital success could be achieved through conflict management. As if in anticipation of chaos theory, family systems theory acknowledged that the smallest change in one portion of the family's universe—a daughter joining a rock band, say—could throw the entire institution into spasm. This required identifying a family support system within the services to which one could return for periodic checkups.

Feminist writers such as Jean Baker-Miller (1976) went further still. Because the basis of the family is a structural inequality that privileges men over women and transmits a diminished sense of self through women's gender roles, family conflict is inevitable. Indeed it is desirable, at least so far as women are concerned, because psychological well-being requires challenging these roles and the power inequality that is their base.

If family conflicts were normative, it was nonetheless obvious that family preservation required that all parties agree to limit their means. Because there was no apparent reason why someone would voluntarily yield through negotiation what they could seize by force, to succeed, families needed a contract outlining compromises by both sides. This implied the relative equality of contending parties, the bone of contention in the first place. In assessing family breakdown, researchers returned to extreme behavior that made conflict and negotiation unworkable, physical violence as a cause of divorce, victim-precipitated homicide, and acquaintance rape (Levinger, 1965; O'Brien, 1971; Wolfgang, 1956). Often cited today as initiating the interest in family violence, the studies of Levinger (1965), O'Brien (1971), and Wolfgang (1956) were initially designed to show that resorting to force was an aberration that contrasted markedly with the relative durability of conventional families.

If failure to manage conflict led to breakdown in middle-class homes, studies also revealed that the key to pathology among the poor was a lack of impulse control, a biological deficit expressed through displays of inadequate socialization, such as delinquency, drunkenness, and street crime. In social work, the conflict paradigm devolved into the multiproblem family, a low-income household network apparently joined by mutual deviance. In practice, the image of the multiproblem family had less to do with the reality of particular families than with the projected inability of multiple agencies competing for dominance over the family terrain to reach agreement on how problems should be understood, interventions prioritized, or tasks allocated. "Territory" was assigned on a first-come, first-serve basis at periodic case conferences. With myriad specialties crying for access to families in trouble, it seemed positively un-American to highlight a single cause—such as racism or sexual inequality—as the source of family violence.

## FROM FAMILY CONFLICT TO FAMILY VIOLENCE

The urban riots, the Vietnam War, and the continued flight of women and youth from conventional families forced social knowledge and social therapy to reconsider their stand on family management. The first policy response to these events was more of the same. The Great Society programs introduced in the wake of the 1960s riots, for example, promoted the belief that social conflict could be institutionally contained through the maximum feasible participation of the poor in parallel structures of governance (a form of conflict management). As the diffuse demand for rights and resources was redirected toward intragroup competition for a larger share of the existing social service pie, collective anger turned inward. The result was an interpersonal calculus focused on trade-offs (e.g., schools for garbage collection) and again susceptible to Keynesian demand management.

The material ground for the attempt to use reasonable demands to open the political process quickly eroded, however, and with it the optimistic view of conflict and conflict management as a legitimate policy goal. Although real wages continued to rise through the 1960s, international competition, military spending, and President Lyndon Johnson's refusal to seek tax hikes or cut social consumption to support an unpopular war combined to close whatever space had existed earlier to integrate black and other groups of working poor into the economic mainstream. With the notorious Green Amendment to the Poverty Act, Congress turned the Great Society programs over to the entrenched, racist city bureaucrats they had been designed to supplant; the exclusion and repression of outsiders quickly followed. No longer would political violence or undisciplined social imagination be publicly interpreted as "social conflict by other means."

The multiple links between social policy and family policy in the 1970s are too complex to trace here. Suffice it to say, to paraphrase sociologist C. Wright Mills (1959), that public issues—including the change of official heart about urban militancy—were read back into the family as private troubles. With no economic place to put the urban poor, their political aggressiveness was reinterpreted as alternately criminal and deviant. A parallel reading was made of women's behavior, particularly in minority and other low-income households, and the mother-headed family was targeted for frontline observation and management. The connection was straightforward. The absence of strong fathers led inextricably to street violence by sons and pregnancy among teens. In the capable hands of Senator Daniel Patrick Moynihan (1973) and other policymakers from the Nixon years on, this connection was sufficient to justify reframing Aid to Families With Dependent Children (AFDC) as a quasi-pathological status requiring a new level of scrutiny and control.

It would be 20 years before the same rates of pathology and breakdown observed by Moynihan (1973) among black families in the 1960s would appear among white and middle-class families (Stark, 1992). In the meantime, policymakers sought a generic model of family functioning—a new social knowledge—compatible with new levels of therapeutic intervention. This was the problem that Straus, Steinmetz, and their colleagues addressed.

## THE FAMILY AS A CRADLE
## OF VIOLENCE: CONSTRUCTING THE THEORY

The announcement by sociologists Steinmetz and Straus (1973) that "the family is a cradle of violence" originated with a 1970 meeting of the National Council on Family Relations and the subsequent publication in November 1971 of a special issue of *Journal of Marriage and the Family* based on this meeting. Although neither the council nor its journal had taken previous notice of domestic violence, the pronouncement was based not on startling new research but on an ideological reformulation. What Steinmetz and Straus accomplished was to pull together research on conflict between various subgroups (peers, parents and children, husbands and wives) with fringe studies about family homicide and spousal violence that had been done to support the conflict model of family management. Next, they turned the conflict model on its head. Where the original work had sharply distinguished violence from the sorts of conflict believed fully compatible with family survival, researchers now placed these studies on a continuum, with parental discipline, spanking, and sibling fights presumably escalating over time into child abuse, wife battering, and spousal homicide. Admittedly, families hosting all these pathologies constituted a deviant subtype (the violence-prone family). But data indicating that at least some of these behaviors were virtually universal—with upward of 80% of families admitting to spanking, for instance—suggested that all families could be defined in terms of violence.

If behavior heretofore considered legitimate conflict was a precursor to brute force, conflict management was a doomed strategy. The distinction between conflict as a means to achieve change and violence outside the system had been key not only to the feminist analysis of family relations but also to the Great Society strategy of racial integration. Now, however, conflict was declared violence by other means. This meant that protest politics were a ruse. Worse, as the Republicans had insisted, it was preparation for civil strife. Identifying violence as a universal component of family dynamics also implied that its causes lay deep within the genealogy of family relations. Indeed, although Steinmetz and Straus (1973) highlight a number of contributing factors previously identified with family conflict (such as individualism and aggression), they place their major emphasis on the transmission of violence from one generation to the next through social heredity, the *intergenerational transmission of violence theory.*

The implications for therapeutic management were enormous. Because conflict was different than more severe violence only in degree, the latter could be prevented only if the former was suppressed. This implied an alliance between the softer therapeutic sciences, such as social work and psychiatry, and the police. Because women were a major victim of violence, they could hardly be charged with identifying or suppressing conflict. Thus, insisted the researchers, violence in the home deserved as much attention as crime in the streets (Steinmetz & Straus, 1974). Like Moynihan (1973) and the Nixon White House, moreover, researchers also implied that violence in the home deserved the same kind of surveillance and restraint. Second, because the potential for violence was universal and transmitted intergenerationally, surveillance and restraint must themselves be universal and ongoing.

In sum, the announcement that the family is a cradle of violence converged with and supported a parallel inability in the political arena to manage what had heretofore been seen as legitimate conflict initiated by women, youth, minorities, and the poor. In this reframing, the repressive and ameliorative functions of social therapy vis-à-vis families become inextricably linked. Set in the context of the collapse of Keynesian optimism, the invention of the violent family as a prototype mediated the routinized management of political conflict by the helping services at the level of interpersonal relations.

## THE VIOLENT FAMILY:
## CONSTRUCTING THE DATA

We have shown how Gayford (1975a, 1975b) in England constructed his research to produce results that supported the victim-blaming theories of Pizzey (1974) and Sir Keith Joseph. A parallel construction process in the United States supported the conclusion that some form of violence will occur in almost every family.

First, violence was completely abstracted from any juridical or historical framework and given a moral reading. Because almost any open instance of aggression in the home (from spanking through expressing anger as a form of release) was either violent in itself or led to violence, all had to be contained. Any implied or direct use of force, no matter how harmless in intent or consequence and no matter by whom, was violent and therefore undesirable. Sibling rivalry might be most common among children under 8 and spousal homicide might occur in fewer than 1 family in 10,000. No matter. As part of a single picture, these events bounded a world in which violence is as common as love (Steinmetz & Straus, 1973).

Next, the continuum was rooted by social genetics, symbolized by the claim that violence begets violence. Subsequent work generalized from risk ratios of very low probability events—such as witnessing severe violence as a child—to conclude that exposure to violence in childhood led ineluctably to adult violence. This same theory suggested, as one text announced, that "the family was a training ground for societal violence" (Steinmetz & Straus, 1973, p. 54), even for war (Owens & Straus, 1975). This helped explain the cliché that America is a violent society.

By this point, the family had lost all specificity. No longer a hierarchical structure of unequal authority materially based in work performed primarily by women, it had been reduced to a space in which rates of relative pathology were generated, a depoliticized terrain where human purposiveness in general and female subjectivity in particular were replaced by statistical probabilities of behavior fragments.

As in the work of Gayford (1975a, 1975b), the measurement tool called Conflict Tactics Scale replicated the researcher's underlying bias, in this case that violence was simply family conflict by other means. The politics of gender roles that led to woman battering—the fact that most violent episodes were initiated to enforce male control (i.e., to suppress conflict) rather than resolve disputes—disappeared behind a research tool that combined threats with actual hitting and considered these events apart from context, intent, or actual consequence (Straus et al., 1980). Female aggressiveness and the fights it precipitated were reduced to alternating statistical points on a seemingly naturalistic continuum with the use of a gun or knife to enforce patriarchal privilege. Looking at hitting rather than the cumulative control achieved through coercion, researchers calmly announced that the population of battered men actually exceeded that of battered women (Steinmetz, 1977-1978).

As in Britain, the development of a social knowledge of domestic violence in the United States was less a discovery of a heretofore hidden reality than a means of imagining partner violence that obscured the very inequalities it was given credit for revealing.

## Conclusion: Cobbe's Dilemma Reconsidered

Cobbe (1878) believed that state intervention to prevent violence against women was more likely to aggravate than ameliorate the problem, rationalizing wife torture while exacerbating sexual inequality. This was because the state's interest in preserving women's status as male property, the ultimate source of wife torture, would override the state's commitment to benevolence. We added two points, that the dynamics involving inequalities of class and race follow parallel and interrelated patterns and that the specific constellation of ideas, interventions, and policies surrounding domestic violence is related to the historically specific challenges mounted around these inequalities, particularly those involving women's rights. The issue we raised is whether Cobbe's critique deserves serious consideration today. We think it does.

In Britain, the prevailing view was that abuse resulted from an individual history of multiple pathologies, including a predisposition to violence, and was carried by immature personalities from one generation of poor to the next. This image was constructed from three elements: the cycle of deprivation theory developed by Sir Keith Joseph; the experience of Chiswick House, whose founder, Erin Pizzey, is a popular expert on abuse; and the findings of John Gayford (1975a, 1975b). Joined with the real-life stories presented by Pizzey (1974), Gayford's biased findings became the basis from which the Select Committee on Violence in Marriage supported the deprivation thesis of Sir Joseph. But the story only began here, because the political thread that joined social knowledge, social therapy, and social policy on wife beating in Great Britain was the desire to reconstitute the militancy of the immigrant poor as so many individual deficits requiring casework rather than social reform. By organizing the facts about domestic violence into a problem (the cycle of deprivation) whose solution seemed to lie in expanded intervention by the welfare state, the social knowledge of battering in Britain helped conceal the role of patriarchal benevolence in preserving social inequalities. The larger political role of social knowledge became particularly apparent when, after the Brixton riots in April 1981, the image of dependent subjects needing protection against their own violent impulses was extended from social science to police science and from a deprived minority to the entire immigrant population.

If the caseworker model advocated in Britain was a response to political unrest among the immigrant poor, the policing of family relations proposed in the United States was a response to an equally broad-based crisis in the basic unit of socialization. Despite the influence of feminism on the rhetoric of social research, the view dominating treatment was constructed in response to two contradictory pressures: the need to identify the family as a distinct sphere of private life in which social problems originated and the need to combat women's self-directed efforts at independence by reimagining and therapeutically reconstituting the family's inner life. By reading women's struggle for individuality as formally identical to the use of force to stifle their individuality and by interpreting wife abuse as a chronic aspect of the multiproblem character of the family as such, researchers reconciled these seemingly contradictory pressures, suggesting that the family's distinctiveness lay in its dependence for stability (and rationality) on interpretation, aid, and management. The image of the violent family whose inner tendencies toward fragmentation must be constantly monitored and repressed legitimated larger policy initiatives to police and ultimately to capture the unfolding subjectivity of women and youth.

In encompassing virtually all interpersonal conflict in its definition of the violent family, U.S. researchers invoked its opposite as an ideal: the peaceful, harmonious, and repressed family of yore. By the 1950s, economic and social changes in the United States had so destabilized this traditional family structure that the myth of family life as a haven from a heartless world could be sustained only with the full complicity (or management) of those to whom it was most transparent: housewives. The contradictions in this strategy were dramatically evident in the strata of family maintenance professionals that emerged off the income and mental health problems of women who tried to stay the course. Once the structural imbalances endemic to family life were acknowledged, so was the inevitability of conflict, hence of conflict management by women as the principal means of maintaining families. Family violence, in this view, was the outer limit at which conflict-management failed, usually when, in response to levels of conflict a partner or parent found intolerable, otherwise legitimate authority was abused.

All this changed as the women's movement and civil protests on an unprecedented scale politicized the options available to women and youth outside the traditional family structure. Even the conflict-management model appeared to have underestimated family instability. When the battered women's movement made it apparent that violence and coercion by men in response to conflict was so common as to be almost normative, researchers interpreted this in a linear rather than a dialectical way, concluding that conflict, fighting, and woman battering were part of a new constellation, the violent family, that required constant surveillance and constraint. If Gayford's (1975a, 1975b) denigrating imagery in Britain took life from media accounts of Pizzey's clients, the authenticity of social knowledge in the United States derived from evidence garnered from the numerous service settings where battered women went for help.

In both cases, as Cobbe (1878) predicted, the political logic from which wife battering arises—the attempt by men to use women as their personal property—was obscured by the conception of the battered woman as pitiable and self-destructive and of family life as a multifaceted battleground. Instead of revealing female subjectivity as intensely purposive and rational, the dominant images of wife torture showed it to be irrational, drawing its purposes by social heredity from an environment in which all struggle was defined as pathological.

## Postmortem: Social Therapy

Although social scientists often equate abstraction with any idea not immediately drawn from data, the classic meaning of the term is to take a phenomenon out of its context, to think it apart from the material reality through which it takes shape. In this sense, the social knowledge of domestic violence is abstract because it employs a dense account of events to conceal their historical and political determinants, mystifying the political basis of the knowledge itself and its potential use to dislocate, even to silence, the subjectivity of those it claims to save from silence.

This process of silencing occurs because the ways in which domestic violence is imagined are widely incorporated in therapeutic practices that constrain how women (and their assailants) understand and live their lives. As in Cobbe's day, protectionist policies in the courts distinguish "worthy" victims from "viragos," base intervention on a calculus of harm that throws relatively minor acts of coercion and control into relief as normal and forces women to defend themselves in criminal cases by claiming to have suffered permanent deficits—such as learned helplessness—rather than having responded rationally (with force) to domination. The process is vampiric. From neglect, medical labeling, mental hospitalization, and medication with tranquilizers through the removal of at-risk children from violent homes, there is a draining of life, a silencing, as stereotypic images of women's experience are deployed through the material constraints of multiple service encounters. The cycle is complete when the deadened result of a history of mistreatment is called on to validate the initial image of women who are either childish and dependent or willfully self-destructive. Even in the shelters, these constructs are the basis for dichotomizing women into those who are authentically battered (e.g., present impressive bruises, exhibit learned helplessness, etc.) and those who are not (Loseke, 1992), hence determining who will survive. So does social knowledge, like social therapy, develop through a distinct and negative correspondence to the subjectivity of its objects.

The fetishistic process extends to women in the population at large. As images circulate through the media and helping systems, victims of violence forget their own initiative, deconstruct their history into discrete episodes of assault, and adapt genetic rather than proactive views of their fate. Batterers too become estranged from their purposes, losing what restraint they have by learning to be out of control. Nonbattered women come to see themselves through the projected imagery as lucky to have suffered only domination as usual.

The body of the battered woman receives the bruises. But it is women's unfolding capacity to discard conventional family roles that is being attacked, re-cognized, and disciplined by the new patriarchal benevolence. Herein lies the quintessence of domestic violence that genetic explanations fail to grasp. Like battering, femininity is a single social practice rooted in continuous historical activity, in collective material and imaginative struggles to earn a living, to reproduce a community of loved ones, and to gain and sustain sexual pleasure. Like battering, femininity emerges from a complex of social relations through which the personal is joined with the political and conceptual. Whereas battering destructures the claims of a female subject to autonomy, however, the dynamic of femininity lies in the unfolding of this subjectivity on a broad front that extends far beyond the grip of individual men, even of social knowledge or social therapy. It was this knowledge—not her faith in patriarchal benevolence—that made Cobbe (1878) optimistic about the future.

## Note

1. Lest this be seen as idle rhetoric, consider the 1879 murder of Elizabeth Glover by William Hancock outside the Black Swan Tavern in London. Though Glover was repeatedly thrown to the ground in front of a crowd that included both a waiter from the tavern and a policeman, the crowd avoided intervening, according to the policeman, because everyone thought "they were man and wife" (Ross, 1993, p. 85).

# Part II

## Health Consequences

# Women and Children at Risk

*A Feminist Perspective on Child Abuse*

Feminist thinking has had a tremendous effect on how society defines and approaches woman battering, marital rape, and child sexual abuse. As a result, these phenomena are generally understood to be gender-specific crimes committed by men and rooted in sexual inequality. Feminist theory has had far less influence on the interpretation of child abuse, however. The prevalent view is that child abuse results from some combination of maternal pathology, inadequacy, and environmental stress. Where child abuse occurs against a background of other types of family violence, the presumption is that the violence is transmitted intergenerationally. A man who was beaten as a child now beats his wife. Unable to cope, she uses the child as a scapegoat. Because mothers are culpable—pathology is the key here rather than sexual politics—and because women appear as villains rather than as victims, feminist theories simply do not apply.

AUTHORS' NOTE: This chapter is adapted from Stark and Flitcraft (1988c). Reprinted with permission of the *International Journal of Health Services*.

There are exceptions. Williams (1980) suggests that sexism and pronatalism have taught abusive women that motherhood is the only fulfilling activity, which they resent. Breines and Gordon (1983) implicate a number of other gender-related issues in child abuse, including the fact that women are the primary parent, the lack of well-paid work alternatives to mothering, and the inadequacy of sex education (as well as contraceptive methods) leading to a large number of unwanted pregnancies. But even these analyses share the assumption that guides current child protection policy: Women are primarily responsible for child abuse, albeit provoked by sex stereotyping and the limits of their mothering role as well as personal deficits or a lack of coping skills.

To determine whether these assumptions are correct, we assessed the link between child abuse and woman battering and weighed evidence that abusive behavior reflects some combination of pathology and stress (the dominant view) against the possibility that it arises from a power struggle between partners.

A related issue involves the response to child abuse by the child protective service (CPS) system, a huge state bureaucracy that expends hundreds of millions of dollars annually to protect children by reeducating and servicing mothers and by removing children to foster care. How does this system respond when a woman's access to the resources needed to mother are forcibly denied her by her partner, that is, when she is battered? More to the point, if it turns out that violent men are primarily responsible for child injury rather than "sick" mothers, how does one explain the exclusive focus of child abuse research, services, and legal intervention on women and children? Finally, what are the prospects for reform?

## Child Abuse and Woman Battering: Gender Politics or Female Pathology?

### MOTHERS OR FATHERS?

A classic vignette of the physically abused child has been that of an undernourished infant with multiple musculoskeletal traumas inflicted at different times by his or her depressed mother. Child abuse has been variously traced to maternal violence or neglect in the family of origin (Steele, 1976); current psychological dynamics such as role reversal (Kempe & Kempe, 1976); a lack of parenting skills (Newberger &

Cook, 1983); poverty or other environmental deprivations (Gil, 1973); the absence of needed institutional supports (Newberger & Bourne, 1978); or some combination of provocation, psychological predisposition, and environmental trigger events (Helfer, 1976). Whether female psychology or a malfunctioning family system is emphasized, whether "destructive, disturbed mothers" are identified or merely "sad, deprived, needy human beings," the fact that abuse results from a breakdown in appropriate mother-child bonding is taken as self-evident. The normative character of female domesticity and mothering is an unquestioned presumption in child psychology, pediatric medicine, and children's services. Thus, the social consequences of adapting these images in problem solving remain unexamined.

But are children typically hurt by their mothers? Representative sample surveys indicate that fathers may be as likely as or more likely than mothers to abuse children. Director of the National Center for Child Abuse and Neglect (NCCAN) Bersherov (1978) testified that males were the perpetrators in 40% of all officially reported child abuse and neglect cases, and an American Humane Society (1978) survey concluded that males were the assailants in 55% of reported cases. Smaller surveys have produced somewhat different results, estimates of abuse by fathers running as low as 25% (Baher et al., 1976).

Once the division of child care responsibilities and the proportion of children raised by single women is taken into account, even the smaller estimates of men's overall involvement in child abuse are significant. More important, there is little doubt that if a man is involved in a relationship, he is many times more likely than a woman to abuse the children. For example, national survey data in the 1970s indicated that men were responsible for two thirds of reported incidents in which men were present (Gil, 1973). Surveys measure single acts without taking their consequences into account and cannot distinguish documented from alleged abuse or identify abuse resulting in severe injury or death. Of equal importance, punitive welfare regulations and fear of violence lead many women to conceal relationships with men and so to underreport. A study of hospital and medical examiners' records indicates that men bear the overwhelming responsibility for serious child abuse and fatality. In comparing the records of child abuse cases for two time periods, 1971 through 1973 and 1981 through 1983, Bergman, Larsen, and Mueller (1986) reported that although the incidence of hospitalized cases did not change, the proportion of severe injuries increased dramatically. The proportion of known male perpetrators reported also increased, rising from 38% to 49% for all cases and from 30% to 64% for severe cases. Meanwhile, the proportion of female perpetrators for all cases decreased from 32% to 20% and for severe cases from 20% to 6%. Fully 80% of the fatal cases in the most recent group were attributed to men; 20% were "unknown." None was attributed to women. Finally, if a male perpetrator was identified, there was a 70% chance that the child's injury was severe, up from 25% a decade earlier. The authors wisely suggest that the apparent increase in severe abuse by men—and the corresponding decline in cases categorized as unknown—reflects a growing willingness to report male friends, not an actual shift in violence.

## THE TRAUMA SAMPLE

Because men commit most domestic violence as well as most serious child abuse, there is a strong likelihood that these events are related.

In work comparing battered and nonbattered women using an emergency medical facility (Stark, 1984; Stark & Flitcraft, 1988b; Stark, Flitcraft, & Frazier, 1979), we found that child abuse occurred disproportionately in battering relationships. Whereas child abuse or fear of child abuse was noted among approximately 6% of battered women, fewer than 1% of the nonbattered women appeared to be mothers of abused children, a highly significant difference. Twenty-five of the 28 child abuse reports identified appeared in the records of battered women rather than controls. Extrapolating to the emergency medical population as a whole suggested that as many as two thirds of the patients who were mothers of abused children might be battered women. Information from a British shelter revealed that 54% of abusive husbands and 37% of abused wives had also abused their children (Gayford, 1975b). This would make domestic violence almost coterminous with child abuse and certainly its single most important context. Hilberman and Munson (1977-1978) also noted the connection between woman battering and child abuse, and one research team, using a volunteer sample of women, reported that 70% of batterers abused children (Bowker, Arbitell, & McFerron, 1988).

The rare estimates of spouse abuse in the child protection caseload have been markedly conservative. Based on official data from 25 states analyzed by the American Humane Association, Bersherov (1978) concluded that "spouses" were assaulted in only 20% of reported child abuse cases. The abusive male was responsible for the child's abuse in 70% of these cases, and the victim of spouse abuse was responsible in the other 30%. Despite the association, however, because the spouse abuse and child abuse did not necessarily occur in the same incident, Bersherov cautioned that "these data . . . should not be taken to establish a causal relationship between spouse abuse and child abuse" (p. 5).

Children in battering relationships face immediate risk of becoming covictims during an assault on their mother as well as suffering psychological consequences because of exposure to violence. Information from a British shelter revealed that 54% of abusive husbands and 37% of abused wives had also abused their children (Gayford, 1975a). Hilberman and Munson (1977-1978) report that one third of 209 children exposed to marital violence exhibited somatic, psychological, and behavioral dysfunctions. Meanwhile, in his local medical practice, Levine (1975) found that difficulty coping with children was a common presentation of woman battering. If the batterer's relation to the children was nonviolent, their response was limited to psychiatric problems. In instances in which children attempted to intervene and became surrogate victims, they became more aggressive in their other relations. Rosenbaum and O'Leary (1981), however, found no differences for male children among violent, discordant, and satisfactorily married couples on the behavior problem checklist. Interestingly, although Rosenbaum and O'Leary found no differences between abused and nonabused children in these families, 70% of the children whose mothers had been victims of spouse abuse were above the mean for a normative sample, suggesting that the psychological consequences of spouse abuse may be more serious for children than those of child abuse itself. Since this early work was undertaken, a substantial descriptive literature has developed on the long- and short-term effects of children's exposure to parental violence (Jaffe, Wolfe, & Wilson, 1990), though case control studies remain rare.

ALTERNATIVE THEORIES

How is the probable connection of domestic violence and child abuse best explained? A once common view, now largely discredited in the domestic violence field, was that psychiatric disease or severe behavioral problems (such as substance abuse) led women to enter and remain in abusive relationships as well as to abuse or neglect their children (Scott, 1974). Research has failed to identify a distinctive psychological pattern among battered women or to distinguish traits that predisposed women to accept violence. In our trauma study, we found that battered women experienced disproportionate rates of psychiatric and psycho-social problems but only subsequent to the onset of abuse, suggesting that the problems are a reaction to the battering, not its cause (Stark, 1984; see also Chapter 1, this volume).

A more plausible psychiatric case could be made that batterers are motivated by mental illness because research shows them to be emotion-ally distant, dependent, uncommunicative, jealous, obsessive, and fre-quently addicted to drugs and alcohol (Gondolf, 1990). Because these same characteristics typify nonviolent men in distressed relationships, however, they are most likely modal traits associated with male sociali-zation rather than indications of disease (Stark & Flitcraft, 1991).

A third argument is that family violence is a conflict resolution tactic partners have learned in childhood. Measuring conflict tactics, a nation-al violence survey indicated that women and men were equally prone to use force with one another and that abused women were 150% more likely to use severe violence with their children than were nonabused women (Straus et al., 1980). Other researchers argue that learning to use force to resolve conflict is culturally and racially patterned in violent families (Gelles & Straus, 1988) or "cultures of violence" (Wolfgang & Ferracuti, 1967), identifying inner-city, minority, and low-income groups as violence prone (Gelles & Straus, 1988; Schmidt & Sherman, 1993; cf. Stark, 1993).

Although men or women may use violence to resolve family conflicts, mounting evidence suggests that partner violence against women typi-cally occurs against a background of intimidation, isolation, and control over resources perceived to be scarce (Dobash & Dobash, 1979; Jones & Schechter, 1992; Stark, 1992). In this context, men initiate violence in lieu of or to suppress conflict, not as its extension. Although cultural mores obviously affect when, where, how, and with whom violence is used, race and class differences in domestic violence are small (Schulman, 1979) or nonexistent (Centerwall, 1984). We can hypothesize, therefore, that the pattern of coercion and control explains the link of domestic violence and child abuse. As important, because the coercion involved in battering is "gendered" (Dobash & Dobash, 1979; Stark & Flitcraft, 1991; see also Chapter 1, this volume), we can also anticipate that the motive for hurting the child is part of a larger strategy to undermine a woman's moorings as mother, wife, worker, and the like.

Hardest to dispel is the belief that both wife beating and child abuse are caused by a third factor, childhood exposure to violence that is transmitted intergenerationally. Empirical support for this proposition comes mainly from secondhand or anecdotal reports, psychiatric studies of unrepresentative or deviant populations (such as presidential assassins), and reports that use vague equations with "abuse" and "neglect," such as a "lack of empathetic mothering" (Steele & Pollock, 1974) or "a variety of less than ideal responses of the caretaker (usually the mother) to the infant," which lead to "a lack of confidence or trust" in the child as an adult (Steele, 1976). Although in better designed research Spatz-Widom (1989) found abused children statistically more likely than controls to be arrested for subsequent violence, the actual differences were small (29% versus 21%).

On the basis of their national population survey, Straus et al. (1980) report "a clear trend for violence in childhood to produce violence in adult life" (pp. 112-113). What their data actually show, however, is that although boys who experienced violence as children were disproportionately violent as adults, 90% of all children from violent homes and 80% from homes described as "most violent" did not abuse their wives. Conversely, a current batterer was more than twice as likely to have had a nonviolent than a violent childhood and seven times more likely to have had a nonviolent than a "most violent" childhood. Reviewing studies in this genre, Kaufman and Zigler (1987) conclude that no more than 30% of those who experienced or witnessed violence as children are currently abusive, an estimate we believe is too high. Even in Spatz-Widom's (1989) sample, for instance, 71% of the abused children were not currently violent. Although there is no way to extrapolate from Spatz-Widom's case controls to the larger population of currently violent individuals, presuming that the child abuse group is a small minority leads us to conclude that the vast majority of currently violent individuals were not abused or exposed to abuse as children.

THE FEMINIST THEORY OF BATTERING:
MALE CONTROL AND THE HELPING RESPONSE

The feminist theory of woman battering is distinguished by its emphasis on coercion and control as well as violence (Jones & Schechter, 1992; Stark, 1992), by the importance it places on how structural inequalities mediated by institutional discrimination against women support interpersonal dominance by men (Dobash & Dobash, 1979; see also Chapter 1, this volume), and by a critique that links the gendered nature of male authority to the oppression of females at all stages of the life cycle, from childhood to old age (Kelly, 1988). In developing this theory, we have also emphasized the role of the helping institutions in frustrating and even blocking women's attempts to escape from abusive relationships and entrapping them in ways that increase their vulnerability.

The conventional view is that women remain in violent relationships because their upbringing, personality, or behavioral problems, some the direct result of violence, predispose them to do so (Gayford, 1975a; Walker, 1979). Though psychological ambivalence is no less frequent in abusive than in other distressed relationships, the reality is that most battered women employ a range of escape, survival, and help-seeking strategies—including moving in and out of the relationship—before leaving. These strategies reflect three realities apart from any indecision— that the physical risks to women and their children are as great or greater if they leave than if they stay; that the control and isolation components of battering substantially reduce their resources; and, as important, that attempts to extricate themselves from the batterer's violence and control are frustrated, blocked, and subverted by those to whom they turn for help and protection. Despite the fact that the women we studied used a range of medical services for assaultive injury or related problems, clinicians rarely identified their problem correctly, minimized its significance, inappropriately medicated and labeled abused women, provided them with perfunctory or punitive care, referred them for secondary psychosocial problems but not for protection from violence, and emphasized family maintenance and compliance with traditional role expectations rather than personal safety (Kurz & Stark, 1988; see also Chapter 1, this volume). These interventions converged with the batterer's pattern of denial, minimization, and blaming the woman and reinforced the woman's sense of isolation, desperation, and entrapment. Behind clinical pictures of chaotic or multiproblem families, battered women came to know themselves as they were known, that is, as "crazy," seemingly verifying this diagnosis by self-medicating with drugs and alcohol.

## CHILD ABUSE: RESPONSIBLE MOTHERS, INVISIBLE MEN

Can child abuse be understood as an extension of this entrapment process, as a problem rooted in the politics of gender inequality, occasioned by male violence and aggravated by the institutional response? What role does the knowledge of child abuse—and the social service practice that follows from this knowledge—play in women's entrapment?

As the issue of domestic violence surfaced, sexist interpretations and practices were quickly challenged by a grassroots political movement. In contrast, child protective services appealed to stereotypic and patronizing imagery of women (Nelson, 1984). The result is that men have remained invisible in the system and mothers are held responsible for child abuse, even when the mother and child are being battered by an identifiable man.

Despite the overwhelming evidence that men are a significant subset and perhaps a majority of abusive parents, at this writing, excluding child sexual abuse, there are no articles in the child abuse literature specifically targeting male abusers. In her literature review, Martin (1983) found only two individual case reports about males. Even in the minority of studies that consider both parents, women are almost always the source of direct information, no attempt is made to control for gender or to differentiate parental behavior or motivation by sex, and "abusing parent" is often a euphemism for mother.

Men are equally invisible in programs for abusing parents. Starting with images of appropriate gender behavior such as mother-child bonding, interventions proceed as if noncompliance with these norms reflects a character deficit that puts mother and child at risk. Varying combinations of parent education, counseling, peer pressure, and sanctions are used to instill appropriate maternal behavior, presumably so that the mother will adequately care for and protect the developing child.

Broad moral conceptions of women's responsibility for violence are implicit in state laws criminalizing "the failure to protect." Typical is New York's statute defining an abusing parent to include one who "allows to be created a substantial risk of physical injury to the child." This is routinely interpreted to mean "allowing" a child to become a covictim of or to witness violence against the mother. In Connecticut as well as many other states, cases are filed under the mother's name (even if she is deceased) and only women are interviewed by child protective services in determining foster placements, a practice linked to high rates of child abuse in foster homes.

If violence is evoked by women's struggles to change and men to sustain traditional sex roles, the practical result of programmatically reinforcing these roles may be to restrict a woman's perceived options, increase her vulnerability to violence, decrease her capacity to protect her children from violence, exacerbate her frustration and anger, and increase the probability that she will be destructive to herself and others, including her children. This is what feminist theories lead us to predict.

## Battering and Child Abuse: A Study

Until now, our knowledge of links between domestic violence and child abuse has come solely from studies of battered women. As a result, there is no direct evidence of whether domestic violence is a significant precipitant of child abuse overall or, if so, how significant. It is possible, for example, that although children are at risk for abuse in battering relationships, battering is a relatively minor etiological factor in child abuse.

To develop a more complete picture of the relationship between child abuse and domestic violence, we studied a population of abused children and their mothers in the medical setting.

### STUDY POPULATION

At Yale-New Haven Hospital, the medical records of children suspected of being abused or neglected are specially marked or "darted" and the children are referred for investigation and disposition to a special hospital Dart Committee. The study population included the mothers of all children referred to the hospital Dart Committee for suspicion of abuse and/or neglect in a single year, between July 1977 and June 1978, 116 mothers in all. Dart Committee reports on children were matched to the medical records of their mothers, and the mothers were then classified as battered or nonbattered based on their adult trauma history and the risk classification described below. The analysis of medical records was supplemented by data from family background notes in Dart Committee reports.

### METHODOLOGY

The trauma screen employed in the study was designed to identify abuse in a population that had not been explicitly identified as battered and to generate sufficiently large groups of abused and nonabused women to permit statistical analysis and comparison. Each adult hospital visit prompted by trauma after the age of 16 was reviewed and women were assigned to a battering risk group according to the following criteria:

- Positive: At least one episode in the woman's trauma history was attributed to assault by a male family member or male intimate.

**TABLE 3.1**  Number of Trauma Episodes Among Battered and Nonbattered
Mothers of Abused Children

| Mother's Battering Risk Group | n | Number of Episodes in Risk Group | Mean Number of Trauma Episodes per Woman |
|---|---|---|---|
| Positive | 29 | 143 | 4.9 |
| Probable | 18 | 61 | 3.4 |
| Suggestive | 5 | 13 | 2.6 |
| Total at risk | 52 | 217 | 4.2 |
| Marital conflict | 6 | 11 | 1.8 |
| Negative | 58 | 64 | 1.1 |

- Probable: At least one episode in the trauma history was an assault (kicked, beaten, stabbed, etc.) but no personal etiology was indicated (note that muggings and anonymous assaults were not included in this category).
- Suggestive: At least one episode in the trauma history was not well explained by the recorded alleged etiology.
- Negative: All episodes in the trauma history were well explained by the recorded injury, including those sustained in muggings, anonymous assaults, and the like.

Data were gathered on (a) the significance of battering in families experiencing child abuse, (b) the identity of perpetrators, (c) whether mothers who were battered came disproportionately from problem homes (as some research suggests), and (d) whether current dispositions responded appropriately to the family situation.

FINDINGS: PREVALENCE
AND FREQUENCY OF BATTERING

Of the 116 women, 52 (45%) had a history that put them at risk for battering and another 6 (5%) had a history of marital conflict, though it was impossible to tell from their trauma history or other medical information whether they had been abused. Twenty-nine women (25%) presented positive episodes, an additional 18 (16%) were probables, and 5 (4%) were suggestive. Fifty-eight women (50%) had no documented trauma history indicating abuse and no record of marital conflict. This information is summarized in Table 3.1.

The 52 at-risk women presented a total of 217 injury episodes during their adult histories, for a mean of 4.2 trauma presentations per woman. Women in the positive group averaged 4.9 episodes each, whereas those in the probable and suggestive groups averaged 3.4 and 2.6 episodes.

**TABLE 3.2**  Problems in the Family Histories of Mothers of Abused Children

| Problem | Number Among Mothers in the At-Risk Groups,[a] N = 52 | Number Among Mothers in the Negative and Marital Conflict Risk Groups, N = 64 |
|---|---|---|
| Alcoholism | 6(12) | 12 (19) |
| Violence | 9(17) | 10 (16) |
| Suicide attempts | 5(10) | 7 (11) |
| Incest | 1(2) | 4 (6) |
| Chaotic family | 12(23) | 12 (19) |

NOTE: Values in parentheses represent percentages.
a. Includes the positive, probable, and suggestive battering risk groups.

By contrast, women in the negative group averaged only 1.1 injury episodes, as one would expect in a normal population. Interestingly, the 1.8 trauma episodes averaged by the six mothers with a history of marital conflict fell somewhere between the suggestive and negative groups (Table 3.1). Conceivably, this group constitutes a battering risk category outside the purview of an identification method based solely on trauma history. At any rate, for battered mothers as for battered women generally, abusive assault is an ongoing process, not an isolated incident.

FAMILY HISTORY

A frequent claim is that the link between battering and child abuse reflects a multiproblem family history that includes violence or other serious problems. This was explored by drawing information on alcoholism, violence, chaos or disorganization, suicide attempts, and incest, common indicators of a high-risk family history, from social services notes in the medical record and from Dart Committee files. To strengthen the conservative bias, women with a history of marital conflict were included with negatives. As shown in Table 3.2, a significant subpopulation of these 116 mothers came from high-risk families of origin. It is evident, however, that abused mothers did not typically come from multiproblem backgrounds, were far less likely to come from a background that included incest and/or alcoholism, and, perhaps most important, were no more likely to have a family background that included violence. In sum, battered mothers of abused children could not be distinguished by a background of family disorganization and, if anything, were less likely than nonbattered mothers in this group to have such a background.

**TABLE 3.3**  Reasons for Dart

| Mother's Battering Risk Group | N | Mother Needs Support | Neglect and/or Suspicious Injury | Abuse |
|---|---|---|---|---|
| Positive | 29 | 15 (50) | 5 (18) | 9 (32) |
| Probable | 18 | 6 (33) | 8 (44) | 4 (22) |
| Suggestive | 5 | 2 (40) | 2 (40) | 1 (20) |
| Total at risk | 52 | 23 (44) | 15 (29) | 14 (27) |
| Marital conflict and negative | 64 | 29 (46) | 23 (35) | 12 (19) |

NOTE: Values in parentheses represent percentages.

## REASONS FOR DART

Most children were darted because a clinician believed they were at risk of abuse, they were neglected or injured under suspicious circumstances, or the mother needed support to help her cope. As indicated in Table 3.3, only a minority were darted because of documented physical abuse. Children whose mothers had a positive history of being battered were twice as likely as the children of nonbattered mothers to be darted for actual abuse, however. Interestingly, they were also more likely to be darted because "mother needs support." At best, this represents a tacit recognition of the mother's predicament, because the battering was almost never noted.

The mothers in this study were selected because their children were darted in 1977-1978, the year before the research was conducted. Not surprisingly, therefore, almost all the at-risk trauma identified among mothers preceded the alleged child abuse. For these women, at least, child abuse developed against a background of ongoing battering. The research design did not allow us to determine whether child abuse might precede battering for another group of mothers who have not yet presented with an injury. Interestingly, the longest history of assault was associated with positive women whose children were also the most likely to be physically abused, suggesting that for this important subgroup at least, overall levels of violence may be an excellent predictor of children's risk, regardless of whether child abuse has yet occurred.

## IDENTITY OF THE ABUSER

Dart Committee reports give the identity of the parent believed responsible for abusing the child. For families in which the mother is battered, the father or father substitute was more than three times more likely to be the child's abuser than in families of nonbattered mothers. Approximately 50% of darted children of at-risk women were abused by the male batterer, 35% were abused by the mother who was also being battered, and the rest were abused by others or by both.

## REMOVAL OF THE CHILD

Of children darted for all reasons, almost one third were removed from homes in which mothers were being battered. This was significantly higher than the percentage of children removed for all reasons from families with nonbattered mothers. This might simply reflect the greater likelihood for children of battered mothers to be physically abused. To control for this possibility, we compared the disposition only for cases in which the children had been allegedly neglected or in which the mothers needed support. Here too, if the mother was battered, the child was far more likely to be removed from the home than if the mother was not battered.

## DISCUSSION

The findings support the hypothesis that woman battering—a dramatic expression of male dominance—is a major context for child abuse. Even a highly conservative definition of battering requiring that at least one abusive injury has been presented to the hospital revealed that 45% of these mothers were battered and another 5% were experiencing marital conflict. This frequency of battered women (45%) is 2.4 times greater than the frequency of battering we found among women presenting injuries to the emergency surgical service (18.7%), twice as great as the frequency of battering found in the prenatal clinic (21%), and greater than in any other group yet identified, including female alcoholics, drug abusers, women who attempted suicide, rape victims, mental patients, women who filed for divorce, or women using emergency psychiatric or obstetrical services (Stark, 1984; Stark & Flitcraft, 1991).

Despite their relative youth, the battered mothers of abused children had presented an average of four injury episodes to the hospital prior to their child's dart, only slightly fewer than the older emergency room sample. This lends credence to the theory that child abuse in these relationships represents the extension of ongoing violence and is an intermediary point in an unfolding history of battering. Further support for this view is provided by the fact that the children of battered mothers were significantly more likely to be physically abused than neglected and more likely to be physically abused than the children of nonbattered mothers. Furthermore, the male batterer appeared to be the typical source of child abuse, not a mother overwhelmed with problems.

A significant subgroup of battered mothers appeared to have abused their children. Even these mothers, however, were less likely to have had a violent or disorganized family of origin than the nonbattered mothers or the mothers of children darted for neglect. The data suggest that the child abuse population consists of two distinct groups, neglected children of mothers with a problematic family history and abused children of battered mothers whose background appears comparatively nonproblematic. The popular stereotype of the mother predisposed by her history to be battered and to abuse her child bears little relation to the women in this caseload.

To those familiar with child protective services, the response to families of battered mothers may be unsurprising. Like the child abuse literature generally, the files of the hospital Dart Committee were silent about domestic violence and the children's records rarely mentioned the man's violence. Instead, emphasis was placed on the mother's failure to fulfill her feminine role ("mother needs support coping"). In this setting, as in the literature, women were held responsible when things went wrong. Even when we looked only at children suffering "neglect," children of battered mothers were more likely than their counterparts to be removed to foster care.

Linked to the ultimate threat—that women will lose their child—were provider requirements that mothers improve their capacity for nurturing and homemaking. In many cases in which the mother was battered and so still at risk, she was labeled uncooperative for failing to identify her own abuse or how the child had been hurt. In these instances, case-workers listed the source of violence to the child as "unknown" or "other." These women may have defined the worker as their adversary, been afraid of the batterer's retaliation if they revealed the violence, or feared the withdrawal of welfare benefits if their relation with an unrelated man was discovered.

The fact that foster placement is more likely when a mother is being battered may reflect the dearth of tools available to manage violent men. Because this is clearly a punitive intervention from the mother's standpoint, it is ironic that it should be used so readily with women who are already at great risk. As a result of foster placement, these women often lose access to whatever meager supports accompany agency involvement. A more profound irony is that, as a group, the mothers most likely to lose their children presented the least danger of physical abuse. Despite the ideal of reunification, once the child was placed, the therapeutic focus shifted from the natural parents onto the child and the new milieu. The underlying problems—including any violence toward the mother—were ignored.

In summary, in the study population, men were primarily responsible for child abuse, not women; battering was the typical context for child abuse, not maternal deficits; battered mothers of abused children were less likely than nonbattered mothers as well as mothers of neglected children to have had a family background of violence or psychopathology; and the response of the child abuse system—including neglect of the violence, support for mothering, and removal of the child to foster care—was ineffective at best and punitive at worst. Given these findings, how can feminist theory help reframe child abuse?

## A Feminist Approach
## to Battering and Child Abuse

Feminists approach the family as a system characterized by inequity, conflict, and contradiction. As a structure of male domination, it shapes intersubjective life into rigid gender identities to which real needs are subordinated (Baker-Miller, 1976). At the same time, the family must also provide the interpersonal and emotional support needed for subjective differentiation, autonomy, and independence (Chodorow, 1985; Flax, 1985). The link between battering and child abuse can be framed by this dilemma.

Self-fulfillment is not attainable within gender roles defined solely by dependence on and service to others. Thus, it is inevitable that women will struggle to expand their options, including the option to engage openly in conflict, and it is appropriate for them to do so (Bernardez, 1987). Nevertheless, many men read these struggles as a threat to their control and respond with force and intimidation, seeking to subjugate children as well as their mothers or to subjugate mothers by hurting their children. As Baker-Miller (1976) writes, "Inequality generates hidden conflict around elements that the inequality itself has set in motion" (p. 14). In the context of gender inequality, every fight concerns both the issue at hand and the larger—and usually unspoken—issue of who will decide.

Ideologically, battering and child abuse are connected by the presumption that women's responsibilities as wives and mothers supersede their personal needs and social rights, including their need for independence and physical safety. By normalizing these responsibilities through theories of women's character and mother-child bonding, psychology provides health and social services with a rationale for basing the delivery of vital resources on women's acceptance of this ideology. Subsuming a woman's personal development to the stability of her family and her children's well-being jeopardizes both family stability and children's welfare.

## THE KNOWLEDGE OF MOTHERS

Research on child abuse continues to be dominated by pediatricians, child psychologists, and other professionals linked to the child protection bureaucracy. As a result, the knowledge base and practice of child protection form two dimensions of a single paradigm in which moral prescriptions about women's responsibility for child abuse are rooted in the alleged "evidence" of women's propensity for nurturing and mothering.

The psychological knowledge of women as mothers was largely developed through observational and interpretative studies that removed mothering from its political context, reinforcing pronatalist beliefs. The process is self-fulfilling. The dominance of pronatalist ideology is evident in the absence of adequate day care, health benefits, or educational opportunities for women; in huge wage inequities and job segregation by sex; in constraints that shape the structure, content, and intensity of women's relationships to their children. Housewives subjected to these constraints exhibit high rates of situational depression (Brown & Harris, 1978). Behind housewife depression lie "high levels of anger and conflict towards husband and children in families" (Weissman, 1983, pp. 102-103).

Theories of mother-child bonding find support from videotapes of middle-class parent-child interaction. In the laboratory, environmental factors are invisible (Henriques, Holloway, Urwin, Venn, & Walkerdine, 1984), making intra- and intersubjective factors loom larger than life. Denuded of the social context that isolates mother with child, reliance on one another—*bonding*—appears to derive from immanent principles rather than from external necessity. So are the intellectual myths constructed that normalize women's work as mothers.

This methodological short-sightedness may seem benign. But the diffusion and administration of the resulting knowledge in maternal and child health services is not. The alleged science of mothering is surrounded by expectations of appropriate parenting derived from patterns presumed to typify middle-class (i.e., healthy) families. Extrapolated to behavior among working-class, minority, or poor women, these expectations form the ground on which pediatrics, social, and protective services shift child abuse from the realm of politics to pathology and trace the violent suppression of women and children to deficits in women's ability to parent (the so-called failure to protect). Thus, pediatric texts, popular advice literature, and psychological research blame mother when things go wrong (Caplan & Hall-McCorguodale, 1985; Ehrenreich & English, 1979; Howell, 1978). Child abuse is alternately attributed to a failure or an exaggeration of the maternal function, a lack of parenting skills, or an inappropriate dependence on or resentment of a vulnerable other. If a man harms the child, this is because the mother is not present when the child returns from school, because adults other than the mother care for the child when ill, or because unsatisfactory care arrangements have been made by working mothers (Garbarino & Sherman, 1980; Robertson & Juritz, 1979). The approach is not limited to the United States. In a London survey, More and Day (1979) are explicit:

> "In the 20 cases where the father or step-father had hit the child, the following pattern emerged. . . . In 7 of these cases, the mother's behavior acted as a trigger for the assault. Either she had provoked her husband in some way and then made sure—perhaps by going out—that the child got the full weight of the anger produced, or she had complained to her husband about the child's behavior (sometimes, perhaps, to take the spotlight off herself in an explosive situation)." (Martin, 1983, p. 300)

Holding women responsible for male violence against themselves and their children reinforces the batterer's common tendency to deny or externalize responsibility for his behavior.

## PATRIARCHAL MOTHERING: THE PRACTICE

The knowledge of mother-child bonding, of the mother's responsibility for abuse, and of how violence evolves across generations of pathology unreflectively incorporated into child protective services. The administrative practices that follow include parent aides, homemaker services, hotlines, Parents Anonymous, outpatient counseling, crisis management, and, if these fail, intensive intervention ("family preservation"), voluntary placement, legal prosecution, and, in extreme cases, the termination of parental rights. Behind each intervention, the governing assumption is that without institutional support for the parenting role, the family unit will dissolve into its multiple pathologies, hopelessly compromising its protective function. There is no thought given to the possibility that this strategy may also stabilize a pattern of destructiveness, including child abuse.

Assigning responsibility for child abuse based on stereotypic notions of women's role engenders conflict between CPS representatives and women perceived as deviant mothers, encourages mothers to conceal the real risks to their children, and evokes resentment among women toward their children. Mothers are defined as people without needs of their own, who do or do not live up to their child's expectations and needs as service providers view them. Women whose behavior differs from the projected expectations frustrate service providers and rationales are sought to "help these women shape up" through punitive contracts and aggressive case management. This response is frequently justified by retrospective reinterpretation, where deviance from perceived gender norms is joined to other presumably dysfunctional factors in a woman's history or environment and the resulting complex is forged into an overall image of pathology. Nonspecialist peer groups also interpret conflicts in women's social identity as illness. Thus, Parents Anonymous literature insists that child abuse stems from a problem that is "within us as a parent" and holds that the woman is "a destructive, disturbed mother." Not surprisingly, when a battered mother is offered therapy and support for parenting instead of protection and food stamps, she is likely to transfer some portion of her anger to her caseworker and her children (Kott-Washburne, 1984).

## THE BATTERED MOTHER'S DILEMMA

Battered women cannot fully protect their children from the assailant. To protect themselves from the stigmatizing reception they anticipate from CPS, however, they pretend they can. When they encounter the caseworker, both mother and caseworker join willingly in a charade. Homemaking punctuated by violence can hardly be "normal." Thus, home visits become exercises in mutual impression management. If the woman answers the door with a black eye, the caseworker knows how she got it. But if the woman threatens to reveal the real source of the trouble, or even to expose the risk a partner's violence poses to the child, she is reminded either directly or with a disapproving look that a failure in maternal responsibilities could easily lead to the child's removal. So the mother lies, the worker is aware of the lie but accepts it, and, if pressed, the caseworker reenacts the charade to satisfy her supervisor. Although all parties are equally invested in this concealment process, if the child is severely hurt, the worker and supervisor assume a studied naiveté and the client is scapegoated.

Behind this tragic comedy lies the most profound dilemma a battered mother can face. She cannot protect her child unless she herself is protected. But if she asks for protection for herself, her child may be removed. In the matrix of power in which the woman finds herself, one way to seek aid is by drawing attention to her problems with her child whether or not these are particularly significant. As a result, many women project an image of themselves as unable to cope hoping that, by accommodating the preconceptions of child protective services, they will be given the support needed to protect themselves, obviously a dangerous gambit.

But it is not merely her own safety that is at stake. An equally important facet of the battered mother's dilemma is whether to expose the assailant's behavior and lose her child or to conceal it and risk her assailant's extending his abuse to the child, a situation we term *tangential spouse abuse*. Here, being a good mother (having her child removed to safety) means admitting that she has been a "bad" mother in the eyes of the world (i.e., she has been battered). Exposure of the battering relationship and subsequent removal of the child often have tragic consequences. Apart from the risk of neglect and abuse to children in foster care, the effects of foster placement on a battering relationship include a depressive reaction, self-blame, a reduction in a woman's survival defenses, the internalization of anger formerly directed at the child scapegoat, attempted suicide, and an escalation in abuse because the batterer has also lost his potential scapegoat. Another tragic sequelae of removal is that battered women immediately become pregnant to prove their readiness for a new child and to compensate for depression.

## PATRIARCHAL MOTHERING AND
## ABUSE BY MOTHERS: THE LIVED EXPERIENCE

The battered mother's dilemma goes deeper still. If women's situation was simply paradigmatic of the weak and the governed, to borrow Elizabeth Janeway's (1971) phrase, then the complex system of social interventions constructed to manage their behavior would be largely superfluous. Women confront male domination as active subjects, legally free and independent, struggling to shape reality to their needs. The women are not mere pawns, but their initiative has been displaced so that they must realize their gender identities in their relations with their children. As French feminists have shown so eloquently, sexism in liberal societies rests less on open bias than in privileging certain definitions of feminine behavior within which women are constrained both to find themselves and to survive (Irigaray, 1977). As women (and children) internalize these limited meanings, they come to know themselves as men would have them known. They become locked into the knowledge of themselves as mothers, the process we term *patriarchal mothering.*

In the laboratory, mother-infant bonding is observed devoid of its political context, that is, with no room for women to change themselves or their relations with children by manipulating the parameters of the world around them. As isolated episodes of woman abuse evolve into battering, women's available space closes in on them and their psychological as well as physical mobility is restricted. Now they experience the same diminished sense of themselves in relation to the social world that is projected by the psychological paradigm. As the mothering role becomes their only route to self-expression, they experience it as both essential and alien, as a source as well as a way out of their confinement.

Administrative transactions with CPS aggravate the process of role closure by simultaneously encouraging women to view the world through the prism of motherhood and to question whether a good mother would have an abusing partner. A situation akin to the psychological double bind that anthropologist Gregory Bateson linked to schizophrenia is created when coercive control leaves a battered woman no alternative but to define herself through mothering, the very frame in which it is impossible for her to be good. Forced to choose between liking herself as abused or acknowledging she is bad (thereby confirming the batterer's view), she becomes myopic to the political dimensions of her predicament, denying her own battering by building a fool's paradise of power over her children while at the same time feeling completely powerless or overwhelmed. Child-abusing women themselves "yearn for good mothering" (Steele, 1976, p. 14); they suffer low self-esteem because of a felt incongruence between how they view themselves and how they would like to be (Rosen, 1978) and turn to their children for company and nurturing (role reversal) (Helfer, 1976; Steele & Pollock, 1974). Researchers trace these characteristics to a "breakdown in the maternal affection system" (Steele, 1976, p. 14). At least in homes in which women are also being assaulted, however, quite the contrary process is at work. Here women strive for selfhood (how they would like to be) and nurturing (good mothering) within the constraints of the mothering role. In part, this is because children are the only source of nurturing in violent homes and in part this is because, as battered women define their options within a world bounded by a male telos, they lose access to the strains of resistance and initiative through which to establish themselves as something other than "his." In the most extreme cases, women appear to be living examples of Irigaray's (1977) account of "Ce sexe qui n'est pas un," as so constituted by their oppression that they have no authentic voice in which to speak.

Thus, the matrix of power in which the battered mother is situated finds a parallel in a narrowing of the cognitive frame through which she perceives the world and is perceived by it. Ideally, the woman can separate her commitment to nurture a dependent other from her personal needs for power, anger expression, control, attention, and the like. In the throes of an abusive relationship, however, these needs must be mediated through mothering; the result is that dependence and nurturing become fraught with psychological conflict, another dimension of patriarchal mothering. Ironically, it is the totalization of mothering among battered women, not its abandonment, that can lead mothers to hurt their child.

There is an additional pathway by which the administrative response links the knowledge of battered women as mothers to their becoming abusive. We have seen that prevalent interventions to stop child abuse, like the responses to battering, are inattentive to the needs of battered women, holding mothers responsible for the child's predicament and making their rights as parents contingent on suppressing the urge for self-development and survival. In numerous instances in our caseload, women's capacity to survive in a battering relationship depended on getting a job, going to night school, taking in piecework for "pin" money, secreting away money given to them for the children's needs, or maintaining an active social life outside the house. Ironically, particularly where young children were involved, these behaviors were often interpreted as evidence that the mother put her own needs before the child's, even resulting in a judgment of neglect in several cases. On the other hand, women who dutifully stayed at home were both more vulnerable to abuse and more likely to hold their children responsible for their own blocked opportunities. One way out of this bind is to deny the battering; another is to hold the child responsible for the partner's violence. By scapegoating their children, battered women momentarily reconcile the dilemma in which loving the child, being a good mother, means putting themselves at risk. By imagining the child is bad and doing just enough to affect his or her removal, women are able to gain some independence with a minimum of internal conflict. Here, as in the previous examples, child abuse by the battered mother is a survival strategy evoked by entrapment.

## Conclusions

### FROM ENTRAPMENT TO EMPOWERMENT

In the lives of many abused women, when assault and coercion are met with an inappropriate or punitive response from helpers, the result is entrapment in a syndrome of escalating destructiveness. Isolated within the relationship and blocked from without when she pursues alternatives, the battered woman seeks to meet her needs within an ever-narrower realm that includes the constricted realm of the mother-child relationship. Her resentment and anger mount alongside the suppressed need for independence and autonomy. Self-medication with addictive substances, depression, multiple suicide attempts, homicidal rage, and violence against vulnerable others may result.

The same process of entrapment appears to be the major context for child abuse. Men are the typical child abusers; in at least half of all child abuse cases, men are battering the mother as well. In the modal situation we studied, child abuse appeared as tangential spouse abuse, that is, as a stage in the perpetrator's attempts to control the mother. But whichever parent abuses the child in a battering relationship, the woman's capacity to protect is compromised by a continuum of control that extends from the violence at home through inappropriate clinical interventions to punitive interventions by CPS. When a battered woman sacrifices her child to be hit instead of her, becomes enmeshed with her child, or scapegoats the child to prompt removal by CPS, she often does so to break a bind in which personal identity is equated with intolerably rigid gender roles.

Training in parenting does nothing to break this bind. To the contrary, by defining her from the vantage of the child's need for mothering, parental support often aggravates a woman's mounting rage. The obligations of mothering reappear as rules imposed by an alien force, converge with the rules the batterer seeks to instill at home, and undermine the very sense of responsibility and control over her environment that CPS hopes to elicit. Anger emerges as a defense against helplessness and child abuse emerges as a desperate way to exert control in the context of little or no control. But though rage is a political emotion, to paraphrase Bernardez (1987), it is often expressed symptomatically. Resistance to mind control may evoke dissociation, resistance to isolation may evoke imaginary companions, and resistance to guilt and shame may evoke a false self that performs chores obediently, even cheerfully (Herman, 1987) but is dead to the world. Or rage may find direct expression in killing the assailant.

If battering is the major context for child abuse and female independence is a basic issue in both problems, female empowerment is the best means to prevent child abuse. As practiced by the battered women's movement, interventions to facilitate empowerment involve (a) advocacy (to protect and expand women's entitlements), (b) collective support (to overcome isolation, normalize estrangement, focus anger, and provide the political basis for change), and (c) enhanced control. The interventions begin with safety planning for mother and child, including independent planning if the child is old enough. Enhanced control means helping battered women clarify their needs and options, then allowing them to select the option that best suits their situation as they know it, even when they have hurt their child.

The decision to support a battered woman who has put her child at risk or may do so is one of the most difficult decisions battered women's advocates must make. It must obviously be made within the confines of the agency mission and with full communication to the mother of the risks to the child as the caseworker or shelter advocate sees them. The philosophical basis for the decision to trust the mother is that, when women are treated as women first, they become better mothers. The pragmatic basis is also clear that mothers will provide accurate information about their children's risk and plan accordingly only if they trust—and believe they are trusted by—the caseworker or advocate. Many shelters now employ child advocates, some run groups for mothers and children (Alessi & Hearn, 1978; Rhodes & Zelman, 1986), and some child protective service (CPS) and other victim-oriented agencies run programs for families in which battering and child abuse coexist. In these settings, a mother who is not able to leave an abusive relationship may nevertheless decide she cannot make the same decision for her child. Although empowerment is more problematic if a woman chooses to remain in a violent relationship, at least temporarily, clarifying the parameters of her situation as a woman can help restore a sense of options as a mother, including the option to use her anger in constructive, self-protective ways.

In its emphasis on equity and its political analysis of social ills, its community base, its willingness to take responsibility for problems few want to tackle, the excitement it communicates, and its capacity to dramatize issues and to mobilize constituencies, the battered women's movement has won over large segments of the social welfare audience. Yet although the battered woman's shelter is an important piece in responding to the crisis of family violence, providing for the long-term security and autonomy of women and children is a task that requires an integrated communitywide effort to which CPS are also crucial. Evidence that dialogue is beginning includes cross-training between battered women's services, CPS, and family preservation services; the assignment of CPS advocates to shelters and the employment of battered women's advocates by CPS; and CPS contracts for community-based groups to serve the battered mothers of children identified as high risk. Many aspects of the feminist approach, however, are anathema to a child protection system that sees itself as advocating for children but not their mothers; that believes the politics of gender inequality lie outside the appropriate domain of treatment and protection; that defines women reflexively, in terms of the needs of others; that holds women accountable for situations in which nurturing the child may be impossible; and that relies heavily on interventions to change individuals in the face of glaring social ills, such as male violence.

Acknowledging that child abuse originates in the politics of gender in no way diminishes personal responsibility for violence. On the contrary, as women are released from rigid role stereotypes and become more comfortable with their social power, they will be better able to accept real responsibility for the range of unresolved, ambivalent, and angry feelings all parents share.

# Killing the Beast Within

*Woman Battering and Female Suicidality*

## Background

This chapter explores the importance of woman battering for female suicidality in the medical setting, paying special attention to the link among black women. As in previous chapters, we examine data from women's medical records both to illuminate a clinical dilemma (in this case suicidality among a population of seemingly normal women) and to critique the gender bias in current formulations of the problem. Gender bias in clinical practice is not benign. As with domestic violence generally, we suspect that with female suicidality, interventions framed by this bias actually aggravate the situations they are meant to manage. As in the previous chapters, we approach the evidence from a presumption that is the opposite of medicine's own—namely that, unless proved otherwise, health problems form around social inequalities and, particularly for women minorities and other oppressed groups, around the imposition of and resistance to these inequalities.

AUTHORS' NOTE: This chapter is adapted from Stark (1995). Reprinted with permission of the *International Journal of Health Services.*

SUICIDE ATTEMPTS
AMONG BATTERED WOMEN

In an earlier study of trauma patients (Stark, 1984; see also Chapter 1, this volume), we found that 18.7% to 25% of female injury patients had been battered, a finding that has proved conservative compared with subsequent research in other medical settings (Appleton, 1980; Gin, Rucker, Frayne, Cygan, & Hubbell, 1991; McLeer & Anwar, 1989; Rath, Jarratt, & Leonardson, 1989). Other research, meanwhile, has established that women in abusive relationships suffer a substantial risk of serial victimization (Klaus & Rand, 1984), homicide (Kellerman & Mercy, 1992), and general medical and psychiatric problems, including pregnancy-related problems, alcoholism, drug abuse, rape, and child abuse (Stark & Flitcraft, 1991). Studies with shelter, convenience, or volunteer samples of battered women have also indicated that a substantial number, 35% to 40%, attempt suicide, far higher than in the general population (Gayford, 1975a; Walker, 1979). Control comparisons taken at a Swedish hospital indicate that battered women may have a far greater relative risk of attempting suicide than nonbattered women (Bergman & Brismar, 1991). In a study of trauma patients at Yale-New Haven Hospital, we found that one battered woman in six (17%) had attempted suicide and a significant proportion had done so multiple times (Stark, 1984; Stark et al., 1981). Suicide attempt rates differed significantly between battered women and nonbattered controls only after the first recorded abusive injury, suggesting that battering might be a key to suicidality in this population. In the Swedish sample, however, alcoholism, possibly stimulated by the abuse, was an important mediator. Although the Swedish women mentioned relational conflict as the precipitant of their attempts, few presented with injury, suggesting that their suicidality was not provoked by an acute episode of violence (Bergman & Brismar, 1991).

Among minority women, the link between abuse and suicidality has been studied only among teens and with contradictory results. Whereas Bayatpour, Wells, and Holford (1992) report a strong association between physical or sexual abuse and suicidality among predominantly black pregnant teens, Blum, Harmon, Harris, Bergeisen, and Resnick (1992) found no correlation among Native American and Alaskan youths.

## THEORETICAL PERSPECTIVE:
## BATTERING AS COERCIVE CONTROL

Despite two decades of public concern with abuse, there has been little analysis of why it should evoke the range of psychosocial problems identified among battered women.

Clinical and survey research have focused almost entirely on physical injury, the most immediate consequence of partner assault. Given high rates of injury, feminists and other activists argue that wife abuse exemplifies a pattern of patriarchal violence against women rooted in the male desire for control (Dobash & Dobash, 1979; Schechter, 1982; see also Chapter 1, this volume). In contrast, more traditional family researchers argue that male violence is an inappropriate but nonetheless learned cultural means of conflict resolution linked to other types of family violence, such as elder abuse, child abuse, or spousal violence by women (Straus et al., 1980). If partner violence is merely a means to resolve conflict, however, it is unclear why it should generate a psychosocial profile among women that includes severe problems such as addiction and suicidality, particularly because no similar pattern has been identified among men who are victims of stranger or partner assault. Research has failed to show that battered women have distinct psychiatric or demographic characteristics, suggesting that the explanation for their behavioral problems lies in the relationship itself.

Because the battered woman's problems appear among women who stay in abusive relationships, psychologists have been prompted to emphasize the traumatic role of repeated assault. The symptoms clustered under headings such as *battered woman's syndrome* or *posttraumatic stress disorder* (PTSD) emerged, it is believed, because severe violence overwhelms the individual's normal coping mechanisms. The theory of battered woman's syndrome developed by Lenore Walker (1979, 1984) emphasizes a depressive pattern of learned helplessness elicited by a woman's feeling there is nothing she can do to escape the violence. The theory of PTSD encompasses a broader range of psychological responses, including a number that mimic severe psychiatric disease (such as dissociation), but emphasizes the adaptive function of these responses given the inability of the psychic system to manage the stress inflicted by repeated trauma in any other way (Herman, 1992). In these theories, battered women are thought to be at increased risk for suicidality either because they believe nothing can help them or, in the PTSD model, because they are overwhelmed by intense fear, unbearable anxiety, loss of control, and a sense of annihilation.

Traumatization theories broadened the early emphasis on physical violence by emphasizing a range of internal and behavioral harms and correctly fixed responsibility for these problems on the violent male. But they provide an incomplete picture of how these problems developed, particularly in relation to external and objective components of the situation. As a result, they overemphasize the extent of women's victimization, mistakenly predict that battered women will fail to report their problems or try to escape from the abuse, leave the impression that male dominance is established primarily at the interpersonal rather than the political level, and suggest that a range of responses that women have developed to survive ongoing abuse are really psychic reactions to the unbearable pain of past trauma. However useful in explaining a clinical syndrome found among a subgroup of battered women, in the end the images conveyed by these theories fail to confront the central paradox posed by the emergence of dependent and self-destructive behaviors among otherwise normal assertive and even physically aggressive women.

An alternative account attempts to explain both why women stay in abusive relationships and why they develop the behavioral problems associated with battering, such as suicidality. In this view, the distinctive feature of battering is that violence is merely one means—not necessarily the most salient from the victim's standpoint—by which partners coerce isolated and intimidated women; control over material and social resources is the means, not merely the object, of the process identified as battering (Dobash & Dobash, 1979; Jones & Schechter, 1992; Okun, 1986; see also Chapter 1, this volume). Although violence could certainly have devastating physical and psychological effects, a woman's peculiar vulnerability to secondary problems, such as addiction or suicidality is a function of the degree of entrapment that results from coercive control exercised over a wide range of her activities, from access to money to her right to decide when, where, and how sexual relations occur (Jones, 1994; Stark, 1992). Institutional barriers that limit women's access to vital sources of assistance intensify this entrapment process, evoking ever more desperate pleas for help, including suicide attempts.

## BATTERING AS A FACTOR IN FEMALE SUICIDALITY

The fact that suicide attempts are often prompted by domestic violence does not tell us what the overall significance of male violence is for female suicidality. Studies in India (Pillay & Vawda, 1989) and Greece and Denmark (Arcel, Mantonakis, Petersson, Jemos, & Kaliteraki, 1992) report abuse as a factor in as many as 44% of female suicide attempts. To date, however, domestic violence has not been explicitly identified as a factor in female suicidality in the United States.

A retrospective reading of the suicide literature leaves the strong impression that domestic violence is often important etiologically. For instance, up to 80% of those who attempt suicide give marital or boyfriend or girlfriend conflicts as their reason (Bancroft, Skrimshire, Casson, Harvard-Watts, & Reynolds, 1977), an explanation that was often a euphemism for violence among battered women in our trauma sample. Researchers frequently note family conflict as a background factor, reporting that women who attempt suicide have " 'problems almost entirely with their mates' " (Maris, 1971, p. 114) and feel afraid predominantly in connection with their husbands (Vinoda, 1966) and that "acute conflict within a close relationship" is an important precipitant to suicide attempts among depressed females (Weissman, Fox, & Klarman, 1973, p. 450). Rather than explore the role fear, friction, and acute conflict might play in suicidality, however, these researchers trace the complaints to personality problems, such as general hostility, depression, or "rigid personality." The Epidemiological Catchment Area study of the National Institute of Mental Health found a strong correlation between suicidality and a range of violent behaviors, including victimization in a violent incident. But the association was ascribed to a violent repertoire of behavior and examined no further (Earls, Escobar, & Spero, 1991).

The sociological aspects of female suicidality are also suggestive of battering. Whereas the typical suicide is committed by a middle-class older white male outside the family context, the typical attempt is made by a younger (and increasingly by a black) female who is either married or of marriageable age (Committee on Cultural Psychiatry, 1989; Gove, 1972; Henry & Short, 1964; Rico-Velasco & Mynko, 1973). This profile also characterizes women at highest risk for domestic violence.

## ONCE AGAIN, WOMEN FAIL

Given these leads, why has a link to male violence not been suspected? One answer is that female suicidality has been framed with a distinctly male bias. At least since Emile Durkheim (1951) argued in *Suicide* that family life offered women "a coefficient of preservation" (p. 286) against anomie, the main factor that places men at risk for suicide, suicide attempts (a predominantly female event) have been conceptualized as failed suicides. To explain this failure, the literature relies heavily on gender stereotypes, alternately emphasizing the buffering role of women's involvement in family life or characteristic feminine weaknesses, such as fear of pain, inherent ambivalence, a propensity for situationally induced (i.e., transitory) depression, and an inability to use handguns (Turner, 1984). Despite the fact that young black women may now have the highest rate of serious suicide attempts (Garrison, McKeown, Valois, & Vincent, 1993), the literature focuses on the low rates of suicide among blacks, emphasizing protective factors, such as a high degree of community integration, church membership, and involvement with extended families and informal social networks (Earls et al., 1991; Martin, 1968; Neighbors, 1984; Thompson & Peebles-Wilkins, 1992). Not surprisingly, a recent study failed to identify such stress-buffering factors in young black females (Brown, Powell, & Earls, 1984). In reality, unless low-income or minority women are frankly psychotic or acting out violently themselves, they are unlikely to be defined as having the sorts of mental health or situational problems that require outpatient support.

The research approach has a self-fulfilling effect on practice. Assessment instruments used to distinguish high-risk patients are based on the problems associated with completed suicides (i.e., on profiles of isolated middle-class white males) and highlight traditional risk factors, such as the severity of the attempt, alcoholism, previous attempts, and the concurrence of serious medical or psychiatric disease (O'Carroll, 1991; Turner, 1984; Weissman et al., 1973). From this vantage, female suicidality appears "not serious," and factors that indicate an emergent social situation such as partner abuse are discounted. Anger and frustration, feelings often associated with interpersonal conflict, as well as environmental stressors, such as a recent divorce, family conflict, or the loss of a loved one, are considered background factors whose presentation in a client's complaint indicate the problem is transitory (Hamdi, Amin, & Mattar, 1991; Turner, 1984). Recent reports reiterate this emphasis.

The Epidemiological Catchment Area study found that depressive symptoms (particularly hopelessness, drug use, and multiple somatic symptoms) correlate more strongly with female suicidality than an unstable marriage, unemployment, poverty, or lack of education (Earls et al., 1991). As a result, the possibility that suicide attempts have a distinctive social etiology rooted in some aspect of women's experience has been neglected.

The research reported in this chapter explores the significance of battering among a general population of women who attempted suicide, assesses the special significance of battering for suicidality among black women, and considers the appropriateness of the medical response. On the basis of a literature review and our findings in the trauma sample, we hypothesize that domestic violence is a significant and perhaps even a causal factor in female suicidality overall, particularly for black women. We further expect that clinical assessments discount domestic violence as a situational factor and so will fail to appreciate or appropriately manage the emergent nature of the woman's situation. Although the dynamics here are complex, by failing to identify abuse or by targeting intervention at a battered woman's alleged pathology rather than her predicament at home, clinicians can contribute to her sense of hopelessness, isolation, and entrapment and thereby increase her risk of further suicidality.

## The Research Study

### POPULATION STUDIED

To investigate the association between abuse and attempted suicide, we reviewed the medical records of women who came to the emergency service at Yale-New Haven Hospital as attempted suicides over a 1-year period. A woman was identified as a suicide attempt if her presenting complaint was suicide attempt or included an intentionally self-inflicted injury or an attempted overdose. Cases in which no self-destructive intent appeared involved or in which suicidal ideation or threat was not accompanied by suicidal behavior were excluded.

Using these criteria, 176 women were identified as having attempted suicide at least once during the study year. The full medical records of this group of women were accessed and reviewed by trained abstractors who recorded pertinent demographic, medical, and obstetrical information as well as information about all suicide attempts in the patient's history, including precipitating events, the method and context of each attempt, the timing of the event in relation to reported injury episodes, and relevant medical social service and psychiatric responses.

## STUDY INSTRUMENT

Although the significance of battering in health settings has been well documented, the problem is rarely identified and is still not a recognized diagnosis. Therefore, retrospective case identification requires an index of probable risk that is independent of provider judgment. The specific technique used here to determine the probability of abuse was the adult trauma history screen (ATHS). Developed by Flitcraft (1977), validated by Stark (1984), and used widely to identify battering among medical populations, the ATHS was used here to classify each episode of injury in the patient's adult history according to the following criteria:

- Positive: Record states that injury was inflicted by male family member or intimate.
- Probable: Record states that injury resulted from a punch, hit, kick, shot, or similar and deliberate assault by another person but no personal etiology was indicated and it was not a mugging, anonymous assault, or robbery.
- Suggestive: Alleged etiology did not appear to account for the type, location, or severity of the injury.
- Reasonable negative: The pattern of injury was adequately explained by the recorded etiology. Injuries sustained in muggings or anonymous assaults were included in this category.

Next, the injury visits within each record were aggregated into a single trauma history and each woman was assigned a battering risk group indicating the greatest likelihood of battering according to the injury. A woman with at least one positive injury was considered positive for battering.

The historical reading of the medical record also established the temporal relation between incidents of reported or apparent abuse, provider interventions, and the presentation of other problems, including suicide attempts.

For the purpose of the study, a woman was identified as battered if, during the year of her suicide attempt, she could be classified as positive or probable according to her trauma history. This meant that she had

**TABLE 4.1** History of Battering Among Female Suicide Attempts, Psychiatric Emergency Service, July 15, 1980 to July 14, 1981

| History of Battering | Percentage | (N) |
|---|---|---|
| Positives | 22.2 | (39) |
| Probables | 7.3 | (13) |
| Total at risk | 29.5 | (52) |
| Nonbattered | 70.4 | (124) |
| All | 99.9 | (176) |

arrived at the hospital with at least one abusive injury prior to the attempt or following the attempt but during the sample year. To minimize subjective aspects of methodology, women with suggestive injury profiles were incorporated into the negative category. As we have reiterated in other chapters, the method is extremely conservative, demonstrating a high degree of specificity but low sensitivity.

## DATA ANALYSIS

Chi-square tests were used to discover in what ways battered women who attempted suicide differed from nonbattered suicide attempters in terms of demographic background, nature and frequency of the suicide attempt, pregnancy status, and response elicited from medical personnel. The precipitating complaint and the proximity of an abusive injury were used to assess a possible causal link of battering to women's suicide attempts.

## FINDINGS

The medical histories of the 176 women who attempted suicide during the sample year reveal that 29.5% ($N = 52$) were battered (Table 4.1); 22.2% ($N = 39$) of the women had at least one documented incident of domestic abuse in their records (positives); and 7.3% ($N = 13$) had at least one injury that resulted from assault, although the assailant was not named (probables). Women with a suggestive or negative history of battering injury either prior to the suicide attempt or after the attempt but during the study year made up 70.4% of the suicide attempt sample ($N = 124$).

## DEMOGRAPHIC PROFILE

### Age, Education, and Marital Status

Battered women were comparable to nonbattered women who attempted suicide in terms of age, educational attainment, and marital status. The women ranged in age from 16 to 69, with a mean age of 30. The modal educational level was a high school diploma. Importantly, marital status did not distinguish battered from nonbattered women. Most women (70%) in both groups were single, divorced, or separated.

### Race

Black women who attempted suicide were significantly more likely than whites to have a history of battering. Blacks made up 25.6% of all suicide attempts for the period ($N = 45$). Whereas 22.2% of the white women who attempted suicide ($N = 28$) were identified as battered, 48.8% of the black women ($N = 22$) in the sample were battered ($p < .001$). In other words, battering was a possible factor in approximately half of all suicide attempts by black women in this population.

### Pregnancy and Miscarriages

Battered women were significantly more likely than nonbattered women to be pregnant when they attempted suicide. Only 5% of the nonbattered women were pregnant at the time of their attempted suicide compared with 19.2% ($N = 10$) of the battered women ($p < .001$). Conversely, of the 16 pregnant women who attempted suicide during the study year, two thirds (62.5%) were battered.

The battered women also had a significantly greater number of miscarriages than the nonbattered women, both in prior pregnancies and in the current pregnancy: 36.5% of the battered women (positives, 44%; probables, 17%) had at least one miscarriage compared with just 2% of the nonbattered women ($p < .001$).

## TIMING, NATURE, AND
## FREQUENCY OF SUICIDE ATTEMPT

Table 4.2 summarizes information on the most recent hospital visit for an abuse-related injury by battered women who attempt suicide.

**TABLE 4.2**  Most Recent Battering Presentation Among Female Suicide
Attempts, Psychiatric Emergency Service, 1980 to 1981

| Most Recent Injury Presentation | Percentage | (N) |
|---|---|---|
| Greater than 6 months prior to suicide attempt | 19 | (10) |
| Less than 6 months prior to suicide attempt | 28.8 | (15) |
| Same day as suicide attempt | 36.5 | (19) |
| Within 1 year after suicide attempt | 15 | (8) |
| Total battered | 29.5 | (52) |

Because the case-finding method employed here was largely retrospective, considering injuries during and prior to the year when the suicide attempt occurred, it is not surprising that the vast majority of the battered women who attempted suicide—85%—had visited the hospital for treatment of a battering injury at least once prior to their suicide attempt. The greater the proximity of an abuse-related injury to an attempt, the more likely it is that the two events were related. Suggestive of current battering is the fact that 65.3% of the battered women had visited due to at least one battering injury in the 6 months prior to the current suicide attempt. Remarkably, 36.5% ($N = 19$) of the battered women in this population visited the hospital with an injury attributable to abuse on the same day as their attempt. This represents 11% of all female suicide attempts. Among positives, 43% were battered on the same day as their attempt and 71% attempted suicide within 6 months of an assault. The 15% who had not visited the hospital because of a battering injury prior to their suicide attempt did so at least once either immediately after the suicide attempt or between the attempt and the retrieval of the record. Although some portion of this group may have entered a battering relationship after their suicide attempt, current or subsequent abuse probably indicated that battering was an ongoing concern at the time of the attempt.

Overall suicide attempts by traumatic means are relatively rare. Yet battered women accounted for 42% of all traumatic attempts—as opposed, for instance, to overdose or poisonings. Although these attempts were occasionally life threatening, they were typically interpreted as gestures.

As in the earlier sample of battered women that we studied, battered women who attempted suicide did so more frequently than nonbattered women. Indeed 21.1% ($N = 11$) of the battered women had attempted

**TABLE 4.3**  Variables Significantly Associated With Battering History Among Female Suicide Attempts, Psychiatric Emergency Service, 1980 to 1981

| Variable | Percentage | (N) | p |
|---|---|---|---|
| Three previous attempts | 21.1 | (11) | .02 |
| Marital conflict as precipitating complaint | 44.2 | (23) | .001 |
| Pregnant at time of suicide attempt | 19.2 | (10) | .001 |
| Previous miscarriage | 36.5 | (19) | .001 |
| Medical referrals home | 65.3 | (34) | .001 |
| No referrals | 22 | (11) | |
| Total battered | 29.5 | (52) | |

suicide three times or more. This compared with 8% of the women who were not battered ($p = < .02$; see Table 4.3).

PRECIPITATING COMPLAINT

Mention of a marital conflict or a lover's quarrel proved to be the single best predictor that a woman who attempted suicide also had a recorded history of at-risk trauma. Marital conflict or a lover's quarrel was noted as a precipitating cause on the records of 11% of the nonbattered women who attempted suicide. By contrast, 44.2% ($N = 23$) of the battered women mentioned such disputes ($p < .001$; Table 4.3). Conversely, if a woman who attempted suicide described a conflict with a husband, ex-husband, or boyfriend as the precipitating cause, there was a 61% chance she had visited this hospital for treatment of a battering injury.

THE MEDICAL RESPONSE

When a battered woman attempted suicide, her abuse was virtually never selected as the focus of intervention. As a result—in part reflecting the disproportionate number of suicide attempts by battered women that were considered gestures—following initial medical treatment, battered women who attempted suicide were more likely than nonbattered women to be sent home or to receive no referral of any kind. Whereas less than half (42.7%) of nonbattered women were sent home, 65.3% ($N = 34$) of battered women were sent home after their suicide attempt ($p < .001$). Similarly, the vast majority of nonbattered suicide attempters (94%), whether hospitalized or sent home, were referred to mental health services. By contrast, 22% ($N = 11$) of the suicide attempts by battered women did not elicit a referral for mental health or social services of any kind (Table 4.3). Nonbattered women were typically referred for voluntary inpatient care (which could at least offer temporary shelter) or outpatient care or counseling. Meanwhile, battered women were institutionalized at the state mental hospital more frequently than nonbattered women, though the difference was not statistically significant.

## Discussion and Conclusions

The traditional wisdom is that suicide attempts are failed suicides for which medicine bears little responsibility, that they arise at the juncture of individual psychopathology and exogenous stress, and that the disposition should respond to the presenting symptoms and underlying intrapsychic or behavioral problems with little attention to immediate precipitants or the social situation (Klugman, Litman, & Wold, 1984; Schmid & Van Arsdol, 1955). Where attempts are accompanied by complaints about marital distress rather than frank symptoms of psychiatric disease, the attempt is considered a transitory event requiring little in the way of dramatic intervention or ongoing support. In treatment, attention is focused on the suicidal theme; significant others, particularly spouses, are often seen as important adjuncts to intervention who are called on to keep the therapist informed about stresses in the client's life (Klugman et al., 1984). Reports of conflict or fights are presumed to reflect underlying personality issues. As a result, violence is rarely noted and almost never selected as a focus of intervention (Flitcraft, 1977; Rose, Pebody, & Stratigeas, 1991).

The present research casts doubt on several aspects of the conventional wisdom. The study clearly implicates battering, an ongoing criminal and life-threatening expression of women's oppression, as a major determinant of female suicide attempts, particularly among blacks. Only more detailed case analyses could rule out a major causal role for substance abuse or predisposing psychiatric conditions. Nevertheless, such a role is contraindicated by the frequency with which marital conflict is a precipitating complaint and the proximity of suicide attempts to prior episodes of assault. Perhaps the most startling finding is that more than one third of the battered women visited the hospital with an abuse-related injury or complaint on the same day as their suicide attempt, indicating that complaints of abuse were emergent regardless of other factors. We cannot say with certainty that abuse was a factor for the 65% of women assaulted within 6 months of their attempt. We believe, however, that a precipitating feeling in these cases was the sense of entrapment resulting from ongoing coercive control. Even this proximity of deliberate injury and attempted suicide is significant given the conservative nature of the identification method and the fact that many women experience dozens, even hundreds, of assaults without seeing a physician (Stark, 1992).

Interestingly, race and pregnancy status are the only background factors that differentiated battered from nonbattered women. Battering contributed significantly to female suicide attempts irrespective of the age, marital status, or education of the victim. The fact that 70% of the battered women who attempted suicide were single, separated, or divorced supports the feminist contention that men treat women as their property outside as well as within families. Ironically, the conclusion that battering rather than psychiatric disease underlies the multiple attempts, traumatic attempts, and miscarriages that distinguished suicidality among battered women was implicitly supported by the relative infrequency with which the battered women were referred for inpatient, outpatient, or follow-up care.

In contrast to the belief that relationship problems indicate a transitory crisis, most women who mentioned marital conflict or a lover's quarrel as a reason for their suicidality were in an ongoing abusive relationship with attendant risks of injury, further suicidality, and even homicide.

The relative frequency with which the battered women attempted suicide while they were pregnant may reflect the fact that women are at highest risk for partner assault when they are also most likely to be married and bear children. In the trauma study, abuse appeared to escalate during pregnancy. This may also be the case among battered women who attempt suicide. Many women feel particularly vulnerable during pregnancy, a fact that abusive men exploit. This dynamic may explain why battering was present in two thirds of the suicide attempts by pregnant women. The fact that battered women in this sample were 15 times more likely than nonbattered women to have suffered a miscarriage further illustrates the consequences of this exploitation, as it does the central pattern of injury associated with partner abuse.

Evidence linking race to battering is equivocal (Stark & Flitcraft, 1991). However, the dramatic finding that battering was a background factor in half of the suicide attempts by black women raises a number of questions about the special link of partner abuse and self-destructive behaviors in communities that are economically marginal or where discrimination is a barrier to access. Here, women are particularly dependent for support on indigenous networks of family and friends as buffers during crises. Yet it is precisely from these support networks that batterers try to isolate their victims. Suicidality may also reflect the dilemma experienced by many minority women about using criminal justice resources, even where self-protection is involved. Conversely, it may reflect the unresponsiveness of police officers who justify low levels of protection with the argument that violence is normal among minority groups, adding to a woman's sense that nothing can be done (Hawkins, 1987).

## REFRAMING FEMALE SUICIDALITY

Premised on biased assumptions about the relative importance of male versus female suicidality, the epidemiology of suicide constructs a calculus of harms that devalues experiences that women feel are emergent, concealing the etiological role of battering. Reframing female suicidality begins by approaching the phenomenon on its own terms. Only when the isolated suicidal act is put back into its appropriate social context can we understand a modal pattern in which otherwise normal women commit repeated suicidal acts as pleas for help with a desperate domestic or interpersonal situation. Any woman may hurt herself in response to a single traumatic assault. But in most cases, battered women are provoked to attempt suicide by the extent of control exercised over their lives. A case from our files illustrates this pattern:

> Alvin Jenkins first assaulted Amanda Jenkins in 1980, shortly after they married, while he was in the military. Over the next 10 years, if things didn't go exactly as he wished, he would go into a rage, push or slap her, break her belongings, and threaten to walk out. Their finances were in complete disarray at least in part due to his alcoholism, but any questions from Amanda made Alvin feel "abandoned" and he would hit her or withdraw for days, leaving her to make do on the little money she had. She returned to school, but he demanded she drop out. Then he took a job requiring a good deal of travel, leaving her "trapped" in the house with two young girls. After two explosive incidents in which he punched her and threatened her with a frying pan, Amanda had Alvin arrested and

removed. When Alvin returned, the assaults and intimidation resumed and, with the support of a battered woman's group, Amanda filed for divorce and was granted custody and alimony. During the separation, Alvin came to the house daily, begging Amanda to take him back for the sake of the children, appealing to her strict religious upbringing, and promising a new life. Finally, Amanda withdrew the divorce action and allowed Alvin to return, causing several friends to desert her. Now, Alvin told her, "I have you where I want you." He took her car keys, denied her money, and ridiculed her in front of the children. On the day of Amanda's suicide attempt, Alvin was following her around the house with a videocamera to show "how crazy you are." When she tried to stop him, he slapped her. Feeling completely desolate, she told Alvin, "You have won" and took an overdose of pills. The psychiatric note includes a diagnosis of adjustment disorder precipitated by family conflict, inner conflict, and guilt caused by her religious upbringing, her ideal of a family, and an intense anger underlying suicidal ideation. Arguing that her suicide attempt in front of the children proved Amanda was crazy, Alvin moved for and was granted temporary custody of the children.

Amanda's suicidal act was nearly fatal, though there was evidence of neither psychiatric disturbance nor severe trauma. Fortunately, psychiatric staff sensitized to domestic violence were mobilized to support her petition and the children were returned. In many other cases, the most significant indicator of a woman's entrapment—hence her subsequent risk of injury, suicidality, and homicide—is the discrepancy between the felt sense of emergency represented by the suicidal act and the absence of comorbid psychiatric or medical symptoms.

## THEORETICAL CONVERGENCES

Classic theories of suicidality help clarify the construction of affect that leads from coercive control to self-destructive behavior among women.

Freud's (1963) discussion of suicide in his essay "Mourning and Melancholia" helps explain how, in response to intolerable levels of conflict, the ego uses identification (with the aggressor) and regression to sadism to transform the rage evoked by despotism into self-deprecation. Freud never mentions physical violence as a factor. Nor does he imagine external controls that could so completely inhibit outward expressions of anger that turning against the self is the only rational option. But he fully understands that depression is often interpersonal conflict turned inward and identifies the mental constellation of contrition often found among suicidal battered women as an "attitude of revolt." The wish to die that he describes combines a fantasy of escape from an intolerable life situation, intense anger at a love object toward whom the person has ambivalent feelings, and a sense of guilt as punishment for a perceived failure. As in the case example above, these three facets—the wish to escape an intolerable situation, homicidal rage, and an overwhelming sense of guilt or shame—are frequently combined in the presentations of battered women who attempt suicide (Carmen, Rieker, & Mills, 1984).

Durkheim (1951) set himself the task of explaining why men kill themselves in such large numbers. He sensed the peculiar predicament of women, attributing whatever preservation against suicide family life gives women to the presence of children in the home and cautioning, " 'in itself conjugal society is harmful to the woman and aggravates her tendency to suicide' " (quoted in Johnson, 1979). He contrasts anomic and egoistic suicide occasioned by the isolation and rapid change of market societies to the altruistic suicides associated with group loyalties (and the concurrent loss of self) in traditional settings, again referring mainly to men. But Durkheim also speculates that there is a fourth type of suicide—what he terms *fatalistic* suicide—that arises from excessive regulation where futures are pitilessly blocked, passions are violently choked, and physical or moral despotism holds sway. Believing such conditions are incompatible with the full development of market societies, Durkheim relegates the discussion of fatalistic suicide to a footnote. Yet the conditions he describes are virtually identical to women's experience of entrapment in battering relationships.

If Freud (1963) describes the psychic mechanisms that turned anger inward and Durkheim (1951) describes the physical or moral despotism that evokes the anger and constrains its expression, feminist theory shows how both processes are mediated by gender inequality. Baker-Miller (1976) details how unequal power relations in families transform female strengths, such as cooperation, creativity, support for personal development, and a special respect for weakness, into patterns of self-denial, self-blame, and a greatly exaggerated sense of male power. According to Baker-Miller, the process of being devalued evokes a free-floating sense of anger or depression in women that adds to their feeling of being bad and finds expression through manipulative and subtly undermining behaviors. These personality distortions are reinforced by

larger patterns of female objectification and inequality and may mistakenly be seen as validating the batterer's claim that it is the woman
who is "sick" (angry, depressed, disloyal, or overly dependent), not he.

Incorporating these theories into an overall model of coercive control
helps explain why, despite the probable symmetry in the relative capacity
of men and women for aggression, women are overwhelmingly victimized by battering (as well as by other forms of so-called domestic
violence, such as child abuse, child sexual abuse, and elder abuse).
Women are victims, but not merely. They are also adults whose rage at
being dominated is redirected inward by a pattern of instrumental
constraints on their opportunities for self-expression, social connection,
and material survival. These constraints are effective not because men
are inherently more powerful than women either physically or mentally
but because the power men "borrow" from patriarchal institutions and
ideologies allows them to construct a private realm from which there
appears to be no escape. Gordon (1988) puts this concisely: "One assault
does not make a battered woman. She becomes that because of her
socially determined inability to resist or escape" (p. 285).

In the most serious cases, a hostagelike situation of entrapment results
in which the woman seeks self-expression through adaptive somatic and
behavioral responses that may be self-destructive or harmful to others
(see Chapter 7, this volume). Here, male power is a political or material
fact and women's dependence, far from being an intrapsychic adaptation, is a normative status that is continually produced, reproduced, and
resisted at every level of interpersonal and psychic existence. It is in this
framework that we speak of suicidality among battered women as
"control in the context of no control."

## Implications for Intervention

### THE HAZARDS OF INTERVENTION

At best, the clinical response to female suicide attempts fails to
provide needed recognition or support. At worst, the battered women's
dilemma is aggravated by antianxiety agents to help them cope, institutionalization at the state mental hospital with little evidence of
psychiatric disease, and referrals home, often with no follow-up of any
kind. This pattern of response isolates women from resources vital to
their survival, replicates the batterer's pattern of denial and victim

blaming, and reinforces women's sense, to paraphrase Durkheim (1951), that their future is pitilessly blocked, their passions are violently choked, and their life is controlled by physical or moral despotism, the process we term *entrapment*. One battered woman's note from our files illustrates this process:

> I am writing this letter in hope that you will please understand me. Please try. I have two beautiful daughters which I love very much with all my heart plus my husband and my mother and the two best friends I ever had. I love them all, but I can't take it anymore. For the last 9 months, my 2 daughters and my life has been in danger by my husband and I have talked to the doctors, the welfare and detectives, but nothing seems to help me or nobody but my two friends who live at. . . . I had to give my daughters to my aunt this weekend because I don't want them hurt. I don't want to do this or want to be hurt, but I can't find any help. Please let my daughters know I love them. I can't find any other way to protect them. I'm sorry.

Women's pleas for help in counteracting coercive control at home are often misread as gestures or rescue fantasies, supporting the finding by Rose et al. (1991) that self-mutilation (self-cutting) incidents by traumatized clients are often dismissed by mental health professionals as suicidal gestures, even when clients inform workers they are trying to manage the secondary effects of abuse (such as flashbacks or homicidal rage). The sexual inequality that leads to battering is reproduced in the clinical setting. Indeed, even when partners evidence identical mental health profiles, both partners in a couple tend to describe the suicidal partner—usually the female—as psychologically disabled and the non-suicidal partner as well functioning (Canetto, Feldman, & Lupei, 1989).

## CLINICAL ASSESSMENT AND TREATMENT

The neglect of male violence in the literature on female suicidality exemplifies the gender gap in medical and psychotherapeutic practice (Reiker & Carmen, 1984). Although the invisibility of domestic violence in psychiatric settings was initially traced to women's hesitancy to reveal the problem, numerous studies have confirmed the observation by Post and her associates (1980) that "avoidance of knowledge about spouse abuse in psychiatric screening has been more a function of the interviewer's failure to ask about it than the patient's reluctance to talk about such problems" (p. 975).

The prevalence of battering in the background of female suicide attempts underlines the importance of routinely questioning all women in the health and mental health setting about possible abuse regardless of their marital status, presenting complaint, or the presence of psychiatric symptoms. At particular risk are black women, pregnant women, and those who mention marital conflict or a lover's quarrel as the precipitant of suicidality.

More important than the risk factors identified here, however, is an understanding that a woman's vulnerability is typically a function of coercive control (moral despotism in Durkheim's phrase) exercised over a wide range of activities, from access to money to access to family and friends (Stark, 1992). For this reason, the subjective level of fear and the extent of entrapment are as important in assessing whether a situation is emergent as assessing the severity of the suicide attempt, prior injury, current physical abuse, or current psychiatric status. Clinicians must be particularly sensitive to the discrepancy between the perceived emergency expressed by the client and a relatively unimpressive suicidal gesture. Rapid restriction of the individual's contacts with family and friends (commonly noted as a symptom of suicidality) is also frequently associated with the escalation of coercive control. Conversely, when a woman's suicide attempt is related to battering, referrals home or the use of significant others to monitor stresses in the client's life may exacerbate the woman's vulnerability.

Women's adaptive responses to the violence, stress, and isolation of an abusive relationship can mimic frank psychiatric disease, particularly depressive and anxiety disorders. For the suicidal battered woman, depressed mood, hopelessness, codependency, low self-esteem, psychomotor retardation, constriction of thought or complete immobilization, inappropriate affect, sleep disorders, reexperiencing of traumatic events, problems with appetite or overeating, disorganized activity states, paralyzing anxiety, agitation, homicidal rage, depersonalized affect, splitting, obsessive attention to detail, even what appear to be delusions of persecution bordering on paranoia may all be reframed in terms of a strength's perspective as survival oriented (Rapp & Wintersteen, 1989).

Symptoms presented by battered women who attempt suicide often support a *Diagnostic and Statistical Manual of Disorders* (*DSM-III-R*) diagnosis of PTSD (Herman, 1992). When used in combination with advocacy and peer support, such a diagnosis can externalize responsibility for the victimization, reduce self-blame, and enable clinicians to focus on the misuse of power in the battering relationship. Rose and associates (1991) caution, however, that "operationalizing PTSD as a secondary diagnosis without developing advocacy strategies to change provider systems unintentionally prolongs the experience of abuse" (p. 412), a process they term *disguised betrayal* or *false charity* because it emphasizes pathology or disease-based, problem-defining practices that incur little organizational resistance at the expense of practices that are more appropriate but may be controversial. In lieu of frank symptomatology, appropriate intervention can be prompted by the nonstigmatizing *DSM-IV* diagnosis of physical abuse of adult.

The presence of comorbid factors such as depression or frank psychosis may require a short period of psychiatric hospitalization. Protective hospitalization may also be required in emergencies. Until the threat of violence is eliminated, pharmacological intervention should proceed on the conservative premise that abuse of medication in subsequent suicide attempts is a high risk. In addition, because battered women often present with long-standing tranquilizer or analgesic use, chronic symptomatology unresponsive to treatment, vague complaints, and frequent clinic visits, they may accumulate a range of pseudopsychiatric labels that identify them as difficult, demanding, or noncompliant patients who do not deserve serious attention, a pattern that can be addressed only through continued reframing and advocacy in the psychiatric setting. Meanwhile, therapeutic modalities such as group work—often avoided with depressed, suicidal clients—can be useful where this profile is evoked by coercion and isolation.

## CASE MANAGEMENT

Once a history of physical abuse or coercive control has been elicited, intervention should focus on safety concerns. Protocols for attempted suicide should include the range of protections and community-based services available for battered women, especially liaison with social service staff, the local shelter, police, and legal services. Counseling strategies include validating the battered woman's disclosure, educating her about the dynamics of abuse, assessing current danger, helping her formulate a safety plan, facilitating access to needed resources, and ongoing monitoring by social services staff (Jones & Schechter, 1992). Intervention should be particularly sensitive to the special significance of battering in minority communities, where abuse may isolate women from indigenous networks of support vital to economic survival. In any case, focusing on the attempt without responding to the situational precipitant of the self-destructive act can aggravate psychopathology. As with any form of hidden abuse, not initiating a discussion of the topic can confirm a patient's belief in the need to deny the reality of her experience, forcing her attempts at expression to take even more indirect paths, leading to increased desperation and further suicidality (Bryer, Nelson, Miller, & Krol, 1987). A comprehensive program to prevent woman battering could dramatically affect the incidence of female suicidality. The initial step is identification, addressing a woman's sense that she must harm herself to get attention to her plight. Given the enormous barriers to addressing male violence against women, the decision to identify abuse, to normalize a woman's experience of a widely committed crime, and to educate her about its significance is an important step toward reducing the differences in power that give rise to battering in the first place.

The frequency with which battered women attempt suicide shortly after a failed helping encounter and often with the medication given them to relax suggests we should reconsider the adage that we bear no responsibility for our clients' suicide attempts. Today, only two decades after the first battered women's shelters opened, most communities in the United States have access to services for battered women. Yet the decision to probe for violence as the source of women's suicide attempts should no more depend on the existence of such resources as should the development of a safety plan with the battered woman who attempts suicide as a plea for help.

Men commit suicide, according to Durkheim (1951), because they feel anomic, as if there are no rules to govern their conduct. The opposite situation, where conduct is governed by inflexible rules against which there is no appeal, vanished, Durkheim believes, with the rise of societies in which men make their own rules. The fact that ongoing battering may be the single most important context for female suicide attempts is a sobering antidote to Durkheim's optimism.

$5$

# Preventing Gendered Homicide

This chapter proposes a homicide prevention strategy based on the gendered nature of violent acts. We document the importance of partner violence in homicide, critique existing models of homicide, and offer a typology of gendered violence suited to intervention.

In the United States, homicide claims more years of life than anything but accidents, cancer, and heart disease. It is the major cause of death among black women under 44 as well as among younger black males (Centers for Disease Control [CDC], 1983). Homicide is the 11th leading cause of death in the United States, and because its main victims are young adults, it is the 4th leading cause of premature mortality, claiming 612,556 potential years of life lost in 1985 (CDC, 1988). The lifetime chance of becoming a homicide victim is 1 in 240 for whites and 1 in 47 for blacks and other minorities. For young urban black males, the danger is even greater, though a 13% decline in homicides among this group prompted the CDC (1988) to recommend that violence prevention also target other groups.

AUTHORS' NOTE: This chapter is adapted from Stark (1990). Reprinted with permission of the *International Journal of Health Services*.

In any international comparison of homicides, the United States ranks near the top: first in the absolute number of persons killed, fifth in overall rate (both sexes at all ages), fourth for young males (aged 15 to 24), and fifth for males who are slightly older (Rosenberg, Stark, & Zahn, 1986). The U.S. homicide rate is many times higher than that of other Western industrial democracies where guns are legal (e.g., five times higher than Italy) or gun ownership is widespread (e.g., Israel and Switzerland). Ironically, the United States ranks second only to the former Soviet Union in the percentage of its population incarcerated, highlighting the futility of relying solely on harsh punishment. Although violent crime in 1992 returned to the high levels of 1981 and 1982, the current murder rate of 9.3 per 100,000 population is nearly identical to the rate of 9.4 per 100,000 recorded in 1973. Furthermore, the most recent Federal Bureau of Investigation (FBI) figures show that serious and violent crime has declined in the 1990s, with homicide decreasing as much as 50% in some major cities in two decades (Morgenthau, 1995).

Because of its effect on younger people, the economic repercussions of homicide extend far beyond the numbers. Publicity about homicides evokes a sense that violence is an omnipresent threat, particularly in cities; that it is unpredictable; and that we can react only after it occurs, not before. Fear of homicide, the sense that one is vulnerable to a fate that may be delivered at any moment without warning, forms a strong undercurrent in how one evaluates the quality of life as well as the legitimacy of those to whom one entrusts governance. Whether we feel safe has become as significant in shaping major life decisions about work, residence, and recreation as whether we are healthy, successful, or happy. Conversely, feeling out of control of this major facet of our environment shapes how we think about a range of public issues, including race relations, crime, education, housing, and human services.

In the past, health providers responded to the traumatic consequences of violence without attending to the problem itself. Working with a medical model focused on disease and keeping a safe distance from the courts, clinicians failed to identify, assess, or report any but the most dramatic violence-related injuries, even when legally required to do so. Public health and epidemiology were equally oblivious. As recently as 1985, the National Research Council and the National Academy of Medicine published a survey of injury in America (Committee on Trauma Research, 1985) that dismissed violence, homicide, suicide, assault, child abuse, and woman battering in a few sentences.

By default, then, homicide prevention has relied on inhibiting criminals through swift and predictable sanctions from the criminal justice system, so-called *deterrence theory*. By all accounts, deterrence theory has been markedly unsuccessful. In fact, homicide reached its highest level in the century in 1980, just as the death penalty was reintroduced. The political Right contends real deterrence has yet to be tried, whereas liberals claim that violence is rooted in the *four Ps* (poverty, personality, pathology, and passion), hence any approach that presumes individuals rationally weigh the costs of their behavior will fail.

Despite its history of inattention, however, the health system's approach to violence has changed dramatically in the past two decades. Responding to a constellation of fiscal, political, and social factors, virtually every major body of health professionals has acknowledged that violence is a public health issue and launched initiatives that target family as well as street violence, emphasize prevention as well as crisis management, and favor an integrated approach that links health care to criminal justice and community-based organizations. Suddenly, violence prevention is hot.

Unfortunately, our understanding of violence has not kept pace with the desire to prevent it. Antiviolence rhetoric is replete with moral platitudes about the collapse of morality, community, and family life in America. At the other extreme, completely neglecting its unique moral and political contexts, public education proceeds as if, like smoking, driving while intoxicated, or the failure to wear seat belts, violence can be stopped simply by telling people not to do it. In some respects, scholarly interpretations of violence are even more frustrating. Psychiatric and social science theories emphasize biological, personality, childhood, or group characteristics that make certain individuals violence prone; structural tensions, such as poverty, racism, or unemployment; and cultural norms that make violence more acceptable in certain communities than in others. However useful in a clinical setting or classroom, the focus on predisposition, irrational behavior, early childhood experience, and social inequality offers little prospect for practical prevention.

Some hope for prevention comes from local innovations, though few programs have been seriously evaluated. Crime rates are political capital, and public officials routinely declare that an increase or a reduction in violence signals the need for more funds. In fact, long-run changes in violence reflect broad economic or demographic trends (as well as resources allocated for detection), particularly in the population of young adults responsible for most violence, and are unaffected by local action. Homicide, meanwhile, is relatively rare, so that changes in local rates usually reflect unique events—a local drug war or a crackdown on gangs, for example—rather than deliberate interventions.

Our experience with disease prevention is instructive. Despite claims to the contrary, medical and public health interventions in this century succeeded in reducing mortality from infectious and communicable disease only after improved living conditions had weakened mortality's underlying social causes (McKeown, 1977; Stark, 1977). To paraphrase Rene Dubos, with the tide rapidly receding due to improved living standards, it was easy to conclude that the small "buckets of water" medicine was carrying away caused the change (Dubos, 1968). Negative evidence for this thesis is the resurgence of drug-resistant tuberculosis as inner-city conditions deteriorate. If, as we believe, recent social changes have made certain types of violent behavior untenable, then, and only then, are deliberate prevention strategies likely to work.

Another important lesson from medicine is that the effectiveness of deliberate measures requires a typology of problems that permits resources to be effectively targeted. Recent examples include the eradication of smallpox, changes in sexual behavior among gay males, and a shift away from a diet high in fat. The parallel to violence prevention lies not in the search for a magic bullet (so to speak) but in unraveling the confusing array of behaviors now grouped under "violence" into an account of how environmental, social, cultural, and personality factors converge in specific violent situations.

Between 15% and 20% of the murders in the United States are secondary homicides, committed during the perpetration of another crime. The rest are primary homicides, in which death results from a deliberate effort to kill, maim, rape, or otherwise violate the physical integrity of another (Gibbs, 1988; Jason, Strauss, & Tyler, 1983). This chapter approaches homicide prevention by focusing on *gendered homicide*, perhaps the largest subgroup of primary homicides, in which the central dynamic is a female's subordination to a male partner. In contrast to the prevailing opinion that homicide is generally impulsive and unpredictable, gendered homicides have a predictable etiology, usually rooted in woman battering. But if battering accounts for a majority of spousal, intersexual, and child homicides, a substantial proportion of intrasexual homicides is also gendered. Although many homicides fall beyond the purview of this chapter, strategies to prevent fatalities linked to gendered behavior offer a realistic way to preserve human life far better than we currently do.

The first section of the chapter assesses the empirical importance of gendered homicide and the relative weaknesses of theoretical models that neglect sexual conflict. The second section analyzes gendered homicide as a form of intense social engagement typified by a history of battering and frequent contact with a range of helpers. The concluding section traces the implications of the analysis for homicide prevention.

## Primary Homicide: Empirical Dimensions

Although they receive a disproportionate amount of publicity, stranger-to-stranger attacks make up less than a third of all fatalities. Of such killings, 43% are associated with another crime, usually robbery; most such killings are with firearms (53% with handguns, 13.9% with another type of gun); the victims and offenders are predominantly male; and the median age of the victim (31 years) is higher than that of the offender (25 years) (CDC, 1988; Jason et al., 1983; Rosenberg & Mercy, 1991; Rosenberg et al., 1986; Straus, 1986; Wolfgang, 1958). In other words, Charles Manson and John Hinkley—strangers to their victims with no motive other than violence—are anything but typical.

Most murders take place in or near the home, during fights between family members, friends, or acquaintances. Of U.S. homicides in 1980, 32.9% were of friends and acquaintances, 15.8% were within families, 12.8% were between strangers, and 34.4% were classified as "relationship unknown" (Figure 5.1). The percentages in 1990 were almost identical (Dawson & Langany, 1994). Many homicides classified as relationship unknown are really murders of strangers, because murders of intimates are usually cleared (i.e., an arrest is made). Yet a study of homicide in eight cities found that stranger homicide accounted for only 14% to 29% (average, 21.4%) of murders (McClain, 1982). Wolfgang's (1958) lower estimate, based on homicides in Philadelphia and using a conservative definition of acquaintance, is that 24.7% involve family members and 28.2% involve relatives or close friends. In sum, between 50% and 80% of all homicides and well over 95% of primary homicides involve persons who either have an ongoing personal relationship (as many as 50%) or are acquaintances.

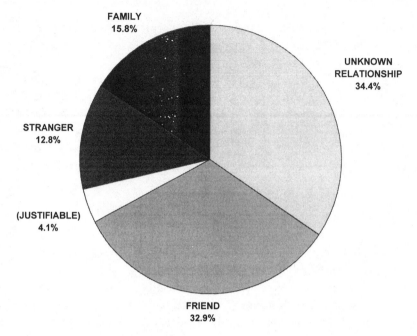

**Figure 5.1.** Percentage of Homicides by Relationship of Victim to Offender, United States, 1980

## RELATIONSHIP OF VICTIM AND OFFENDER

In murders where the relationship was known, a friend or acquaintance was responsible for the greatest number of homicide deaths ($n = 7,504$), a rate of 3.3 per 100,000; with family members next, 1.6 per 100,000; then strangers, 1.3 per 100,000; and finally, "justifiable homicide" by a police officer or citizen, approximately 0.4 per 100,000 (1980 data).

## SEX AND RACE

The ratio of male to female homicide victims is 3.5:1 for each category of victim and offender relationship. Men, black males in particular, are at higher risk in each relationship category, from a rate of 17.7 per 100,000 for murder by a friend or acquaintance to a rate of 2.7 per 100,000 for justifiable homicide, a category in which blacks and other minority males constitute 54.9% of all victims. Black and other minority women have consistently higher death rates than white women and, for homicide by a family member or friend, higher rates than white males

(Hampton, 1987; Mann, 1987; McClain, 1982). Among black females, 47% are murdered by acquaintances and 43% by family members (McClain, 1982). Among black males, 62% are killed by acquaintances and only 20% are killed by other family members, typically wives. Among black youth, from 1976 to 1982, 46% of homicide victims were killed by acquaintances, 20% by strangers, and only 8% by family members (Gibbs, 1988). How race and socioeconomic status contribute to these homicide rates is not understood.

Data from the five southwestern states in which more than 60% of all Hispanics in the United States reside show that the overall homicide rate for Hispanics (20.5 per 100,000) was almost three times the rate among whites (7.9 per 100,000; 1980 data). The most striking differences occurred among young male age groups, possibly the result of gang violence. Street violence is a major cause of death only among Hispanics.

## FAMILY HOMICIDES

The United States has a higher rate of intrafamily homicide than the overall rate of homicide in European countries, such as England, Germany, and Denmark. Most family homicides involve spouses, occur at home, and progress through a series of assaultive incidents. From 1976 to 1985, 17,241 homicides involved spouses or ex-spouses, approximately 9.2% of the homicides for these years (Mercy & Saltzman, 1989). FBI data indicate that approximately 55% of family homicide victims are white and 43.7% are black, suggesting a far higher ratio of homicide to proportion in the population among blacks. Blacks also account for 45.4% of all spousal homicide victims (Mercy & Saltzman, 1989). In all probability, however, this has less to do with race than with social class and the bias in police response. Using the number of persons per room to measure social class, Centerwall (1984) found that blacks in Atlanta, Georgia, were no more likely to commit domestic homicide than whites living under similar conditions. Race or social class does seem to affect the sex ratio of offenders and victims in family homicides. White wives are at almost twice the risk of being killed by a spouse as white husbands, whereas black wives have victim rates that are moderately lower than those for black husbands (Mercy & Saltzman, 1989). The median age of family homicide victims is 33; the median age of offenders is 32. Handguns are used in 40% of the cases, other guns in 24%, knives in 17%, and other means in 18%. With greater economic independence, women have been replacing knives with guns as weapons of choice.

ACQUAINTANCE HOMICIDE

At first glance, homicides by acquaintances contrast sharply with intrafamily homicides. Acquaintance homicides are more prevalent among blacks than whites; offenders, whose median age is 23, are usually younger than their victims; handguns are the typical weapon; and victims are younger and more likely to be male and black than in family homicide.

The problem is that the term *acquaintance* subsumes two very different types of relationships, intersexual homicides in which the acquaintance is a lover or live-in partner (but not a family member, spouse, or ex-spouse) and those in which the parties are young, same sex, or friends. For instance, boyfriends and ex-boyfriends are responsible for a significant proportion of the 46% of black female homicides attributed to acquaintances. The notion of gendered homicide also extends to acquaintance homicides among friends. Although a third of these homicides occur in the street and a high percentage occur in bars, the most common site is a private residence (Jason et al., 1983), highlighting the fact that many of these conflicts directly involve or concern female partners. Ethnographic and anecdotal data also suggest that, in homicides precipitated by verbal arguments and occurring in or near the home (the predominant form for black males over 15), proprietary rights over a woman are often the issue.

WORKPLACE HOMICIDE

Assault is a more common cause of female workplace deaths than occupational injury and accounts for 1 in 20 female homicides (Bell, 1991). Although estimates of the percentage of these deaths caused by husbands, ex-husbands, or boyfriends range from 20% to 50%, many others grow out of harassment situations, that is, domestic violence in the workplace. Similar dynamics involving jealousy or harassment are also in evidence in many cases in which males victimize other males at work.

CHILD HOMICIDE

In 1980, child homicide by a family member caused 501 deaths, with black males killed three times as often as white males (6.8 versus 2.3 per 100,000) and twice as often as black females (3.3 per 100,000) (Straus, 1986). Blacks account for approximately 40% of deaths to children under 3 years of age and 24% of all child homicide deaths (Hawkins,

1986). Social class and gender prove more important than race, however. A recent Ohio study found that when socioeconomic status was controlled, racial differences in homicide involving children ages 5 to 14 disappeared (Muscat, 1988).

As is the case with child abuse, child homicide is often attributed to a psychotic or depressed mother, a mother made distraught by a failed relationship, or a woman's failure to protect her child from an outburst by a male friend. In reality, fathers are far more likely than mothers to cause child fatality, accounting for more than two thirds of neonaticides and infanticides (Straus, 1986). White stepfathers are 10% more likely and black fathers or stepfathers 50% more likely than mothers to kill an infant (Straus, 1986). In a Georgia study of 51 fatal child abuse cases, fathers again were the principal culprits. When Bergman et al. (1986) compared medical examiner records in child abuse cases for two time periods, 1971 through 1973 and 1981 through 1983, they found the proportion of known male perpetrators had risen from 38% to 49% for all cases, from 30% to 64% for severe cases, and to 80% in fatal cases.

Though the dynamics here require careful documentation, intersexual (partner) violence is almost certainly the major precipitant of child homicide, reflecting the link between woman battering, child abuse, and child fatality. In more than half of all cases identified at hospitals, child abuse occurs as a stage in ongoing woman battering (Stark & Flitcraft, 1988c; see also Chapter 3, this volume) the more severe the abuse alleged, the greater the probability that a male partner was responsible (Bergman et al., 1986). Informal reviews from New York City, Oregon, and Massachusetts reveal that between 41% and 70% of child fatalities involve domestic violence (Carter, 1995).

## FAMILY HOMICIDE TRENDS

Domestic homicides in general and spousal homicides in particular appear to be decreasing, particularly among blacks. After a sharp increase in family homicide between 1966 and 1980, there has been a significant decline (Straus, 1986). An important component of this decline appears to be a decrease in the spousal homicide rate among blacks. Reviewing FBI statistics from 1976 to 1985, Mercy and Saltzman (1989) found that the spousal homicide rate for whites remained virtually unchanged, whereas the homicide rate for black husbands declined 52.0% (from 12.7 to 6.1 per 100,000) and for black wives declined by 45.8% (from 9.6 to 5.2 per 100,000). A probable cause of this decline, efforts to combat woman battering, is reflected in survey reports from both husbands and wives, indicating a decline in severe violent acts by husbands (Straus & Kantor, 1994).

It is possible, however, that the reported decline in spousal homicide reflects a growing tendency for black partners to define themselves as unmarried. Two studies taken more than 20 years apart suggest that the percentage of intersexual homicides among black partners may actually have increased. Whereas Wolfgang (1958) reports that fewer than a third of the victims in family homicides by black women ($n = 93$) are husbands and lovers, reviewing 1981 data from seven cities ($n = 119$), McClain (1982) found that although the overall percentage of family homicides by black women had dropped, almost 90% of these were husbands or lovers.

Our literature review confirms Lachman's (1978) conclusion that "almost one third of all homicides take place within the immediate family, another 21% in romantic triangles or lover's quarrels, and 27% take place among less intimate relatives and friends" (p. 36). In sum, at least half of all homicides and approximately 66% of primary homicides are directly or indirectly domestic.

## BATTERING AND HOMICIDE BY WOMEN

Women are offenders in 17% of all homicides and are almost six times as likely to commit a primary rather than a secondary homicide (17% versus 3%). The vast majority of these cases involve what Wolfgang (1958) calls "victim-precipitated homicide," that is, a proactive or defensive strike against an assailant. Estimates of how much female violence is defensive range from 42% to 79% (Nisonoff & Bitman, 1979; Suval & Brisson, 1974). Defense attorneys traditionally concealed an abusive history, fearing it would demonstrate a woman's motive to kill her partner. Studies show that 40% to 70% of women in prison or charged with murder or manslaughter were abused by the men they killed (Barnard, Vera, Vera, & Newman, 1982; Browne, 1987). What distinguishes women who kill their partners is the propensity for their partners to use rape, child abuse, and severe and frequent violence as means of coercion (Browne, 1987).

Consistent with the view that female homicide is often victim precipitated, women offenders are significantly less likely than male offenders to come from dysfunctional families or broken homes or to abuse drugs or alcohol, particularly if they are black and their victim is male

(McClain, 1982; Richardson & Campbell, 1980; Suval & Brisson, 1974). By contrast, 35.3% to 44.4% list anger and revenge as the motive for killing, typically an indication of abuse (Hampton, 1987). Several studies report that black female offenders have a lower educational level than whites, but Browne (1987) and Mann (1987) report either no educational difference or that incarcerated female offenders have higher levels of education than nonoffenders. Some studies report violence in the childhood of battered women (Browne, 1987; Stark, 1984), but reviewing this literature, Hampton (1987) concludes that 62.3% to 88.9% of female homicide offenders come from intact homes. Regardless of race, female homicide offenders are likely to be unemployed or to work in an unskilled occupation (Mann, 1987).

HOMICIDE-SUICIDE

Homicide-suicide involves one or more killings and the subsequent suicide of the assailant. Although there are no national data on this phenomenon, a recent study by the Kentucky Department of Health Services (Currens, 1991) reveals that homicide-suicide accounted for 6% of the homicide deaths in that state between 1985 and 1990. The perpetrators of homicide-suicide were almost always male, the victims were almost always female, and the parties were known to one another, usually because the assailant was the husband, boyfriend, or former husband or boyfriend of the homicide victim. In the Kentucky study, 97% of the perpetrators were male; 70% were husbands, ex-husbands, or boyfriends; and 73% of the victims were women. Anecdotal evidence suggests homicide-suicides are almost always the culmination of woman battering.

RACE OR GENDER?

An alternative to the emphasis on gender is the common tendency to focus on racial explanations of homicide. Allegations that black males are overwhelmingly the perpetrators of homicide have elicited a range of theories ranging from the sociobiology of Harvard's James Q. Wilson (1985) through liberal accounts highlighting pathological features of black personality (Poussaint, 1972), family (Palley & Robinson, 1988), culture (Wolfgang & Ferracuti, 1967), and the ghetto environment (West, 1994). In his theory of the black underclass, for instance, sociologist William Julius Wilson (1987) links the structural isolation of low-income blacks in the ghetto to the two primary pathologies in the black community—black-on-black violence and female-headed households. In Wilson's (1987) view, violence-related arrests of unemployed black males deplete the pool available for marriage, whereas the absence of strong male models contributes directly to delinquency and violent crime. Along with other researchers, Wilson (1987) favors economic incentives to strengthen male-headed families, including job programs targeting black males. The analysis is linked to related claims that violence by black youth, out-of-wedlock pregnancy, and drug use in the ghetto are also products of female-headed families.

Elsewhere, Stark (1993) has argued that racial differences in violence have been greatly exaggerated largely due to reliance on arrest data—which are skewed because of police bias—rather than data from victims or self-report studies, which show few racial differences in violent acts. Not only are 75% of violent crimes committed by whites but hard drug use is higher among whites and out-of-wedlock births are increasing four times as rapidly among whites than blacks. There is no strong evidence that children of single mothers are more prone than others to violence. In fact, the group of youth identified by researchers at highest risk are those who have been exposed to violence by a male adult against their mothers or themselves.

Although race may not differentiate who initiates violence, fatal outcomes are far more likely when blacks are involved. So-called black-on-black violence is very real, not because blacks are so much more violent than whites but because the consequences of violence for blacks are likely to be more severe. Society's response to violence in the black community directly contributes to this tragic outcome. Cuts in state Medicaid coverage, the closing of a number of metropolitan hospitals, and the probability that blacks will be employed in retail or small, highly competitive firms that provide inadequate or no insurance coverage have led to a decline in access to emergency and other medical services among blacks in the past decade. Meanwhile, police regulate violent behavior among blacks mainly when it "overflows" into public areas shared by whites, hence the massive arrest rates among black youth and for drug and gang-related offenses but not for crimes that occur in and around the home, such as domestic violence. Hawkins (1987) argues that police harbor stereotypes of blacks as "normal primitives" from whom violence is expected and so fail to respond to intersexual violence, increasing the probability that it will escalate to homicide.

Setting stereotypes aside, gender rather than race (or social class) appears to be the best predictor of interpersonal violence. For instance, although battering is a more common source of female injury than rape, mugging, or auto accidents combined, survey data indicate only a 3% difference between violence against low-income women (11%) and violence against middle-income women (8%) (Schulman, 1979). Surveys suggest that domestic violence may be twice as high among blacks than whites (Schulman, 1979; Straus, 1986). But when income is controlled, blacks rates are found to be equal to white rates (Centerwall, 1984) or lower (Steinmetz, 1974).

Because partner violence is a major source of female fatality, policies that increase women's dependence on men—under whatever rationale—also contribute to the increased probability of homicide. In contrast, highlighting the protective effects of economic independence, the homicide rate among black spouses has declined significantly, as the proportion of black women who are single, separated, or divorced has grown (Mercy & Saltzman, 1989).

## SUMMARY

Eighty percent of all homicides are "friendly affairs" involving family members, close friends, or acquaintances; occur in or near home; and are preceded by a verbal argument. More than 75% of primary homicides involve family members or acquaintances, compared with only 24% of secondary homicides.

Persuasive evidence implicates abuse in the 17% of primary homicides committed by women and in the 20% committed by men where family members are the victim, usually spouses. In addition, because woman abuse is the context for almost half of all child abuse cases, men are the typical assailants in these cases. Men account for 80% or more of all child fatalities. Woman abuse appears to be the major cause of child homicide as well. It is highly likely that battering is also the major context for homicide-suicide.

The dynamics involved in the estimated 60% of primary homicides that are intrasexual are less clear. A certain percentage of these involve same-sex lovers and perhaps one third originate in lovers' quarrels where men kill one another because of jealousy. Violence used to impose male authority over women and children may be a factor in approximately two thirds of all primary homicides and in more than half of all homicides.

## Models of Violence, Theories of Homicide

Three basic models frame our current response to homicide: a biological-psychiatric model, an engineering model, and a sociological or environmental model. Though each could contribute to a useful typology, as presently formulated they confound rather than assist practical efforts at prevention.

### THE BIOPSYCHIATRIC MODEL

The biopsychiatric model identifies genetic, biological, or psychiatric factors that predispose individuals to behave in an aggressive, antisocial, or violent way. Violence is explained as the result when an instinct or drive (sex, aggression, hunger, territoriality) has been frustrated by an external obstruction (Mednick, Pollack, Volavka, & Gabrielli, 1982) or when the processes that normally inhibit aggression are rendered ineffective by an abnormal process (such as child abuse) or mental illness.

At the most general level, the biological model interprets violence as an adaptive expression of innate tendencies to preserve the individual (hence the species) against perceived threats or stressors, the basis for legal notions of self-defense. Animal analogues demonstrate that adverse ecological conditions, such as overcrowding, can stimulate survival-oriented violent reactions in normal individuals. Because what is defined as threatening often involves perceived challenges to sexual privilege, however, the model has important normative implications, implying that persons who fail to respond to these challenges are weak. Thus, in sentencing a man to 18 months for killing his wife 4 hours after finding her with another man, a Maryland judge recently explained, " 'I seriously wonder how many men . . . would have the strength to walk away without inflicting some corporal punishment' " (Lewin, 1994, p. A18).

Biological theories emphasizing abnormality are commonly used to explain the transmission of antisocial behavior, including violence, from one generation to the next. DiLalla and Gottesman (1991) cite adoption studies indicating a genetic component to antisocial behavior, twin studies of antisocial probands that corroborate the adoption studies, and physiological studies that highlight the association between impulsive behavior and low 5 hydrozyindole-acetic acid (5-HIAA), one of the metabolites of the neurotransmitter serotonin. Some investigators believe that a segment of the population whose genetic makeup includes a special form of one chromosome, known as the XYY chromosome, has a tendency toward violent behavior.

Psychiatry also emphasizes the diversion of aggressive instincts but highlights personality disorders originating in rare medical problems, such as temporal lobe epilepsy or exposure to severe trauma, including childhood violence, rape, and wartime atrocities. Starting from unresolved narcissistic and asocial attitudes that are part of the child's original nature, conventional psychoanalytic theory employs the Freudian notion of the psyche to explain how dysfunctional parenting can elicit violence because the id overflows with violent drives, an overdeveloped superego produces a well of repressed rage, or an underdeveloped superego leads an individual to accept violence in himself or herself and the environment (Friedman, 1983).

Like psychiatry, psychology emphasizes the influence of early childhood or the frustration of needs at specific stages of growth (Megargee, 1982). The transmission of violence occurs as individuals internalize and replicate responses to problems they have observed among significant others or been rewarded for imitating, though learning. Spatz-Widom (1989) reveals that abused or neglected children are more likely than their counterparts to be arrested for violence as teens, though the difference is small (29% versus 21%).

### Limits of the Biopsychiatric Model

Extreme or life-threatening insults precipitate only a small minority of homicides. Thus, a broad application of the frustration-aggression hypothesis involves asking how the visceral stimulation of aggressive impulses is linked to the cognitive and cultural processes that make certain events appear threatening to specific groups. Animal analogues are of little use here, because, as Lily Tomlin reminds us, farm life in Idaho can feel as stressful as life in downtown Moscow. Although the biological model is theoretically gender neutral, the *hot blood* defense has been used almost exclusively by men, reflecting the belief that aggression is sex linked. In fact, men appear to be more aggressive than women only in specific situations—for example, where the target of aggression is the same sex as the aggressor—and even these differences wane as the cultural roles of men and women converge (e.g., in low-income and minority communities) or females are removed from arenas in which sex stereotypes are enforced.

## The Role of Aggression in Violence

The basic tenet of the biopsychiatric model, the link between instinctual aggression and criminal violence, is its most problematic. Aggression is a generalized drive that can be expressed in ways that range from competitive sports to wartime atrocities. Even in the classic frustration-aggression hypothesis, violence is not necessarily the most effective means to remove obstacles. By contrast, many types of violent behavior—woman battering, combat, and gang rumbles are examples—involve patterned modes of reacting that have little to do with aggression (e.g., the assailant may be physiologically calm). Indeed, one defining element of intersexual violence is its use to suppress unacceptable levels of female aggression and conflict (Baker-Miller, 1976).

A range of aggressive feelings is often linked to a violence-prone or disturbed personality. Yet because these states can spring from a desire to shape one's environment actively, they have a definite place in normal life. Given the fact that most families are internally constructed around sexual inequality, a certain degree of open conflict around control is both inevitable and desirable. Thus, when Leary (1988) traced the experience of 393 couples from the period just before they were married, he found that the most aggressive couples, including those reporting they had attacked their partner, scored highest on marital satisfaction. The inverse relation between intersexual violence (coercion by males) and other forms of aggression helps explain why assertiveness training has been one of the most successful tools for reducing violence by male batterers.

## Childhood Precursors

In mapping the unique pathways through which couples channel aggression, psychiatry corrects a defect in the frustration hypothesis—that very few of those whose needs go unmet commit criminal violence. However, psychiatry's consistent failure to predict violence highlights the major weakness of its approach; that is, violence-related illness is usually diagnosed after the fact. Meanwhile, models that emphasize the roots of adult violence in childhood trauma are marred by small and unrepresentative samples, lack of controls, and definitions of childhood mistreatment that run the gamut from the use of guns and knives to a lack of empathic mothering (Steele & Pollock, 1974; Straus et al., 1980). In any case, the vast majority of children exposed to parental violence do not become violent adults (Kaufman & Zigler, 1987) and the vast majority of men who commit gendered violence have not experienced violent childhoods (Stark & Flitcraft, 1988c). At most then, childhood experiences are one of the many influences that frame adult behavior.

A social learning model focusing on current reinforcements and inhibitors is more promising. Unfortunately, a familial emphasis on dominance and control is not defined as unhealthy in our society. If coercion "works" to realize socially approved ends or is rewarded, individuals resort to it more frequently (Leary, 1988), regardless of whether violence also meets secondary psychological needs. Conversely, arrest remains the most effective sanction against intersexual violence, suggesting that common processes of inhibition are at work (Berk, 1993). Similarly, the most effective therapeutic models confront the cognitive messages that give men permission to dominate and hurt women. Though it helps explain how habits of dominance are acquired, learning theory cannot explain why violence and coercion are used for sexual dominance.

THE ENGINEERING MODEL

Although not a formal theory, the engineering model offers a straight-forward explanation of homicide: Given a propensity for violence, people kill one another because they have the means to do so. This simple postulate has enormous implications for prevention.

Altering the physical environment to improve health has been a popular public strategy at least since Edwin Chadwick introduced public sanitation as a cure for disease, poverty, and rebellion in the mid-19th century. The engineering approach to accidental injury has been widely employed in occupational and environmental health as well as auto safety, where relying on individual change (such as seat belt use) appeared futile. Because accidents are unplanned by definition, motives are irrelevant. The engineering model insulates those at risk from the immediate mechanical hazard (e.g., through the use of air bags or safety bumpers), removes the hazard altogether, or protects or repairs the object of damage (Haddon, 1980).

*Gun Control: Engineering in Action*

Gun control extends the engineering approach to deliberate injury. Guns are involved in 60% of the deaths due to homicide and suicide in the United States (Rosenberg et al., 1986) and are responsible for an ever larger proportion (Sloan, Rivera, Reay, Ferris, & Kellerman, 1988). Without claiming to explain the dynamics or motives for violence, the engineering model seeks to prevent firearm injuries and deaths by restricting access to handguns and ammunition.

How effective is gun regulation? At first glance, the answer is not very. For instance, a study of a Detroit law stipulating 2-year mandatory sentences for felonies committed while possessing a firearm showed no effect on gun assaults, armed robberies, or homicides not involving a gun (Loftin & McDowell, 1981). Harsher sentences for drug-related firearm violence were quickly incorporated into the cost of doing business on the street. Besides, because handguns account for three fourths of gun-related homicides, the emphasis on semiautomatic weapons makes little difference.

From the vantage of the typology developed here—particularly of gendered homicide—the engineering approach looks far more effective. For example, although a 1976 Washington, D.C., law strictly prohibiting the purchase, sale, and possession of firearms made no reduction in felony-related homicides, it did dramatically reduce primary homicides (Jones, 1981). A subsequent study indicated the law was responsible for a 25% overall decline in gun-related homicide and suicide in Washington, D.C., preventing an average of 47 deaths each year. A comparison of Vancouver and Seattle, cities with relatively similar socioeconomic and crime profiles, revealed that limiting access to handguns was associated with significantly lower rates of aggravated assault and homicide in Vancouver between 1980 and 1986. Beyond this, virtually all the difference in the relative risk of homicide in Seattle (1.63) was due to a more than fivefold higher rate of homicide by firearms (Sloan et al., 1988). The rate of homicides with weapons other than firearms did not increase in Vancouver to compensate for the restriction on handguns, suggesting that the availability of a weapon is the crucial issue, not the strength of intent, as critics of gun control often claim. Meanwhile, although there is some evidence that the presence of a gun in a robbery decreases the probability of nonfatal injury (because resistance is less likely), Kellerman (1992) shows that the presence of a gun in a household significantly increases the probability of homicide.

The present incentive for gun control stems from dramatic instances of public violence. But even limited local gun regulation would significantly reduce injury and fatality in intersexual and familial homicides.

## Limits of the Engineering Model

Obviously, if an activity is socially desirable—such as driving a car—then it is morally palatable to support the least noxious means of carrying it out. Although limiting fatality is good in itself, an engineering approach to intersexual violence would do nothing to affect the availability of a range of other means regularly employed to dominate and harm women. Thus, in countries with low rates of homicide and significant control of firearms, murder is overwhelmingly a domestic crime in which men typically kill their wives, mistresses, or children, though rarely with guns. In England, for instance, of the murder victims over 16, 70% are female; of those females, nearly half are killed by their legal husbands and a quarter by other relatives or lovers (Morris & Blum-Cooper, 1967). Of course, there would be many more domestic homicides without gun control. Still criminologists have neglected Verkko's (1967) fascinating observation, based on historical and cross-national data, that as overall homicide rates change, the number of female victims of murder remains relatively constant, again suggesting a distinct etiology for gendered homicide.

The greatest weakness of the engineering reformers is their political naiveté. The model fails to address why resistance to its application is often strongest among the very corporate and political interests that profess to favor public health and safety. Thus, the promise of the engineering model to provide a quick fix that leaves the underlying causes of conflict undisturbed is its Achilles' heel, particularly when the harms involved benefit those who are privileged by social inequality.

## THE SOCIOLOGICAL APPROACH

Sociological explanations for homicide range in focus from the microdynamics of criminal behavior to the systems that link violence to structural, historical, or cultural factors. Theories that emphasize microevents contend that violence is the consequence of certain types of interaction, for instance, the intense family (Straus et al., 1980), ganging (Jankowski, 1991), tavern culture (Gibbs, 1986), or even relationships with police in which being labeled elicits criminality (Cicourel, 1967;

Luckenbill, 1977). A popular macrodynamic theory holds that disadvantaged groups adapt illegitimate means (such as violence) to realize their goals when they are denied access to legitimate means by poverty, unemployment, racism, relative economic disadvantage, or the absence of a marriageable pool of young men (Cloward & Ohlin, 1960; Curtis, 1975; Wilson, 1987). Note that whereas individualistic and interactionist theories presume that violence is a form of deviance, the environmental, structural, and cultural theories contend that violence is a normative means to reach socially valued ends, particularly in America. Thus, with respect to intersexual violence, a popular argument is that violence is endemic in family life because "a marriage license is a hitting license" (Straus et al., 1980).

These theories suggest a potpourri of prevention strategies, ranging from legalization of heroin and cocaine (to prevent labeling) to wholesale restructuring of public education, the media, and the economy. Although specific economic reforms (such as eliminating the wage gap between the sexes) are crucial to preventing gendered violence, recent analyses of homicide rates in large metropolitan samples found that poverty alone was not a significant predictor of homicide rates (Blau & Blau, 1982; Messner, 1982). The key variable was social inequality.

Sociological theories are as compatible with conservative as with liberal agendas. For instance, the image of a black underclass has convinced some policymakers to draw a line in the sand behind which they write off (i.e., deprive of services) low-income communities. Furthermore, if "violence is as American as apple pie," or built into the economic structure, then little can be done to prevent it.

## SUMMARY

Prevailing approaches to homicide illuminate important facets of the problem. Genetic as well as environmental factors undoubtedly interact in the formation of disorders that predispose individuals to antisocial behavior. But the vast majority of violent acts are unrelated to psychiatric disease or biological predisposition and may have nothing to do with aggression at all. Conversely, as the young couples studied by Leary (1988) indicated, fighting itself is not the problem and, if used creatively and within bounds, may actually enhance a capacity to resolve conflicts. Gendered violence, on the other hand, is often methodical and manipulative rather than impulsive and is aimed at suppressing rather than resolving conflict. The biopsychiatric model tells us almost nothing about the facets of violent behavior that are most readily modified—the where, when, how, and how often of violence—or about who (in the sense of which groups) are defined as appropriate victims. Conversely, because the right of males to dominate women is supported by a range of social messages, the current approach of teaching young people to resolve their differences nonviolently is morally palatable only if people are simultaneously dissuaded from using other means of coercion to subordinate partners on the basis of sex or race. Ironically, reducing violence used to control vulnerable individuals or groups would enhance a capacity to use aggression creatively—a positive outcome—and to direct (legitimate) anger at the forms of inequality and domination that frame so much suffering in our society.

Although mental illness is hardly a precondition for gendered violence, a disproportionate amount of criminal violence is perpetrated by young people requiring psychiatric care (Gibbs, 1988). At present, these youngsters are likely to be processed through the prison system rather than through the mental health system, particularly if they are black, a disastrous approach. Furthermore, between 30% and 50% of the in- and outpatient mental health caseload have histories of violent behavior, victimization, or both (Herman, 1986; Hilberman & Munson, 1977-1978; Post et al., 1980), and percentages are even higher among psychiatric subpopulations of substance abusers or attempted suicides (Gondolf, 1990; Stark & Flitcraft, 1991). Unfortunately, the present psychiatric system is unlikely to screen for this history or deem it relevant to treatment decisions unless it is linked to psychosis or violence is directed at staff (Gondolf, 1990). As a result, most disorders linked to violence are identified only after a crime is committed. Indeed, psychiatry's insensitivity to victims or perpetrators of violence is reflected in inappropriate diagnoses and treatments that actually increase the probability that subsequent violence will be fatal. Even at best, psychiatry has a minimal role in preventing intersexual violence because the vast majority of offenders and victims are not mentally ill. Recognizing this, the latest version of the *Diagnostic and Statistical Manual of the American Psychiatric Association* (*DSM-IV*) classifies physical abuse by/of an adult under conditions that may be the focus of clinical attention but are not attributable to psychiatric disease.

With respect to violence, learning theory finds only limited support in prospective data (Spatz-Widom, 1989) and even here the link between early childhood exposure to abuse and subsequent violence is asserted rather than proved. For the minority of violent adults who were exposed to childhood trauma, a question remains about why parents (which usually means mom) play a much more important role than school, peers, or other influences. For the rest, the most parsimonious explanation for intersexual violence is that coercion secures real material advantage, at least in the short run. As a deterrent to violence, the value of early parent-child ties of love, nonviolent parenting, and experiences that reinforce the child's positive attachments, minimize frustrations, and encourage flexible role models or inner controls are emphasized. However beneficial, this agenda is unlikely to reduce adult criminal violence. Learning theory is more persuasive when it shifts to current inhibitors and reinforcers of violent behavior. Predictable sanctions for offenders, reeducation programs that challenge male control, and empowerment learning for women are among the strategies believed to inhibit intersexual violence successfully.

Proponents of engineering remind us that homicide remains a crime of opportunity (i.e., a murderous weapon must be present) and that we can restrict violent means without changing personality or beliefs. Ironically, the probable effect of gun control would be to reduce homicide by ordinary citizens, that is, where the National Rifle Association (NRA) denies there is a problem.

Finally, though its alternating emphasis on micro- and macrodimensions of violent behavior leaves the huge middle ground of situational dynamics unchartered (cf. Cambell & Gibbs, 1986), sociology recognizes that the means, victims, intensity, and cultural meaning of violence are rooted in group life rather than nature and are patterned by one's race, gender, and class.

## TOWARD A TYPOLOGY OF HOMICIDE

The challenge to homicide prevention is to capture the insights of existing models in a typology that describes and allows us to modify the relations involved in murderous encounters. To start, we must abandon the popular belief that criminal violence arises from conditions or passions that make rational calculation impossible. From Othello through Bigger Thomas in *Native Son,* classic literature abounds with characters who kill because they are mad or driven mad by jealousy, drink, or social disadvantage. In fact, none of these is a significant cause of homicide. Alcohol has been consistently linked to domestic violence, as both a precipitant for men (Gondolf, 1990) and a consequence for women (Stark, 1984), but substance use does not distinguish battering situations terminating in homicide from those that do not end in homicide (Browne, 1987). Conversely, the cessation of violence and of alcohol abuse are unrelated (Richardson & Campbell, 1980). Although jealousy and other sex or power passions are omnipresent, psychoanalysts remind us that jealousy—like violence itself—is a means to control the object of anger or guilt. From rural Greece through suburban Westchester, norms of status and authority provide the political subtext for the language of passion. Far from being irrational, young men who lose control and attack wives, lovers, or strangers in a paneled basement in wealthy Glen Ridge, New Jersey, or at night in Central Park are exhibiting a highly ritualized, gender-specific, and widely practiced means to attain approved ends, an affirmation of their identity, social role, family name, or honor and proof of dominance, whether over women or other men. The issue is not impulse control, but the right to treat human beings as property.

## Gendered Homicide

As many as half of all homicides involve attempts to impose, defend, or resist sexual stereotypes. Theoretical models that trace these fatalities to broad aspects of biology, personality, environment, or social structure lack the specificity needed to devise practical prevention strategies. Instead, we propose a situational typology based on the gendered nature of these violent acts. To be gendered means more than an infusion of sexual imagery. In addition, the gendered typology ascribes the intensity typically associated with sex or passion, hence with some combination of biology and psychology, to the power and privilege associated with socially constructed sexual differences. Challenges to these constructed differences may elicit a visceral response. Specifying that gendered homicides are crimes of coercion and control rather than of passion opens an arena for prevention not afforded by the emphasis on sexuality, emotion, or mental illness.

Gendered homicide will persist as a type as long as domination is rooted in real inequalities. Practical prevention efforts, however, can focus on the major components of the phenomenon. Three dynamics distinguish gendered homicide from secondary homicide and homicide between mere acquaintances: The fatality is proceeded by a history of partner assault and coercion that culminates in a situation of entrapment; the assaults involve intense social engagement about appropriate gender role behavior; and both the victim and the perpetrator have a history of encounters with helping agencies. These components are mutually reinforcing. The failure to identify, assess, or intervene early in the abusive situation contributes to a woman's entrapment and strengthens the male's sense of entitlement. Interventions that affect any one component also reduce the risk associated with others.

## A HISTORY OF ASSAULT AND COERCION
## THAT CULMINATES IN A SENSE OF ENTRAPMENT

Regardless of who is killed, gendered homicides are almost always the culmination of a prior history of violence and coercion.

When Amma, age 19, married Albert Harris, 23, in 1976, Amma's parents declared the Harris family "dead" to them because Albert was black. Once, while the couple was still living in West Virginia, Albert broke Amma's nose. But the couple went on to have three boys and two girls and, hoping to find the economic opportunity and support they could not find at home, they moved north. The violence continued against Sean (the oldest boy) as well as Amma. From April 1986 until Amma found her own apartment, she stayed in shelters and emergency housing. On the day he was supposed to appear for violating one of many restraining orders, Albert raped Amma in her apartment. He was imprisoned, then released when his bail was significantly reduced. He told Amma he would never let her have "his" children, a threat he repeated during the divorce proceeding, when he was awarded the sword he had used in the rape. Shortly after the divorce, he "hitched" a ride with Alma and her new boyfriend to a local shopping mall where he fatally stabbed Amma.

During the course of the 6-year marriage before she fatally shot her husband, Dila was raped; slapped; punched in the head, arms, and legs; strangled; and "kicked across the room." These assaults were accompanied by threats with a gun and by a pattern of control over sex, money, friendships, communication with family, Dila's physical appearance, and minute details of everyday life. Symbolic was a "log book" in which Dila was forced to keep a record of how she spent each day, including all expenditures and meal plans for the month. At night, Mic would interrogate her about her entries in the log book, then beat her. "If I said something he didn't like, he would hit me. If I couldn't account for exactly where I was, he would hit me. If I forgot I saw someone, just a friend, no big deal, it would be like, why didn't you tell me you saw him?"

In a third or more of all homicides, and in an even higher percentage that occur in urban areas, at least one prior assault has been documented by police or court records, as in the case of Amma (Teske & Parker, 1983). With gendered violence, the percentages are far higher. A report from Kansas City reveals 80% of domestic homicides were preceded by one or more complaints of assault to the police and 50% by five calls or more (cited in Browne, 1987). In Connecticut, of the 18,483 domestic violence arrests during 1993 for which this information was available, there were prior domestic violence arrests and court orders for 3,381, almost one in five (Family Violence Reporting Program, 1993). Between 51.6% and 90% of women who kill have been previously arrested, usually for assault (McClain, 1982). Hawkins (1986) obtained information on previous arrests for assault during the 18 months preceding homicide. At least one prior arrest had been made in half the homes where black women were killed and in 38.5% of the homes where the victim was a black male.

Many partner assaults presented to the hospital are not reported to police. Estimates based on medical records reveal that between 19% and 50% of various female patient populations have been assaulted by a social partner and that 85% of these women have an ongoing history of multiple episodes (for a summary of these data, see Stark & Flitcraft, 1991). The importance of partner assault throughout the life cycle is illustrated by hospital research showing that 34% of the injuries to girls 16 to 18 years old are caused by partners, as are 18% of injuries to women over 60 (McLeer & Anwar, 1989). Even these data are extremely conservative, however. The fact that the vast majority of domestic assaults are reported to neither police nor medicine is confirmed by surveys indicating that, as in Dila's case, between 25% and 30% of abused women suffer serial victimization, many beaten as frequently as once a week (Klaus & Rand, 1984; Teske & Parker, 1983). Women typically fail to report because the vast majority of abusive episodes do not involve medically significant injury and because partner control often extends to help seeking by the victim. In our experience, however, the risk of homicide is predicated on the accumulated history of abuse and control regardless of the severity of prior injury.

With the exception of child fatality, where a prior history of domestic assault is often documented, there are no studies that consider whether a history of partner assault precedes homicide in situations in which men kill other men. Suggestive evidence is available, however. Among a population of 644 batterers arrested in Quincy, Massachusetts, 43%

were found to have prior records for violence against persons. Reviewing these prior arrests, Klein (1993) found that almost two thirds had prior crimes against males as well as female victims and that the average number of prior crimes against persons was a startling 4.5.

Despite the dramatic nature of physical assault, the single most important risk factor for gendered homicide is the level of entrapment established when physical domination through beatings and sexual assault (rape) is supported by intimidation, isolation, and control over money, food, sex, work, and access to family and friends. Dila's case illustrates the extent of control that typifies such situations: Her every movement was watched, recorded, and critically reviewed so that she became a virtual hostage in her own home. The pattern of coercive control is so lethal because it closes off sources of potential escape or support, eliciting adaptive responses that range from numbing, self-medication with alcohol or drugs, and suicidality to the Stockholm syndrome, whereby the victim develops a childlike dependence on the abuser. Women entrapped in this process are extremely vulnerable to homicide and may kill their assailants (or themselves) as a matter of survival.

Although partner violence is almost always accompanied by the pattern of coercive control, prior to the commission of a homicide, the assailant often shifts his coercive tactics from control to destruction, freeing himself of the ambivalence normally associated with hurting someone on whom he also depends. Even when males kill one another, destruction may be a point in a developing intersexual struggle for control over a woman, as in the case that follows. The same shift to destruction is evident in many infanticides or neonaticides, workplace homicides, and homicides-suicides.

## INTENSE SOCIAL ENGAGEMENT
## ABOUT SEX ROLE STEREOTYPES

The first episode of assault occurred several months after Miguel moved into Rachel's home, when he was drunk. He agreed to do his drinking at the boarding house where David (Rachel's former boyfriend and Miguel's cousin) lived. One evening, when Rachel went to pick Miguel up at the boarding house, David came downstairs and tried to talk to Rachel. She asked Miguel's permission and he replied, "You do what you think is right." Rachel was 6 months pregnant at the time with David's child. An argument ensued during which Miguel told David, "She's mine, she does what I tell her," and ordered Rachel into the car. He told her to relax and stop crying, then suddenly slapped her across the mouth. Rachel was shocked. Then he told Rachel to kiss him, which she did. On the way home, Miguel broke the dashboard and the windshield with his fist. Several months later, David was fatally stabbed in a fight with Miguel.

Sexual politics frame every aspect of intersexual homicide, from the identity of appropriate victims to the intensity of encounters that culminate in death. In Dila's case, apart from the log, beatings focused on common facets of sex role stereotypes such as her right to talk with other men, her right to control the money she earned, being overweight, cooking, and cleaning. Mic would send Dila to Weight Watchers (which she liked), but then put her on a scale and beat her because she was "too stupid" to lose weight. What many men consider provocation is often, for women, a way of negotiating for resources or opportunities for self-expression by trying to meet their needs within and against the boundaries of gender stereotypes. For Dila, eating was one of the forms of control she could muster, an example of what we call *control in the context of no control.* In these instances, men become assaultive with women because they cannot tolerate the costs or the intensity of negotiations around power and control.

Rachel's case illustrates that the same expectations about possessiveness, dominance, and control may prompt homicidal violence against males. Although this fatality was reported as involving acquaintances, Miguel's assault on David was no less gendered than his attacks on Rachel. Violence in these instances is not merely a means to secure prerogatives associated with masculinity (such as Rachel's loyalty). Violence is also a vital component of masculine identity and as such has an expressive function (as it does in the media, in sports, and in various rites of passage) independent of the goals for which it is employed. Sexual identity is often implicated in other forms of violence, including military combat. But in gendered violence, male sexual identity is explicitly established at the expense of femininity, even when, as in the fight with David, the issue is which man will dominate.

Ironically, this social component of gendered violence—that it is a zero-sum game in which masculinity is established against the personhood of a particular woman—lends it an intensity unknown to other forms of criminal activity. These normative facets of coercion by males also lend credibility to the essentialist notion that violence in defense of sexuality is intrinsic to male nature, the basis for the so-called hot-blood defense. Accordingly, society recognizes a number of occasions, some officially, others through custom, when male violence can be expressed with relatively few restraints. Violence on these occasions has a quasi-sacred quality, illustrated by the fact that observers of wife beating traditionally maintain the same respectful distance from the parties as the audience for a boxing match.[1] The combination of sexual inequality, essentialist notions that violence expresses male nature, theories of why it is unmanageable, and the designation of spaces where sexual identity can be forcefully expressed explains the durability and intensity of gendered violence.

## VICTIMS OF ASSAULT AND COERCION
## ARE KNOWN TO HELPING AGENCIES

When her boyfriend began to batter her, Nathaline moved in with her sister. Over the next 18 months, he broke into her house, smashed the windows and the door, tried to drown her in the bathtub, raped her repeatedly, and beat her with a club. She went to the hospital and called the police on numerous occasions, and he was arrested three times, then released after a short time in jail. She was diagnosed HIV-positive, was assigned a caseworker through a local church, and got a protection order. But when the order was served, he told her he would kill her. Fearful that this would happen or that her children would be injured, she went out into the street, confronted him, challenged him to "do me" now, and, when he repeated that he would get her that night, stabbed him fatally.

Few myths have been more damaging to the health of battered women than the belief that they fail to seek help. For almost a decade, discrepancies between the high numbers of battered women identified through population surveys and the few who appeared in institutional records were explained by learned helplessness, a depressive syndrome that leads persons subjected to repeated frustration to give up hope (Walker, 1979). As battered women entered shelters in droves and researchers probed more deeply, however, it became clear that victims (and perpetrators) of gendered violence show up in large numbers at every service site imaginable.

What has also become apparent is that health, justice, and service professionals respond to gendered violence in ways that actually increase the probability of entrapment, hence of homicide. Studies of police as well as of medical and mental health providers consistently report a failure to identify partner violence or, as in Nathaline's case, to recognize its prognostic significance for further injury, a range of psychosocial problems, or death (Buzawa & Buzawa, 1990; Kurz & Stark, 1988). Physicians and psychiatrists fail to follow assault victims (or perpetrators) clinically (even when they attempt suicide), prescribe inappropriate pain medication or tranquilizers, describe them with stereotypic terms such as *crock* or *hysteric,* and refer them for help with secondary problems (such as depression or substance abuse) but not violence (Dobash & Dobash, 1979; Stark & Flitcraft, 1988b). The children of battered mothers are routinely removed to foster care, further isolating the mother (see Chapter 3, this volume), whereas battered women who attempt suicide are more likely to be sent home with no social service intervention than nonbattered women who attempt suicide (see Chapter 4, this volume). Traditional police practice followed a similar pattern (Buzawa & Buzawa, 1990). Unless there was serious injury or an officer was insulted, police failed to arrest, a response pattern that directly increases the risk of homicide, particularly in communities where partner violence was considered normal (Hawkins, 1987). Virtually every state has reformed its domestic violence laws, leading to a sharp increase in the number of men arrested for partner assault. Even so, as Nathaline's case illustrates, because battering is evaluated solely as an assault crime, neither its repetitive nature nor the cumulative risk posed by coercion and control are considered relevant. As a result, even where arrest is mandatory, few perpetrators go to jail. On the contrary, as the experience of battering is fragmented into myriad personal problems for police, medicine, psychiatry, and social work, these systems identify and respond to what they perceive as a pattern of demanding or inappropriate use, distancing and protecting themselves from the victim, or, as with Nathaline, responding in a purely perfunctory way. Ironically, because it increases a woman's susceptibility to entrapment, this strategy elicits the very history that distinguishes battering from other crimes.

By blocking women's access to help, undermining their credibility, increasing their isolation, and aggravating harmful behaviors such as alcoholism, these interventions reinforce the pattern of coercion and control by partners, increasing the probability that violence will escalate to homicide.

## Conclusion

We owe to Karl Marx the adage that problems can be fully conceptualized only after the solutions already exist. A variation on this
proposition applies to homicide: Prevailing conceptualizations have
actually inhibited effective solutions. The theory of homicide is dominated by the four Ps—pathology, personality, passion, and poverty—
reinforcing the sense that violent events are unpredictable and can be
managed only reactively, the foundation of deterrence theory. Feelings
of impotence are reflected in the myths we construct around violence,
for instance, in the obsession with horrific violence in the media, the
designation of young black males as scapegoats for what criminologist
William Chambliss calls our "moral panic," and the search for a solution
through harsher imprisonment, get-tough sentencing ("Three strikes
and you're out"), and the death penalty. In channeling an inchoate
discontent through greatly exaggerated images of crime and the criminal
element, we deify criminal violence, turning it into a national totem we
simultaneously worship and dread.

Fear leads to denial, and the result is that knowledge of how to
prevent homicide is far less extensive than knowledge of its scope and
effect. Only 17 of the 364 items on homicide reviewed by Rosenberg et
al. (1986) deal with prevention. An important step toward demystifying
homicide is to emphasize its roots in ordinary life, that is, in conflicts
likely to affect any or all of us.

This chapter has outlined a typology of homicide based on the
frequency of various violent acts, the relationship among the parties,
the motivation for the violence, and the proximate structure that
supports the violent acts. The typology distinguishes the 80% of homicides that are primary, in which violence but no other crime is intended.
In common parlance, these "friendly" homicides are precisely those
believed to be governed by the four Ps. We viewed the data on primary
homicide through the prism of intersexual violence, showing that
gendered homicide accounts for the vast majority of spousal homicides,
homicides committed by women, child homicides, homicides in the
workplace, homicides-suicides, and a substantial proportion of male-
male homicides, ultimately encompassing approximately half of all
homicides and as much as two thirds of primary homicides.

The typology shifts the explanatory focus from the four Ps to the
components of male domination in private life. From this vantage,
gendered homicides share three characteristics: They are the culmina-

tion of an entrapment process consisting of coercion and control; their intensity and chronicity reflect the imposition of stereotypic sex roles to establish male status; and the parties—but not usually the coercive pattern—are known to service providers.

The analysis clearly implies that gendered homicide should be a primary target for homicide prevention; that young adults should be identified as at highest risk; that public education should target male attitudes toward privilege and control, particularly with respect to women and children; and that health, mental health, police, and social service providers should be trained to identify victims of assault and coercion and to intervene before women (or children) become entrapped in battering relationships. Because partner violence responds to and effectively prevents women from realizing the life chances made available by legal rights to formal equality, a prevention strategy must also include a range of sanctions for threatening, coercive, or assaultive behavior; community education to challenge sex stereotypes; and active support for survivors of domestic violence. Federal and state laws supporting battered women's shelters and mandating arrest in cases of partner assault provide an important basis for this strategy. Meanwhile, although the network of battered women shelters in the United States offers vital support during crisis, survival apart from the assailant requires a broader strategy of empowerment that includes access to independent housing, child care, legal services, reproductive and other health services, job training (or retraining), and job placement.

Each of the components of gendered homicide requires a distinct response. The importance of prior assaultive and coercive behavior suggests the need to change criminal law to encompass the repetitive nature of domestic violence as well as the deprivation of basic liberty caused by coercive control. Incorporating the potential lethality of domestic violence crimes into sanctioning decisions early on could affect the entire continuum on which gendered homicides fall. In addition to a history of coercive control, child abuse against a background of partner violence requires a strong deterrent. Conversely, prevention also requires that medical and social service assessments of children's risk be revised to highlight the absolute level of coercion in the home, even if there is no child abuse. In homes in which partner violence is identified, safety planning for children is as important as planning for the mother.

The historical nature of gendered violence also provides a strong argument for handgun regulation. The NRA argues that regulation would prevent gun use by ordinary citizens, not by criminals. Evidence on intersexual violence suggests this is the strongest rationale for gun control because the great proportion of gendered homicides are committed by ordinary citizens during unplanned assaults that have gotten out of hand.

One facet of sexual inequality that prevention could address is the essentialist presumption that violence is inevitable in certain situations—and therefore to be accepted—given the masculine propensity for aggression. Community education must challenge this presumption by promoting zero tolerance for the choice of women and children as appropriate targets for male aggression and by promoting a broader array of behaviors deemed acceptable by women and men. Public enthusiasm for the traditional father-headed family should be tempered by publicity targeting the health hazards inherent in normal male socialization, the risk of gendered violence in all intersexual situations, and the importance of safety first for women and children in efforts at family reunification or preservation.

Ironically, the most ominous component of gendered homicide provides the greatest opportunity for prevention, its occurrence amid a complex history of help seeking. Developing uniform instruments to screen for early onset domestic violence and routinely questioning women (and men) about coercion and control at all service sites could help identify the vast majority of potentially lethal relationships. The next step depends on the institutional setting, but the key skills, safety planning, advocacy, and support for independence are easily integrated into existing regimens. Apart from communitywide screening, the array of services required to support the independence of battered women can best be developed by client-driven, community-based networks that develop coordinated violence prevention strategies. Another mechanism for implementing systemwide, prevention-oriented change is the *domestic violence morbidity and mortality review team*. Loosely modeled after hospital-based fatality reviews and comprising representatives from health, domestic violence advocacy, criminal justice, and child protection services, the multiagency team helps identify circumstances surrounding domestic-violence-related deaths and near-fatal injuries that could be prevented in the future.

Recognizing that professional intervention contributes to the entrapment of women in violent relationships takes us full circle, back to the pillars of homicide prevention, female empowerment, and male accountability. Changing professional practice can help. Preventing gendered homicide involves curtailing what is widely considered the legitimate realm of male authority and closing gender and generational gaps that are reflected as much in a paucity of alternatives for violent men as by professional complicity in assaults against women and children.

## Note

1. An early literary instance of this appears in Henry Fielding's classic novel *Joseph Andrews*. Fanny, the hero's fiancée, is kidnapped and beaten by a captain who is taking her to be raped by a local squire, when a stranger approaches, responding to the woman's cries. When the captain explains she is his wife, however, the man turns around and leaves without a word.

# Part III

## Clinical Interventions

# Personal Power and Institutional Victimization

*Treating the Dual Trauma of Woman Battering*

This chapter describes the dimensions, consequences, and appropriate treatment of woman battering in mental health settings. Its major theme is that the distinctive psychosocial profile identified among battered women is elicited by a *dual trauma* consisting of coercive control and inappropriate clinical intervention. Accordingly, effective intervention requires a dual response, combining reformulated trauma theory with the advocacy and empowerment strategy used by community-based domestic violence services.

In his 1980 presidential address to the American Psychiatric Association, Alan Stone (1980) considered the extent to which racial injustice, homosexuality, and the movement for women's rights challenged psychiatry's hidden values, particularly the assumptions of scientific neutrality behind which psychiatry dismissed the relevance of important

AUTHORS' NOTE: This chapter is adapted from Stark and Flitcraft (1988a). Reprinted with permission of Brunner/Mazel.

political issues (such as women's rights) for clinical practice. Stone questioned whether, as a consequence of more directly affecting personal as well as professional identities, "the issues raised concerning women cut deeper in American psychiatry than even racism and homosexuality" (p. 13).

Woman battering represents one of the gravest challenges the struggle for women's rights poses to mental health. Since male violence became a major focus of the women's movement in the early 1970s, survivors of rape and woman battering and their supporters have opened more than 1,500 community-based programs in the United States, won dramatic improvements in civil and criminal protections, and elicited widespread support from professional medical, nursing, mental health, and social work organizations. In particular, by promoting a model of practice in which women conventionally portrayed as helpless and pathetic are encouraged to take collective responsibility for their futures, the battered women's movement offers a viable alternative to reductionist and largely unsuccessful professional interventions with a significant subpopulation of mental health clients.

Despite these developments, 16 years after Stone's speech, it is unclear whether mental health has seriously considered the relevance of violence against women for clinical practice. Twenty to fifty percent of the clients seen at inpatient and outpatient settings have been identified as victims or perpetrators of woman battering (Herman, 1986; Hilberman & Munson, 1977-1978; Post et al., 1980). Domestic violence has been implicated in one in four female suicide attempts (see Chapter 4, this volume), in almost half of all child abuse (see Chapter 3, this volume), in a third or more cases of female alcoholism, and as a major factor in drug abuse, homelessness, female depression, panic disorder, and an array of related problems that often extend to children (Stark & Flitcraft, 1991). Yet mental health professionals are still unlikely to ask about violence unless it is part of the presenting problem (Jacobson & Richardson, 1987). As a result, probably fewer than 1 case of domestic violence in 10 is so identified and in even fewer is the abusive relationship the focus of intervention. Even when patients identify partner violence during an interview, enormous confusion remains about how to differentiate it from other assaultive situations, how to assess its severity, how to determine its role in psychiatric illness or other psychosocial problems, and what interventions might prevent the recurrence of violence or address its multiple sequelae (Herman, 1992).

A lack of basic knowledge about battering is reinforced by the difficulty of shedding much light on the problem using the traditional psychiatric model of disease. Specialists in the field emphasize the roots of the problem in a pattern of external restraints, the instrumental use of violence to sustain male dominance, and the importance of advocacy, empowerment for victims, and interagency collaboration that ensures safety for the woman and accountability of the assailant through the joint efforts of justice, health, and community-based advocacy organizations such as shelters. In contrast, mental health practitioners are more likely to see links between battering and other forms of aggression or interpersonal conflict; to emphasize its expressive functions vis-à-vis internal disorders, organic deficiencies, or a multifactorial personality profile; and to target the core psychiatric disorder, often pulling other family members (including the perpetrator) into treatment as more dramatic symptoms subside (Snell et al., 1964). Observing the psychiatric response to violent patients, Gondolf (1990) found that perpetrators of family violence received a very low priority, in part because, compared to those who assaulted strangers or hospital staff, the batterer was less likely to be psychotic or to be accompanied by a family member insisting on hospitalization. Although "harm toward others" is a criterion for involuntary hospital admission, and hospital protocol and policy suggest a thorough assessment of violence, Gondolf concludes, "there is no mention of family violence services except those dealing with incest" (p. 438).

In highlighting the internal consequences of external restraints, the recently formulated paradigm of posttraumatic stress disorder (PTSD) and a variant termed battered woman's syndrome (BWS) (Walker, 1979, 1984) attempt to bridge the gap between the traditional psychiatric approach and an approach that fixes responsibility for the consequences of violence on its source, the abusive partner. Initially devised to explain psychological disturbances, cognitive distortions, and dysfunctional behavior patterns among otherwise normal adults primarily during wartime, the model has recently been extended and adapted to victims of domestic violence by psychiatrist Judy Herman (1992). In extending the notion of psychological trauma to the affects of institutional maltreatment, this chapter attempts to adapt this framework to the broad political issues posed by battering.

A clear implication of Stone's (1980) challenge is that, by not responding appropriately, the mental health professions already play a political role in shaping women's experience. A major factor inhibiting an appropriate response to battered women is what Reiker and Carmen (1984) term *the gender gap* in psychotherapy. This refers not merely to the omission of women's concerns from professional training or overt prejudice but also to the invisible barriers to access posed by conventional responses to women's concerns. Identifying these barriers, recognizing their contribution to women's entrapment in abusive relationships, and developing intervention strategies to overcome them are other key goals of this chapter.

## Defining Terms: Domestic
## Violence, Abuse, and Woman Battering

Among the expanded rights accorded to women, children, the elderly, and the disabled, none is more important than physical safety from partners, parents, and caretakers. *Family violence* is a broad term that subsumes two very different phenomenon: *domestic violence,* or the coercion of partners in marriage or other intimate relationships, and *abuse,* or the violent exploitation, mistreatment, or neglect of persons who are dependent because of their age or physical incapacity. In recent years, domestic violence and other forms of abuse have been widely criminalized. Apart from criminal prosecution, which remains uncommon despite a proliferation of new laws, intervention takes different forms: protective services when children, the disabled, and the frail elderly are abused and support, advocacy, and empowerment when independent adults are victimized. What is assumed to be healthy for children, a temporary inequality in which dependency and protection meet developmental needs for autonomy, has the opposite implication for healthy adults, for whom an emphasis on dependency or protectionism can inhibit development and instill a sense of lesser worth. For the battered woman, subordination itself is the main source of humiliation, not the abuse of an otherwise legitimate position of dominance. Indeed, it is the pattern of coercion and control used to establish subordination that elicits the major mental health consequences associated with battering.

Domestic violence laws differ widely in the types of acts (assaults, threats, stalking) they cover and which relationships constitute a domestic crime. In clinical settings, however, the most effective operational definitions employ an inclusive notion of violence or coercion regardless of the severity or frequency of injury inflicted or whether the current presentation involves injury, medical, or psychosocial problems.

Family violence crimes are distinguished from other assaults because force is used in close or blood relationships and perpetrators usually have continued access to the victim. Unlike child abuse, however, where residential or foster placement can prevent access, in woman battering available legal protections are far less effective. As a result, partner assault is an isolated episode in only an estimated 25% of cases (Teske & Parker, 1983). Ongoing access also makes it possible for the perpetrator to control numerous aspects of his victim's life, another important difference from stranger assault. Finally, like many other fights, domestic violence is rooted in norms about how certain persons (parents, males, lovers, husbands) should behave given various occasions or provocations. This fact is significant in shaping how all parties—including treaters—perceive and even rationalize domestic violence. At the same time, most perpetrators deny, minimize, or blame their victim for the assault. These characteristics—the intimate and ongoing nature of the violence, its link to coercive control, the normative character of the relations from which the violence and coercion stem, and confusion about accountability—frame the experience of domestic violence and demarcate its trauma from the consequences of extreme episodes of violence (such as rape or wartime atrocities) about which there is little ambiguity.

As used here, *battering* describes the dynamics of partner assault as a pattern of coercive control. Battering encompasses the range of behaviors employed to hurt, intimidate, coerce, isolate, control, or humiliate a partner.

## The Battering Syndrome:
## From Injury to Coercive Control

### GENERAL PREVALENCE

Due to differences about whether domestic violence should be identified with couples or include any partners and whether its hallmark is severe assault or the pattern of repetitive violence and control, there is disagreement about its true prevalence (the overall number of cases at any one time) and incidence (the number of new cases). Two national household surveys limited to intact couples suggest that between 1.1

and 1.8 million wives are severely abused by husbands each year (kicked, bit, hit with a fist or some other object) and that another 3 million are pushed, grabbed, shoved, or slapped (Commonwealth Fund, 1993; Straus et al., 1980; Straus & Kantor, 1994). Other research indicates that 50% to 75% of battered women are single, separated, or divorced, however, and that current risk is established by a pattern of repetitive acts and control even where there is no immediate violence. For clinical purposes, therefore, more relevant are data from national and state surveys indicating that between 25% and 30% of adults have been assaulted one or more times during the course of marriage (Stark & Flitcraft, 1991; Straus & Gelles, 1986; Teske & Parker, 1983).

## PHYSICAL CONSEQUENCES

Early research on woman battering focused on injury. In the Yale trauma study, Stark (1984) and Stark and Flitcraft (1991) reviewed the medical records of 3,676 randomly selected women presenting with complaints of injury at a metropolitan hospital. The study revealed a group of heretofore unidentified victims of partner assault that was larger than any other population of injury patients. The hallmarks of injuries among this group were their frequency, duration, and sexual nature. The battered women identified in the emergency room averaged one injury visit per year. Other research reveals that many were assaulted once a week or more, so-called serial abuse (Klaus & Rand, 1984).

The vast majority of abusive injuries are not serious enough to prompt medical or police attention, highlighting the emergent nature of the relationship rather than a given assault. Hospital studies show that, although battering may present as a physical emergency, battered women constitute an even larger segment of nontrauma caseloads. For instance, 20% to 25% of the obstetrical caseload have a history of battering (Helton & Snodgrass, 1987). Estimates of prevalence in nonemergent settings range from 28% of the female patients in primary care clinics (Rath et al., 1989) to 38.8% reporting ever having been beaten in a midwestern family practice setting (Hamberger, Saunders, & Harvey, 1986).

## PSYCHOSOCIAL CONSEQUENCES

Compared to a baseline population of nonbattered patients, the battered women in the Yale trauma study were 5 times more likely to attempt suicide, 15 times more likely to abuse alcohol, 9 times more likely to abuse drugs, 6 times more likely to report child abuse, and 3 times more likely to be diagnosed as depressed or psychotic (Stark, 1984). Absolute numbers were as significant as the relative frequencies. For example, 19% of all battered women attempted suicide at least once, 38% were diagnosed as depressed or having another situational disorder, and 10% became psychotic. Even among the psychiatric emergency caseload, battered women presented with a distinct profile. For instance, battered alcoholics had 10 times as many trauma episodes as nonbattered patients, were younger than other alcoholics, and were 3 times as likely to have gone through short-term detox. Almost a third of psychiatric inpatients and outpatients have a history of domestic violence (Carmen et al., 1984; Herman, 1986; Hilberman & Munson, 1977-1978; Post et al., 1980). These women carry diagnoses of personality disorder primarily (Post et al., 1980) and evidence low self-esteem and homicidal rage (Carmen et al., 1984).

A key issue is whether these problems proceed or follow the onset of abuse. Although battered women in the Yale study were slightly more likely to be alcoholic than controls even before the onset of abuse, in each case, including alcoholism, more than 60% of the problems post-dated abusive injury. In other words, the battered women were psychologically normal individuals who developed a complex psychosocial profile in the context of ongoing partner assault.

POLITICS OR PATHOLOGY?

The complex psychosocial profile presented by battered women led observers like Erin Pizzey, founder of the Chiswick refuge in London, to conclude that battered women were violence prone (Pizzey & Shapiro, 1981). This confirmed early mental health accounts that described abused women as masculine, rigid, overemotional, with weakened ties to reality, and as having inappropriate sexual expression (Contoni, 1981; Scott, 1974; Snell et al., 1964) or as accepting victimization owing to their immaturity, childlike nature, or socialization (Gayford, 1975a; Walker, 1979).

Contrary to these stereotypes, careful control comparisons show few, if any, personality differences between abused and nonabused women. Indeed, abused women often have a better sense of reality than their assailants, are more social and sympathetic than controls, are less masculine though not necessarily more feminine, and exhibit greater ego strength (Finn, 1985; Graff, 1980; Star, 1978). A high rate of suicidality indicates that some abused women turn anger inward. But a substantial number of abused women are outwardly aggressive, independent, or overtly hostile to their assailants. Even Lenore Walker (1983) reports that battered women are generally independent, aggressive, and highly motivated, rather than helpless (see also Campbell, 1989).

The myth that battering results from individual dysfunction exerts a strong hold on service providers trained to provide therapy rather than to advocate for systems change. Because of their many problems, abused women are often mistaken for victims needing rescue. Many batterers, meanwhile, have suffered pain in childhood, often including physical maltreatment, leading to easy—but usually unfounded—generalizations about the roots of their violent behavior. It is safer professionally, however, to trace male violence to childhood neglect and focus on impulse management rather than target the community roots of male dominance. Because legal protections for women are so precarious, those who leave a violent relationship may be in no less danger than those who stay. Indeed, the Yale study found that risk was higher among separated than married women (Stark & Flitcraft, 1991). Given these realities, linking the decision to stay in an abusive relationship with characterological dependency blames victims for problems they are desperately trying to resolve. Yet this is precisely how medical, psychiatric, and even shelter staff rationalize the frustration and anger they feel when a woman returns to or remains in a violent relationship (Loseke, 1992). No challenge to mental health is greater than identifying the strengths of women who are entrapped in battering relationships.

## INSTITUTIONAL VICTIMIZATION

A superficial reading of women's medical histories confirms the belief that battered women are psychologically deficient. Clinical portraits of pathos and personal devastation unfold with tragic predictability. Shortly after an abusive episode, women reappear with a range of medical complaints, then with "alcohol on breath," then with another injury, a suicide attempt, as depressed, or with a presentation of "nerves." This progression seems so automatic, the rhythm with which self-destructive behaviors follow injury seems so natural, and the cumulative effect of professional intervention seems so minimal that even long discredited myths about masochistic or violence-prone women appear valid.

Yet this picture of pathos contrasts markedly with the domestic lence survivors encountered in battered women's shelters. In our research, we realized that the tragic progression from abuse to battering pictured on medical records was less an objective reflection of what clinicians saw than a biased justification for how they responded—or failed to respond—to domestic violence and the consequences of this response.

Providers sometimes wrote that a woman had been "beaten by boyfriend," though more often, they simply recorded "hit with ashtray" or "kicked with foot." Formal designations indicating domestic violence appeared in only 1 abusive episode in 40 and even then had no therapeutic significance. That this is more than professional naiveté is suggested by another fact: Although battered women were not identified as such, clinicians responded differently to them as a group even when they presented the same ostensible problem as nonbattered women. In this implicit diagnosis, problems of omission were accompanied by a failure to follow abuse victims clinically, even when they attempted suicide. Other interventions further isolate women from sources of help, progressing from the inappropriate use of pain or antianxiety medication to pseudopsychiatric labeling to overtly punitive strategies, such as removing children to foster care or hospitalization in the state psychiatric facility even in the absence of convincing disease. Denial, minimization, and punitive intervention also characterize the response to abused women who are alcoholics or who attempt suicide. As problems mount in the face of clinical insensitivity and inappropriate care, abused women are reported to be hypochondriacs, crocks, hysterics, women with vague complaints and "total body pain."

Within health care, labeling is a process of metacommunication that legitimates nonintervention, isolation, perfunctory treatment, and punitive responses. The cumulative effect of these interventions is to reduce women's options significantly by closing off their access to help, reinforcing the picture their partner paints of them as crazy. The result is that some women actually become the victim of tragic circumstances projected in the medical narrative. From the vantage of the activist alternatives in the community, the response seems passive-aggressive in the extreme. The clinical "facts" portray women whose souls have been crushed by an inscrutable and hostile other. But the clinical response is a key factor in eliciting these facts.

## THE TRAUMATIC CHARACTER OF INTERVENTION

In weighing the traumatic effects of extraordinary experiences, re-searchers emphasize cognitive changes, behavioral dysfunctions, and relational problems. Using these criteria, intervention is traumatic for many abused women.

Sexual bias is as common in mental health as in other areas of service. But the real barriers to access for abused women arise when stereotypes regarding female character, appropriate behavior, and normal family forms are embedded in unquestioned assumptions and in systemwide responses to women's help seeking. These responses have direct, severe, and long-term consequences for how victims of abuse interpret their experience, how they behave, and how they relate to others around them, including their abusive partner. Some women have impaired self-esteem to start. But for most, entrapment, despair, and self-blame follow a history of progressive isolation from sources of support and frustrating—even punitive—help seeking. Neglect, inappropriate medi-cation, isolation, blaming violence on secondary problems (such as alcohol), pseudopsychiatric labeling, and punitive referrals undermine women's credibility and reinforce a pattern of behavior that oscillates between submissiveness and compliance on one side and anger, even rage, on the other. That these same responses characterize a woman's reactions at home suggest the convergence of the caretaker and abuser roles in her life.

## THE BATTERING SYNDROME

In the medical complex, battering presents as an evolving configura-tion of physical and psychosocial problems evoked by ongoing partner violence that is interwoven with a history of institutional neglect and inappropriate interventions. This syndrome includes a history of trauma and general medical problems accompanied by a disproportionate risk of rape, miscarriages, and abortion; alcohol and drug abuse; increasing isolation; attempted suicide; child abuse; and mental illness. Casework with women in the community further reveals that physical abuse is almost always embedded in a pattern of coercion characterized by the use of threats, intimidation, isolation, and emotional abuse, as well as a pattern of control over sexuality and social life, including a woman's relationships with family and friends; material resources (such as money, food, or transportation); and various facets of everyday life (such as coming and going, shopping, cleaning, and so forth). Often, to the victim, this pattern of coercive control is the most salient feature of domestic violence.

Physical abuse can lead to disfigurement, incredible pain, fear, and psychological trauma. But the pattern of subordination and psychosocial problems that distinguishes woman battering requires something beyond violence; avenues of help and escape are both literally and psychologically closed and women become entrapped. This was the effect we observed among women whose help seeking was greeted with neglect or no follow up, labeling, inappropriate medication, and referrals that communicated that the women—not their assailants—were the real source of the problem.

THE ISSUE OF VIOLENCE BY WOMEN

Contradicting a common stereotype, there is growing evidence that women also hit their partners as or even more often than they themselves are hit (Straus et al., 1980; Straus & Kantor, 1994; Szinovacz, 1983). Although women are injured in partner assault many times more often than men, women commit just under half of all spousal murders (41%) (Dawson & Langany, 1994). For inner-city girls at least, learning to resolve conflicts through a "fair fight" with fists, feet, and weapons is as much a developmental phase as learning to drive is for suburban girls (Letchner, 1993). Domestic violence statutes cover violence by female partners; women arrested for domestic violent crimes are often included in mandated treatment programs for batterers.

Although we may be approaching sexual symmetry in partner violence, however, there is no evidence whatsoever that any significant proportion of men who are assaulted either by partners or by strangers suffer a pattern of injury, medical, and psychosocial sequelae similar to that identified among battered women. The crucial analytic issue, then, is why abuse elicits the particular psychosocial profile associated with battering only among women who evidence little previous history of disturbance. We believe the answer lies in the convergence of coercive control and the institutional response when abused women seek help. Battering and fighting to resolve conflict are completely different phenomena. Unlike a fair fight, battering results when a process of entrapment makes one partner the unwilling object of the other's authority. What makes it possible for men to entrap women is not their greater strength but the social strength they derive when unequal power relationships are reinforced, rather than countered, in helping encounters.

## Reconsidering Traumatization Theory

Lacking evidence of predisposing personality factors, psychologists have traced the profile observed among battered women to the violent nature of the relationship. In addition to eliciting some of the more dramatic behavioral problems identified in the medical records (such as addiction and suicidality), the trauma of repeated assault can cause severe psychological distress or dysfunction, including major depression; sexual and dissociative disorders; cognitive changes in how one views oneself, the world, and the occurrence of violence; and relational disturbances, most dramatically illustrated by the Stockholm syndrome or traumatic bonding, where escalating violence actually increases a person's attachment to her abuser (Dutton, 1992; Dutton & Painter, 1993; Mullen, Romans-Clarkson, Walton, & Herbison, 1988). Many of these reactions have been clustered under the diagnostic headings of BWS and PTSD. In both cases, the individual's normal coping mechanisms are replaced by adaptive responses designed to manage the feeling that all avenues to escape are closed (learned helplessness) in the case of BWS and, in PTSD, the unbearable anxiety that accompanies repeated violation of one's physical and psychological boundaries.

In its initial formulation by psychologist Lenore Walker (1977-1978, 1979), BWS used a cognitive framework, the learned helplessness model of depression, to explain how cumulative exposure to violence evoked the affective and behavioral components identified among abused women. Walker describes a cycle of violence in which tension builds up (minor abuse), followed by an "explosion" (severe episodes) and then by "loving contrition" when the perpetrator promises to refrain from violence. Living through this cycle, women hope things will improve, though, over time, the cycle shortens, the period of contrition disappears, and hope fades. Meanwhile, repeated violence elicits a depressive syndrome characterized by low self-esteem, self-blame, fatalism, relative passivity, and an unwillingness to seek or accept help even when it is made available. Possessed with an exaggerated sense of their assailant's control, battered women conclude that escape is impossible and concentrate instead on survival, employing denial, numbing, or, in extreme cases, proactive violence to cope.

Since its initial formulation, the concept of BWS has broadened to encompass the spectrum of symptoms exhibited by battered women as well as the array of interpretations allowed in court cases involving domestic violence. Today, BWS is often presented as a special case of PTSD, a set of reactions first defined in *DSM-III* in 1980 and occasioned by exposure to events outside the range of usual human experience. Here too, emphasis is on how the person adapts to feelings with which normal adaptation mechanisms cannot cope, primarily flashbacks (reexperiencing the trauma) and "intense fear, helplessness, loss of control, and threat of annihilation" (Herman, 1992, p. 33).

Recognizing that the official formulation of PTSD fails to capture "the protean symptomatic manifestations of prolonged, repeated trauma," Herman (1992, p. 119) identifies three symptom categories of what she terms *complex PTSD*: hyperarousal (chronic alertness), intrusion (flashbacks, floods of emotion, hidden reenactments), and constriction, "a state of detached calm . . . when events continue to register in awareness but are disconnected from their ordinary meanings" (p. 44). Additional reactions subsumed by Herman and others under a PTSD framework include anger, inability to concentrate, efforts to avoid reminders of the violence, reenactment of the trauma in disguised form, sleep disturbances, a feeling of indifference, emotional detachment, and profound passivity in which the person relinquishes all initiative and struggle (Dutton, 1992). These symptoms almost always support a protracted depression. Emotional oscillation between floods of intense, overwhelming feeling and states of no feeling at all is reflected in personal relationships that vacillate between desperate dependency and complete withdrawal. Over time, Herman believes, intrusive symptoms diminish and constrictive symptoms dominate, leading to a degree of restraint on inner and outer life that may mimic enduring personality characteristics. The fear elicited by the traumatic event also intensifies the need for protective attachments and may lead women to move unwittingly from one abusive relationship to the next.

Traumatic life events, like other misfortunes, have more severe consequences for those with other psychiatric problems. But crucial to traumatization theory is the belief that normal persons exposed to a similarly unbearable reality would seek to manage events in the same general way. Hence, the characteristic effects or reactions are attributed to aspects of the traumatic episode(s) itself—the severity, duration, and occurrence of the violence, for instance, and the availability of buffers (Finkelhor & Browne, 1985). Because the range of potentially traumatic events is so broad, however, the concept of PTSD is increasingly used to frame an equally broad spectrum of conditions ranging from a brief stress reaction where no intervention is required to classic PTSD or BWS to the syndrome of reactions to prolonged trauma Herman (1992) calls *complex PTSD*.

## THE CHALLENGE TO
## TRAUMATIZATION THEORY

How well does the trauma model capture the entrapment process identified with woman battering?

Extreme ongoing assaultive behavior may be sufficiently traumatic to entrap a woman or to elicit the range of psychological, behavioral, and psychosocial disturbances associated with battering. The vast majority of domestic violence episodes, however, involve relatively minor acts (pushing, shoving, hair pulling, grabbing, etc.) rather than severe violence. More important, work with battered women has convinced us that entrapment due to coercive control is the major context for secondary psychosocial and behavioral problems rather than violence per se. Furthermore, although assault from an intimate creates unique psychological dilemmas, this is much less important among the majority of victims who are dating, separated, or divorced.

Thus, partner violence is necessary, but rarely sufficient, to elicit the traumatic response to battering. Rather, this response arises in the conjuncture of structural discrimination, barriers to institutional access, and coercive control by partners. Sexual inequality (reflected in lower wages, fewer job options, etc.) creates a categorical vulnerability among women to dependence, abuse, and control. Even women in nonviolent relationships, for instance, report extraordinary levels of fear and self-inhibition about normal activities, such as going downtown alone or taking a bus (Gordon & Riger, 1991). This vulnerability constrains women's options in family fights. Once abuse occurs, blocked access to sources of help, safety, and support reproduces the relations of unequal power that allow men to use their authority arbitrarily in the first place.

Traditional mental health colludes with this larger discriminatory process (as well as with the batterer) when it minimizes the violence or coercion involved, assigns mutual responsibility to both parties for the problem (as in certain family system approaches), or identifies the major issue as inherited behavioral or psychosocial problems that "belong" to the victim (Imber-Black, 1986). Even models that identify the perpetrator as the sole source of the problem, however, may miss the social origins of female trauma and hence fail to locate coercion and the response it elicits on a continuum of normal control and vulnerability.

The initial description of BWS failed to link social and interpersonal dynamics adequately to learned helplessness. In addition, BWS provided an incomplete and often one-dimensional picture of the victim, portraying her as defeated or passive to her own fate, whereas in fact a much more dialectical understanding is needed to grasp women's aggressiveness, even at the height of adversity, and the complex inner struggle taking place. These limits led proponents of BWS to predict mistakenly that battered women would fail either to report their problems or to try to escape from the abuse, and left the impression that male dominance was established primarily at the interpersonal level rather than as part of a process of social inequality. In addition, the initial conception of BWS mistook a set of psychic responses to an objective situation of entrapment for a psychological syndrome elicited by the unbearable pain of repeated assault. However useful in describing a subgroup of battered women, the theory conveyed an image of pathology that obscured the central paradox posed by the emergence of dependent and self-destructive behaviors among otherwise normal, assertive, and even physically aggressive women.

The original theory of PTSD also emphasized that violence (as in the case of assault), personal violation (as in incest or rape), and kidnapping were sufficiently traumatic in themselves to evoke a predictable constellation of feelings and behavior only minimally related to individual difference. But PTSD encompassed a far broader range of responses than BWS. The work of Herman (1992) replaces the mechanical behaviorism of the learned helplessness model with a complex, even contradictory psychological dynamic elicited in victims who are simultaneously passive and aggressive, enmeshed and withdrawn, empty and "drowning" in feeling. Herman's stance is ethical as well as therapeutic, fixing accountability on the perpetrator and refusing to compromise a person's right to physical safety because she or he exhibits psychiatric symptoms. This is particularly important in battering, where the etiological links between violence and its psychiatric sequelae are often impossible to unravel.

Despite the many advantages of a victim-oriented framework, battering challenges the traumatization approach in a number of important respects.

1. The traumatization model has been applied mainly to cases, such as stranger rape or war trauma, in which the traumatic episode(s) and the posttraumatic reaction(s) can be clearly demarcated. This is often impossible in domestic violence situations, in which intimidation and control over material resources and social supports may be ongoing even with court orders in place. As a result, intratraumatic fears, feelings, and behaviors appropriate to current entrapment can easily be mistaken for posttraumatic paranoia, depression, or powerlessness. Assessing this distinction is crucial for women's safety and mental health.

2. The PTSD framework helps explain how extreme events shock the system to adapt through dysfunctional behaviors (Woods & Campbell, 1993). But it provides a less credible account of how the more diffuse process of coercive control elicits dysfunction. As a result, working within this framework can lead treaters to minimize aspects of coercion and control in relationships that may be most salient for clients.

3. A posttraumatic framework that links current problems with severe acts of assault or violation implies a calculus of harms that discounts the less dramatic and more diffuse problems associated with the onset of domestic violence. Conversely, battered women exhibit a wide range of problems that fall outside the purview of PTSD (Dutton, 1992; Goodman, Koss, & Russo, 1993). Several studies confirm the emphasis on reexperiencing the trauma (Finkelhor & Yllö, 1985), fear of events that remind victims of assault (Hilberman, 1980), and avoidance, numbing, and symptoms of increased arousal and anxiety (Jarrar, 1985; Star, Clark, Goetz, & O'Malia, 1979) and seem to indicate a high prevalence of psychosexual dysfunction, major depression, generalized anxiety disorder, and obsessive compulsive disorders, all consistent with a broad PTSD framework. But there is also evidence from veterans research and population studies that the PTSD constellation is only one of many reactions to extreme stress, and not necessarily the most common (Figley, 1992). As domestic violence case finding is integrated with routine mental health assessment, classic symptoms of PTSD become less common. Too great an emphasis on these symptoms would miss the majority of battered women in the mental health population and result in a misallocation of resources.

4. A posttraumatic framework emphasizing extraordinary shocks to the ego system may miss the key role of institutional barriers in closing off psychological, behavioral, and relational options, hence the extent to which the symptoms of battering function in a wide social interplay that reaches beyond physical assault to the experience of therapy itself.

5. Because it implies that traumatic events are disabling, the PTSD framework can overemphasize victimization at the expense of survival skills, reinforce dependency, and mistake reality-based reactions to the illegitimate exercise of institutional authority for personality problems: justifiable anger at professionals for resistance, real powerlessness for depression, or myriad help-seeking efforts for overinvolvement or enmeshment (Imber-Black, 1986). The abused woman may be in the throes of a compensatory and reactive behavior pattern over which she has little control. Yet by highlighting victimization, a posttraumatic stress model can undervalue a woman's quest for autonomy and suggest she be rescued rather than supported in her choices. It is far easier to accept an abused woman as the dependent victim who first appears in the office than as the aggressive individual who emerges after we elicit and read back into her experience a history of persistent help seeking. Nothing is more difficult during the recovery process than separating this aggressiveness—without quashing it—from the rage and violence it may evoke in a particular man (or helper).

6. Despite its attention to external responsibility, the PTSD framework conveys an image of pathology to both the woman and the world outside. This image can retraumatize a woman by undermining her fight for child custody, for instance, or by reinforcing the batterer's claim that she, not he, is crazy. In the absence of frank symptomatology of ongoing PTSD, a nonstigmatizing classification is *DSM-IV* "Physical abuse of an adult" (coded 995.81).

7. In the hands of politically sensitive therapists, a PTSD framework suggests that symptoms that mimic underlying depressive, dissociative, or borderline disorders may be reactions to male violence, hence appropriate objects for advocacy and crisis intervention as well as longer-term treatment. For a range of more conventional treaters, however, it may signify a category of chronic disturbance for which little can be done immediately. Rose et al. (1991) caution, "operationalizing PTSD as a secondary diagnosis without developing advocacy strategies to change provider systems unintentionally prolongs the experience of abuse" (p. 412), a process they term *disguised betrayal* or *false charity* because it emphasizes pathology or disease-based, problem-defining practices that incur little organizational resistance at the expense of practices that are more appropriate but may be controversial.

8. Traumatization theory has not adequately addressed the social factors that shape the cognitive reception of domestic violence. Although extreme trauma can elicit unconscious defensive responses, interpretations

communicated by mental health and other professionals can profoundly shape components of a victim's secondary appraisal, such as attributions of blame, coping strategies, future expectations, and ascription of gender roles.

9. The time-limited situational interventions required to deal with the traumatic consequences of battering appear to be relatively straightforward compared with the complex issues raised by long-term psychotherapy. Paradoxically, however, trauma-oriented practitioners are often ill-prepared to confront the personal, ethical, and professional dilemmas raised by battering, particularly where its prominent elements are coercion and control rather than extreme violence.

In summary, PTSD provides an important bridge between conventional psychiatry and the advocate's insistence that responsibility for violence be fixed squarely on the perpetrator. Questions remain, however, about how adequately PTSD grasps the broad pattern of adaptive strategies women devise in response to the dual and intratraumatic stress of ongoing coercion.

## Treating the Dual Trauma of Wife Battering

The modal experience of battering is a dual trauma: fear and anger induced by violent subjugation combined with a sense of increasing entrapment. A process of institutional victimization is combined with partner violence to transform a persistent, assertive woman into a "helpless victim" for whom "nothing can be done." Abused women appear passive and withdrawn or inappropriately hostile, presentations easily misread as signs of inner deterioration. To overcome battering successfully, the victim's response to the violence and to inappropriate and punitive care must be elicited and supported. The first step in differentiating what the patient has done (and why) from what has been done to her is to obtain a full history of interpersonal as well as institutional trauma (Jacobson & Richardson, 1987).

THERAPEUTIC GOALS:
AUTONOMY AND EMPOWERMENT

In battering, the secondary traumatization creates a condition of profound existential risk that requires mental health intervention as surely as underlying psychiatric disease: The battered woman is not safe nor is she free. Therapeutic goals support autonomy and empowerment. Autonomy addresses safety and includes a sense of separateness, flexibility, and self-possession sufficient to define one's self-interest in interpersonal and public contexts. Empowerment addresses the process of entrapment. At a minimum, it implies the opportunity to make significant choices about present behavior and future courses of action. Both goals entail restoring material as well psychological well-being.

A report on domestic violence from the American Medical Association (AMA) Council on Ethical and Judicial Affairs (1992) highlights beneficence and nonmaleficence as the principles to guide clinical intervention. In addition to routine identification, assessment, and treatment, physician responsibilities extend to "participation in efforts to secure a safe place, including offering hospitalization if necessary for patients when there are no available shelters" (p. 3192). Having emphasized safety in the case of woman battering, however, protective services (the basis for intervention in child and elder abuse) are replaced by informative and interpretive encounters "that facilitate patient empowerment and autonomy." Patient consent becomes the basis for notifying spouses, partners, or other third parties, including police, about a diagnosis of battering as well as for using third parties to confirm or substantiate a patient's report of abuse.

Hare-Mustin and Marecek (1986) point out that the psychological goals of autonomy and empowerment may conflict with therapeutic principles, such as beneficence, the desire to serve the patient's welfare by getting her to make the "right" or "healthy" choice. Although many therapeutic encounters pose this dilemma, beneficence must be carefully managed with women who alternately feign dependence (as a means of survival), fear it (because it has put them at risk), desperately need genuine interdependence (to support self-esteem), and experience dependence as the antithesis of safety. Despite the frustration of witnessing a client failing to leave a situation we believe puts her in danger, "rescuing" such women only reinforces their sense of not being able to do so for themselves. Worse, when benign paternalism fails, therapists often behave like rejected lovers, alternately acting out in the treatment process or unwittingly identifying with the assailant's anger.

Autonomy and empowerment are transactional rather than exclusively individual capabilities and are attained through shifts in the context of domestic violence—in the gestalt sense—as well as through developing individual awareness. Even "to hold a traumatic reality in consciousness," writes Herman (1992), "requires a social context that affirms and protects the victims" (p. 9). The alternating hope and fear that characterize the ambivalence of battered women about leaving reflect real as well as perceived shifts in the space, power, and resources that are available for women to maneuver. The probability that a woman will make independent choices depends on how authority is structured around her, including the authority of her helpers. Accordingly, effective intervention seeks to realign power in the home and helping environment and to mobilize resources on the woman's behalf.

Pursuing autonomy and empowerment for battered women in mental health settings opens the proverbial Pandora's box. The treater who decides to respond to domestic violence confronts widespread prejudice against female independence as well as the hostility elicited in colleagues by a client population that may alternately appear overly dependent and aggressive and demanding. The psychosocial problems that accompany abuse make battered women low-status clients, as does the prevailing sense that they are failures (as mothers, wives, and women) for whom nothing can be done. The financial affairs of battered women are likely to be in disarray, particularly if the women are middle class, or they may have little or no access to money at all. Depending on the degree of coercion involved, their access to transport and ability to leave the house, to talk privately on the phone, to keep appointments, or to use referrals may be severely constrained. As the institutional dimensions of entrapment surface, an advocacy-coaching model of intervention comes to the fore that tests the therapist's knowledge of systems against deeply embedded beliefs about the proper role of therapy. Effective advocacy may involve colluding with client strategies to circumvent barriers to help (e.g., concealing work on abuse from the husband's insurance carrier). How to do this without increasing the client's subsequent vulnerability—or the therapist's own—is an important practical art.

## THE POLITICAL CONTEXT
## FOR CLINICAL INTERVENTION:
## COMMUNITY-BASED DOMESTIC VIOLENCE SERVICES

The political context for an improved clinical response to battering is provided by community-based domestic violence services grouped around the battered women's shelter.

A century ago, women stayed with violent men because there was no alternative. Nineteenth-century feminists naively believed that male tyranny in private life would disappear as women gained formal rights to divorce, custody, property, the vote, and equal protection under the law. When battering persisted despite women's hard-won entitlements in the late 1970s, it was first believed that individual personality factors might be responsible. It was both easier and safer to argue that something about the women prevented them from using existing opportunities for help.

The rapid proliferation of shelters that were often started and run by formerly battered women showed that it was the nature of the services offered, as much as anything about domestic violence itself, that explained the absence of battered women on official service rolls and their dependent, passive, or withdrawn appearance in the mental health context. As an antidote to institutional victimization, the supportive milieu of the women's space allowed women to be assertive, examine their predicament realistically, and skillfully negotiate on behalf of themselves and others. By setting self-reliance and advocacy in the context of mutual recognition and collective support, the shelter reawakened women's capacity for social autonomy, including independence in service settings. This highlighted the fact that meaningful access to conventional services required the development of health and mental health programs that were similarly woman oriented and that supplemented standard techniques for case-finding, crisis intervention, assessment, and treatment with peer support and advocacy for systems change. Sensitive to this reality, many hospitals, community mental health facilities, child protective services, and police departments developed programs incorporating the shelter philosophy.

Battered women's shelters have many shortcomings, including low levels of funding (or training), deteriorating physical plants, inexperienced staff, high levels of burnout, and caseloads that force staff to abandon genuine advocacy for sheer crisis management. Shelter staff are often ill-equipped to handle the multiple behavioral problems attendant on unresolved domestic violence, particularly substance use, mental illness, and child abuse. In addition, often in response to pressure from funders or so-called professionalization, many shelters have compromised the early ideals of client-run services, allowing their volunteer base to dissipate, muzzling their political role as advocates for systems change, and looking more like a traditional social service than a women-run alternative. None of these shortcomings discounts the fact that, in less than two decades, a community-based alternative to violent relationships has been created that compares favorably with more conventional treatment approaches on virtually every standard, whether judged by crude recidivism, by cost-effectiveness, or by long-term benefits to women and children.

## THE THERAPIST AND
## THE BATTERED WOMEN'S SHELTER

Treating the dual trauma of battering requires that therapeutic aid be combined with advocacy for systems change; safety planning, including planning with any children; and material and social alternatives to entrapment. Shelters help women regain much of their strength and confidence while, in addition to offering safety and peer support against abuse, they also represent women politically in their encounters with the helping services. For mental health as well, an advocacy-coaching model is essential because denial, minimization, blaming the victim, and isolation by professionals are often hopelessly entwined with the pattern of entrapment by partners. With clients still at risk, effective therapeutic work requires ongoing liaison to shelters, courts, police, and medical services. Such support is crucial to nourish a woman's individualized sense of possibility.

Most battered women will not require emergency shelter; even those who use shelter typically return to the world they have left within a short time. To realize the benefits of peer support, the therapist may cultivate a viable (safe) space within a woman's network of friends, family, and kin or simulate the shelter experience through group work embodying the principles of recovery, safety, support, and empowerment. Isolation is both cause and consequence of abuse and institutional victimization. Yet the abused woman's experience is often symptomatic of more generic female experiences in particular neighborhoods, towns, ethnic groups, or extended-kin networks. Although social connectedness alone will not guarantee safety from an obsessive male assailant or remedy the effects of an insensitive professional response, skillful networking functions both to mobilize indigenous female (and male) prowess against future violence and to transfer advocacy skills to supportive peers. Against a background of protection and accountability for the violence, the relative effectiveness of this strategy for a particular woman is a function of the duration of violence, the degree of entrapment, the complexity of accompanying psychosocial problems, and the woman's history of institutional maltreatment. The social support a woman musters often holds the key to whether she can be both safe and separate.

## EXPUNGING INSTITUTIONAL VICTIMIZATION

Cooper (1971) describes the basic problem in psychotherapy as *progressive depopulation,* helping the vast family that patients bring with them to "leave the (therapeutic) room." Similarly, the capacity for choice so essential to empowerment requires disentangling and exorcising enmeshed relationships that have accumulated during decades of psychological development. With battered women, repeated violations of virtually all boundaries may have created a particularly fragile and diminished sense of self. Embedded in this sense of utter vulnerability are fragments of institutional maltreatment that have accumulated in the patient's psyche over the years, eliciting a dysfunctional relationship to caretakers that must also be exorcised before a healthy interdependence with supportive others can be reestablished.

To offset the emphasis on personal pathology, posttrauma therapy should seek out the complex ways in which subordination in institutional and intimate encounters has developed and converged over time. The story of battering to which we bear witness unfolds around two processes of traumatization and hence yields both the history of assault and coercion—called the *adult trauma history*—that we use to identify and assess coercion and control by partners and the history of institutional care. The trauma history describes the objective basis in coercion and control for current relational difficulties; the experience of institutional maltreatment underlies the gap in trust between client and therapist. Just as we must help patients in other circumstances differentiate their own stories from those that have been projected onto them by significant others who threatened to withhold love, so is the history of help seeking elicited to help abused women differentiate their legitimate responses to institutional neglect and maltreatment from the interpretations of their character and behavior, driven home by inappropriate professional response.

The history of help seeking allows the woman to recover a sense of a public self she can recognize as uniquely hers, a bounded and credible entity that has carried her purposes into the world even at those moments when she was most oppressed. Like the abusive relationship, the experience of frustrated help seeking convinces women they have failed to help themselves and hence are incapable of doing so now.

Rather than focus on a woman's helplessness and victimization, the therapist guides the woman through a reframing process in which even self-destructive behaviors such as suicide attempts are interpreted as survival-oriented given the constraints imposed by the battering situation and the failure of helpers to respond. Conversely, restoring a woman's sense of current capacity entails reframing her unsuccessful help-seeking initiatives as well as the anger, frustration, and sense of impotence elicited by inappropriate institutional responses. In anticipation of effective advocacy, it is important to identify the political dimensions of institutional power that have constrained a woman's choices, including sexism. It is not uncommon to find that treaters, lawyers, police, or caseworkers have cut off contact, violated basic rules of confidentiality, or even harassed or abused clients they recognize as vulnerable. Therapists are often shocked to discover how their colleagues have treated battered women and may disbelieve the client, withdraw from confrontation, or, at the other extreme, become so intent on rescuing a woman from the system that they undermine her sense of personal responsibility and control. Therapists should be as attuned to professional incompetence as they are to partner abuse.

Dorothy Rapp is a New Jersey housewife who killed her husband because of battering. She had repeatedly turned to police, neighbors, family, and doctors (New Jersey Network, 1985). The interviewer below is a news reporter, but she could easily be a professional counselor.

> **Mrs. Rapp:** I asked the police, "Well can't you take me somewhere?" and they said no. I said, "Can't you arrest him because he's hurting me?" and they said, "Only if you come down, sign a complaint."
> **Interviewer:** And you didn't want to do that?
> **Mrs. Rapp:** No, because I had done it before, I had signed a complaint . . ."

Having witnessed the consequences of an assault by Mr. Rapp, the New Jersey police required nothing more to make an arrest. Unlike Mrs. Rapp, who understood that this was a stalling tactic, the interviewer implied that Mrs. Rapp's failure to file a complaint complicated the situation. Rather than confirming the reality, that Mrs. Rapp had tried to stop the violence in every way she could, the interviewer reinforced Mrs. Rapp's insecurity and guilt about the tragic situation.

Over time, as the partner's control becomes more and more destructive, the focus of a woman's help seeking may shift from escape to survival. The desire for independence remains strong but goes underground and must be expressed within the parameters of the partner's control, a process we term *control in the context of no control.* The refusal to yield to domination is evident even in negative or apparently self-destructive behavior.

> **Mrs. Rapp:** He put the shotgun right there (gesturing to her head) and said, "I'm going to do it." I said (lifting her head challengingly), "Go ahead. What are you waiting for?"
> **Interviewer:** Did you mean that?
> **Mrs. Rapp:** You bet I did.

An element of resistance is barely audible behind Mrs. Rapp's attempts to manage her own murder. Instead of supporting empowerment by identifying the strength mustered in this terrifying moment, the interviewer implied that Mrs. Rapp may have been deliberately provocative, again reinforcing what other helpers had suggested, adding to Mrs. Rapp's confusion about who was responsible for the abuse. Later in the evening, Mr. Rapp went outside, promising to shoot Mrs. Rapp when he returned. Unable to control or predict when or how any or all her boundaries would be violated, cut off from all outside sources of support, Mrs. Rapp desperately struggled to see herself through something other than Mr. Rapp's eyes.

> **Mrs. Rapp:** I lay there thinking, "I deserve this because I'm bad. . . . I mean he kept telling me I'm bad.

After she killed her husband and had completed a therapeutic process that emphasized her passivity and victimization, Mrs. Rapp lost touch with the fact that it was she who had sought help and others who had refused it.

> **Mrs. Rapp:** I thought I deserved it. So I didn't do anything to get help. I guess I really loved him.

The learned helplessness model would explain that Mrs. Rapp killed her husband in sheer desperation, believing all other options to be closed. In contrast, a revised traumatization framework would locate her "outburst" on a logical continuum with other forms of resistance she had mounted to entrapment at home and by her helpers. Moreover, it would frame her ambivalence, including her belief that she deserved or even wanted the abuse, in relation to the objective dilemma she faced, namely that assertiveness against life-threatening violence was both self-affirming and self-destructive. By differentiating the external sources of Mrs. Rapp's negative self-image and counterposing them to her actual behavior (e.g., her persistent help seeking, her underground resistance), intervention can reinforce the rational core of autonomy without minimizing victimization and vulnerability.

## IDENTIFYING THE POLITICS
## OF PERSONAL INDEPENDENCE

Even in the most unequal, pitifully traditional, or circumscribed relationships, battered women experience abuse and institutional victimization as part of a power struggle over personal integrity and control. This reflects the fact that issues of sexual inequality and gender stereotypes make every confrontation between a woman, her partner, or the helping system a political as well as a personal encounter.[1] The normally difficult task of disentangling the effects of violence and institutional victimization is compounded if the therapist is uncomfortable with female equality and aggressiveness and is either unwilling or unable to view women's persistence and stubbornness in a positive light.

Sometimes, the political issues are explicit. In one client's words: "It was a second marriage for us both. We pooled our savings to buy a condo. I knew there would be a power struggle. I just didn't expect the violence."

Often, however, as battering develops, the focus of conflict shifts from female independence to secondary problems (such as his drinking or hers) that treaters have identified as primary. The treater emphasizes these issues because, like the victim, the first impulse is to end the violence without threatening the relationship; this can be accomplished using conflict resolution strategies, such as anger management, couples' counseling, mutual contracts, or mediation. These strategies can temporarily suppress secondary problems (including the violent behavior). But unless power relations have been realigned, these strategies will reinforce the status quo, exacerbate coercive control, and increase the probability of severe violence in the future.

Once a safety plan is in place for the woman and any children, the politics and interpersonal dynamics of institutional and partner trauma are best addressed in the same way, by building a woman's capacity for survival or escape around the strategic prowess she has already exhibited through persistent help seeking, aggressiveness, and resistance. Battered women establish moments of autonomy within the experience of subordination to which they attach their fragile sense of identity. Insults to these moments are often the watershed events that elicit decisive action. Although such moments may involve the children, it is because their meaning is intensely personal that they provide temporary refuge. When the truck driver husband of one of our clients returned from a long-distance haul, he would awaken his wife, have her cook him a meal, have sex, then fly into a jealous rage and beat her. She left him, however, only when he refused to let her attend church, an entitlement she had identified since childhood as her refuge from family trouble. For Francine Hughes, returning to school represented the last effort to survive in the relationship. It was after Mickey Hughes forced Francine to burn her school books that she killed him in the so-called burning bed case. Because the extent of the woman's autonomy is usually the most salient issue for both partners, treaters must studiously avoid interventions whose efficacy requires further restriction, even those that are self-imposed or agreed to contractually.

## THE INTERACTIVE ELEMENT

Once a woman's personal strengths have been identified, it is possible to confront the interactive element in violent relationships without blaming the victim. In its emphasis on the gender-specific character of abuse, feminist theory justifiably downplays this aspect. As the history of Mrs. Rapp illustrates, however, abused women repeatedly engage their assailants, seek to control their situations even under the severest constraints, and are often quite direct about their needs.

The claims of abusive men to the contrary, most battered women are not feminists in any programmatic sense and may often cling desperately to traditional gender roles. But when a batterer brings a litany of complaints about his wife's failures to the table, he is expressing something of which both partners are painfully aware, that conventional role behavior does not meet the woman's needs and that her behavior—or the meaning she secretly attaches to it—contradicts her expressed sense of how a woman should behave. The refusal to perform traditional responsibilities assigned to women—such as housework, child care, or meeting a man's sexual needs—is a common context for abuse. Furthermore, given the realities of sexual inequality, women are forced to negotiate for their needs in devious ways that make them ashamed and vulnerable to attack. In such cases, it is far more useful to identify, interpret, and normalize actual behavior in the relationship (by pointing out, for example, that "No one can be happy if all they do is cook, clean, or talk to kids") than to ameliorate expressed concerns by reassuring a woman that she is a good housewife or mother (she may not be).

For many batterers, relationships are a zero-sum game in which each sign of a woman's separateness represents something taken from them (possibly by an imaginary lover) or, alternately, a failure in their ability to provide. She may have long ago recognized the relationship was limited and sought to meet her needs elsewhere, through a job, school, friends, or a lover. He reads such behavior as betrayal and, taking his narcissistic wound as justification, severely constrains her mobility, employing violence and coercion to force her to quit her job, account for all money, stop seeing her friends, prepare perfect meals, or offer elaborate proof that no other man has been in the house. Forced to abandon or to bring their otherwise diffuse quest for self-expression home, many women assume an aggressive posture expressed in open acts of defiance (which often provoke beatings) and passive-aggressive adaptations to the traditional gender role behavior he demands. Uncomfortable with her mechanical compliance but equally threatened by the loss of control implied by her autonomy, he tries to enforce a status quo in which she agrees to present him with only problems (or needs) he can handle. This implicit contract, in which couples' therapists often collude, is repeatedly broken by the myriad disappointments of everyday life—a photo of his mother breaks, the baby cries too long, the phone rings during sexual intercourse—or by periodic violations of his pitiably narrow boundaries ("She really knows how to push my button"). Requests that he recognize feelings other than anger or sex reawaken his sense of inadequacy and are quickly followed by dependence, fear of abandonment, then fury.

> **Mrs. Rapp:** I said, "Gee isn't that a beautiful blue sky and it's so pretty today." And he just hauled off and knocked every one of my teeth out.

Behind a rigid character armor, even physically imposing abusers may imagine their body is tiny and distorted, a self-image linked to their tendency to minimize and shirk responsibility for the pain they inflict and to a Jekyll-Hyde pattern in which the assailant becomes overly solicitous after a violent episode. During this *honeymoon phase,* some women appear tentative in their help seeking, though, contrary to what Walker (1984) argues, we have found this is less often because they are fooled by promises than because they expect his patronizing dominance to be sanctioned positively by third parties, including friends and helpers. Anger management and assertiveness training can be effective ways to stop physical abuse. But modifying the pattern of coercion and control at the heart of battering is much more complicated.

## VICTIM INVESTMENT IN
## VIOLENCE: TWO APPROACHES

Some degree of mutual dependence is the rule rather than the exception in all abusive relationships. The woman's world becomes increasingly circumscribed until she may rely on her partner in every significant facet of her life, including her self-evaluation. The extent to which batterers micromanage facets of women's lives is hard to exaggerate and often extends to food, cigarettes (or illicit drugs), dress, TV, sleep, even access to toilet paper. Women may appear to be invested in the abusive behavior, draw it out, provoke it, comply with its dictates, blame themselves, assume the roles of which they are accused, experience relief when violence occurs, and defend, minimize, or completely deny that they are battered.

These therapeutic dilemmas should be framed in terms of their positive core, the limited control women are attempting to exercise in contexts that permit little or no control. A client who was sent to Weight-Watchers (which she liked because she got out of the house) was put on the scale daily, then beaten because she was "too stupid" to lose weight. Another was sent for cigarettes and beer but always "forgot" something and was beaten as a consequence. As entrapment proceeds, control at home, like control in the helping system, is sought indirectly, through somatization (e.g., overeating, excessive fatigue, "forgetting") or through externally submissive, passive, and dependent behavior. Self-medication with licit or illicit drugs is an expression of control as well as an attempt to medicate stress. Similarly, although self-blame is widely interpreted as a signal of low self-esteem, in battering relationships it is also a strategic way to take responsibility within a limited field, saying, "I called the police. It didn't work. Next time I'll try something else." When Dorothy Rapp thought "I deserve it," she was framing a tactical question to herself that opened a space for action. Overtly, she considered whether she deserved it because "I'm bad" (as her husband claimed). Underneath, however, she wondered whether she was bad because she was waiting passively to be killed. Functioning as a form of control, self-blame allowed her to act decisively in a context of being controlled, saving her life.

Dependent behaviors (compliance, denial, adaptation to the violence) are also infused with aggressive content and strategic purpose. Feminist psychologists who employ an object relations approach believe that women's character structure leads them to rationalize violence by incorporating it into their larger interpretation of the world. According to dependency or relational theories developed by Chodorow (1985), Dinnerstein (1977), Gilligan (1985), and the psychologists at the Stone Center in Wellesley, women are taught to get their dependency needs met through caretaking and their displays of passive-dependency have a protective and systems-maintaining function for significant others. The therapist may focus on a man's cruelty. But the victim feels she must be available for this "fragile" man and becomes invested in his over-compensatory behavior because it reveals his need for caretaking (and so for her).

The apparent normalization of violence by certain abused women reflects both female character and socialization—as dependency theory contends—and the strategic use of dependence to negotiate institutional maltreatment and interpersonal violence—as the revised traumatization framework proposes. An impulse toward personal power and autonomy is often hidden behind what appears to be a self-destructive investment in dependence. As the woman's efforts to supplement the relationship are disallowed, she is forced to seek her independence within the context of this primary dependence, infusing it with aggressiveness. This feeling is hard to disentangle from the mounting anger she feels toward her assailant (and her helpers). Often, abused women interpret the acts of violence—correctly in our view—as a response both to overt acts of independence and to the impulse toward independence concealed beneath a pseudodependent posture. It seems strange or self-effacing to hear a woman we regard as overly traditional suggest "I deserved it," particularly when she has ostensibly been beaten for trying to comply with her partner's demands. Even as we remind her that nothing she has done justifies her partner's behavior, however, we should also identify the strain of resistance concealed by compliance. The client who was beaten because of her "terrible memory" made this admission following a detailed recitation of 10 years of abuse. In the safety of the treatment context, she immediately recognized the survival function of her "memory loss" and that she was neither stupid nor forgetful (as her partner and she had claimed), but furious.

However dysfunctional, the violence may be the only reminder a woman has of an impulse toward autonomy quashed by a man she regards as emotionally limited. Dependency theory relies on the adherence of victims to traditional female roles and values. Oddly, among abused women, dependence (underfunctioning) takes on an almost stylized quality behind which a woman has often become increasingly self-sufficient, less respectful of conventional roles, and, as a result, open to personal change. The price she pays is enormous by any standards. But it is a price we must respect.

Where dependency theory applies, the therapist works to change the conception of a family system so that the woman no longer feels compelled to underfunction to support the pseudofunctioning of the male. But when a strategic conception seems more appropriate, the task is to elicit the aggressive component behind the rationalization of the violence and to distinguish the passive-dependent behavior that women frequently display if not cultivate from the actual level of autonomy and differentiation of self that they have achieved beneath, through, and despite this display.

The strategic substructure of a victim's behavior is not easy to elicit. As victims internalize the punitive response to their self-development, they become ambivalent and confused about autonomy and may even identify their power through the violence rather than with the independent impulse to which it is a response. Moreover, though giving up the violent relationship may be the therapist's measure of success, the victim may conceive of her endurance and struggle as an important phase in her self-development. "After all," she thinks in deciding whether to stay, "with how many men could I even have gotten this far?" In this instance, emphasizing her progressive victimization rather than her personal aims can extend her ambivalence and contribute to a sustained depression. For many abused women, the psychological alternative to strategic dependence is not a healthy dependence but the homicidal rage that made Dorothy Rapp and Francine Hughes strike out against their

partners. The subordination that results from the dual trauma of battering is an adaptive and contradictory process that must not be mistaken
for submissiveness.

For some battered women, violence is the only issue and entrapment
results directly from limited options or paralyzing fear. But although all
battered women want the violence to stop, as paradoxical as this seems,
many victims experience the violent reaction as an integral part of a
power struggle through which they seek to develop their personality
and express their independence. This "investment" is as much political
as psychological and reflects the fact that oppressed minorities must
always seek individuation among lesser evils. These women cannot
conceive of the violence ending without fundamentally compromising
or even abandoning their goals for personal growth. Helping the woman
without inadvertently reinforcing dependence presents an ongoing dilemma during treatment.

## THE VICTIM-THERAPIST RELATIONSHIP

In summary, the challenge to traumatic therapy with victims of domestic
violence is to admit an individual and interactive element without blaming
the abused woman, to recognize the serious threat posed by violence
without compromising personal issues for family peace, and to establish
a sense of current options while remaining respectful and emotionally
unreactive to the woman's choice to change or not to change her living
situation. The therapeutic response must adapt to the complex profile
the abused woman presents of dependence and autonomy, power and
vulnerability, ambivalence toward conventional roles and fear of punishment if she changes. Violence, coercion, and institutional maltreatment
foster an unconscious association of autonomy, aggression, and the
exercise of personal authority with disloyalty, betrayal, and loss. As a
result, abuse victims repeatedly test the degree to which we choose to
see them as dependent and dysfunctional or are comfortable with their
competence and anger. Their history makes battered women hypersen-
sitive to hidden messages that they are bad (or mad), which undermine
explicit offers of support.

Letting the battered woman know she has done the right thing in
talking to a therapist and has behaved reasonably within the constraints
of her situation helps elicit her strategic capacity in the current crisis.
She did not need saving before; she does not need it now. Communication about what behavior is appropriate is equally important. In the

woman's experience, the pursuit of autonomy precipitates anger and violence from loved ones and service providers. When the abused woman presents herself as powerless, even passive, she is testing the therapist's response as well as expressing her real situation. The victim's dilemma—she must choose between being compliant and loved or independent and abused—converges with the therapist's own conflict between beneficent caretaking and support for female autonomy.

Autonomy and empowerment are possible only if the woman can feel both strong and cared for at once. Unfortunately, despite three decades of rhetoric about helping people "get in touch with their feelings," most therapists still identify more readily with vulnerability, depression, and low self-esteem in women than with appropriate aggression. Another problem involves a common fear of strong women and a corresponding tendency to project a male stereotype of how women should be (dependent, helpless) through an exaggerated emphasis on the professional role as helper. Lerner (1984) sees the projected stereotype as a way to devalue the omnipotence of the maternal figure by inverting the therapist's relation to her and treating the patient like a little girl. Apart from this compelling interpretation, the fact remains that therapists typically value autonomy more highly than dependence or caretaking—and as more healthy—while, at the same time, treating it as somewhat abnormal for a woman to be fiercely independent, to behave strategically, or to seek separateness as a primary goal. The result is that the victim can be put in the same double-bind in treatment that she experiences at home. She will get approval only if she behaves in a relatively dysfunctional and ultimately unsatisfying way.

Carmen et al. (1984) highlight a related issue. For disorders that are incongruent with society's idealized image of women, such as alcoholism and illicit drug abuse, women's service needs have been hidden and ignored. Our research confirms that women who experience these disorders as sequelae of abuse are seen as bad as well as mad, hence not as credible victims deserving help. In a critique of a family systems' approach to battered women, Bograd (1986) argues that the projection of a female stereotype in therapy is linked to the use of quid pro quo behavioral contracts in which the husband promises to control his temper for his wife and she agrees to comply with some of his requests. Frequently, the couple agrees that the violence must stop, and the woman accepts certain limits and supplements the relationship. Even if such contracts were not ethically suspect, the compulsive exclusivity that characterizes abusive relationships makes them untenable. Bograd recognizes that separating the couple is a legitimate family therapy move and conveys a powerful metastatement about responsibility. Whatever one may think of the incompatibility of independence with violence, no matter how pitiable a woman seems when she says, "I just want the violence to stop," the therapeutic role is to help her clarify, not compromise, her political goals. Physical safety is the prerogative of every woman, not something for which she should have to bargain.

To understand fully the substance, scope, and limits of female aggression, therapists should be in touch with their own aggression. An account of domestic violence always elicits aggressive feelings, if only as an instinctual defense against the reawakened fear of personal harm. The same process goes on in the therapist and often for the same reasons. A common tendency is to displace aggressive feelings before they surface, in oneself as well as in one's client, supporting a woman's "insight" that "I'm hurt, not angry," for example, or "I'm not enraged at you, I'm depressed at myself." As serious, many therapists share the batterer's inability to differentiate aggression (which is need centered) from hostility, anger, and violence (where the primary impulse is destructive) and mistakenly conclude that if a woman is aggressive, for example, if she fights for what she wants in a way that infringes on another's space, then abuse is the result of mutual combat. Disclosing one's own difficulty with aggressive feelings can resolve some of this confusion.

We have viewed woman battering from the vantage of one issue primarily: How the professional response impinges on, enters, and shapes violent relationships so that struggles for independence that have been met by abusive assault end in battering, the subordination of women's capacity for personal power and autonomy. There is reason for strong optimism about clinical work with battered women that combines a revised trauma model emphasizing a woman's strengths, incorporates the experience of help seeking, and includes liaison with shelter and criminal justice services and advocacy directed at changing the system of which we are a part. Putting an end to coercive control is another matter, however. This entails communitywide initiatives to promote zero tolerance for domestic violence and to challenge what are widely held to be prerogatives of the normal male role. Even as we provide for the personal safety, empowerment, and autonomy of those put at risk by violent partners, therapists can play an important political role by highlighting the paucity of alternatives for men as they expand those available to women.

# Note

1. In many battering relationships, once violence is used, this larger political dimension grows in significance in direct relation to its suppression, so that both sides attribute an importance to disagreements that appears exaggerated to outsiders. One goal of a feminist-oriented intervention is to bring this hidden political dimension to the surface by supporting the woman's perception (which the batterer shares) that "the issue is not the real issue."

# Clinical Violence Intervention

*Lessons From Battered Women*

Recently, a well-known advocate for battered women gave a riveting talk at a conference of grant makers, where Anne Flitcraft was also scheduled to make a presentation. The advocate discussed the progress that the battered women's movement had made over the past 20 years. Gradually, however, she substituted the term *domestic violence* for woman battering and proceeded to discuss *domestic violence services*. When Flitcraft began, she looked out at an audience that was frankly puzzled. Setting aside her written text, she asked, "What do you think of when you hear the term domestic violence?" After a brief discussion, consensus emerged that domestic violence meant family violence, including all those relationships such as child, sibling, partner, spouse, and elder abuse.

Flitcraft's colleague had done nothing more than to bow to conventional usage. But the effect was to lose a key point—that the services she was describing were made by and for women.

---

AUTHORS' NOTE: This chapter is adapted from Flitcraft (1995).

It is impossible to live in the world of violence and violence prevention without sensing that the meaning of the word *violence* becomes blurred periodically. Once we set out to tackle violence as such, the problem seems so overwhelming, to have so many meanings, and to involve so many different groups of people that we naturally gravitate toward common denominators, common experiences that will help us pull these meanings and groups together under a unifying definition. This kind of synthetic thinking can often be useful but it can also be premature and confusing.

An understanding of violence as a public health problem begins by differentiating the experience of violence in ways that support effective intervention and prevention strategies. When violence occurs among persons who are or have been social partners, women are injured and men perpetrate the assault in the vast majority of cases (Rosenberg et al., 1986). Thus, consideration of gender is key to strategies to reduce or prevent this type of violence. With a sleight of linguistic hand, the speaker before Flitcraft had unwittingly replaced the issue of battered women with that of domestic violence. The result was that the distinctiveness of violence against women became invisible to the conference participants. It was invisible not because the home is private—virtually every move women make in the kitchen, bedroom, or bathroom has been the subject of commentary. Violence against women became invisible because the term domestic violence took on a broader meaning. As soon as violence is domesticated, as soon as one talks about the family, women's experience disappears behind the experience of all those for whom they care: children, siblings, the elderly, the disabled, and, yes, husbands as well.

Violence against women becomes "just a part of life." This is true not simply for policymakers or researchers; women themselves can readily put the experience of others before their own experience and think, "I don't care what he does to me. But he better not touch the children. Abuse? You know, I thought it was just life."

Failure to distinguish woman battering from other forms of family violence, such as child and elder abuse, leads to the conclusion that battered women's needs are similar to those of battered children and the abused frail elderly. Without a gender understanding of domestic violence, it seems reasonable to some to address the needs of adult women by adapting mandatory reporting by medical personnel to protective services as well as other medico-legal strategies used since the mid-1960s to address abuse of children and the disabled.

In fact, the health system has established mandatory reporting and protective services for those who are not able to care for themselves. Children, the disabled, and the frail elderly, for instance, are all dependent groups who either lack civil rights or lack the capacity to exercise their civil rights. Women who are victims of domestic violence are socially adult, fully competent individuals; although they may not yet have full equality before the law, including equal protection, they are certainly capable of exercising their civil rights. Most important for a consideration of the health provider response, they are participants in—not objects of— medical care efforts.

Woman battering, spouse abuse, or domestic violence is not just about being hit. Rather, to recognize domestic violence means to understand the dynamics of violent intimate relationships—particularly gendered relationships. In this context, domestic battery includes not only repeated episodes of physical or sexual abuse but also emotional abuse, degradation, limitations on freedom of movement, limitations on freedom of association, the destruction of property, threatened or real child abuse, stalking, retaliation, and isolation from friends and family (American Medical Association Council on Ethical and Judicial Affairs, 1992; Stark & Flitcraft, 1992). Its core is a pattern of coercive control over key aspects of the victim's life. Although these aspects of coercive control form the woman's dominant experience of violence, coercive control in and of itself does not always create the types of injury that excite a trauma surgeon or a crime that piques the interest of a detective. Coercive control, which is the fundamental core of women's experience of domestic violence, then ceases to be recognized as either an important medical or a criminal justice event.

Once the gendered nature of domestic violence disappears, coercive control disappears as the identifiable core, a woman's experience of domestic violence is fragmented into a myriad of more or less serious medical and legal events, and the agencies that are our eyes and our ears—on whom we depend for epidemiological data—cease to be reliable sources of information on the problem. Consider the case of one of our patients. Gloria was nearly blind, with wide scars over her shoulder and abdomen and multiple scars, both traumatic and surgical, over her abdomen and flanks. Gloria's several-volume medical record documented bilateral retinal detachments, burns over her torso from hot grease, a fractured jaw, multiple stab wounds to the abdomen, and a gunshot wound that required emergency partial resection of her liver. In the discharge for hospitalization, house officers through the years had carefully noted the patient as a 22-year-old, a 25-year-old, a 27-year-old with a long and complicated history of trauma secondary to alcohol abuse.

Without a gender perspective on violence, we lose the capacity to recognize the links between one trauma episode and the next, as well as the ability to acknowledge the risk of future harm that Gloria faced. Nor is the confusion limited to medicine. The police and courts are other agencies on whom battered women depend. In the case of Kristen, the police department in her community had received an emergency protective order against her boyfriend. Kristen's boyfriend, who had a long history of violence against previous companions, slipped through parole hearings, court hearings for minor offenses, and batterer education programs during his months of escalating assaults, thefts, and threats against Kristen. Finally, his parole officer advised Kristen to get the protective order but did not remand the assailant's parole, sending him instead to yet another psychiatric evaluation. The police sergeant issued a complaint for assault and battery, larceny, and intimidation of a witness in violation of the state's laws on domestic abuse. However, the complaint remained on the desk in the clerk's office and was still waiting to be processed when Kristen was killed 3 weeks later, 3 weeks after her boyfriend's psychiatric evaluation (Lardner, 1993).

The inability to see the unique dynamics of domestic violence not only blinds us to identifying it but blinds us to the seriousness of the problem when indeed we do see it. These cases illustrate the fundamental challenge that domestic violence poses to both health care and criminal justice, for neither institution has organized a sufficient framework to assess, manage, and effectively ensure safety for women in violent relationships.

The next section shows how, from a clinician's viewpoint, the aspects of violence mentioned earlier unfold over time in the life of a battered woman. Analysis is based on the following parameters:

*Injury.* We begin conceptually with the notion of injury. An important aspect of domestic violence is not necessarily the severity of the injury but the frequency of the injury. For instance, a woman who comes to the emergency room three times with injuries has an 80% chance of being a battered woman, whether those injuries require sutures or not. These injuries tend to be to the central areas of the body, in contrast to accidental injuries to the hands and feet. Frequency and central pattern combine to constitute an adult trauma history typical of domestic violence (Stark & Flitcraft, 1991). If we want to know about domestic violence, we have to ask patients about their adult trauma histories.

*Illness.* Living within a violent relationship is not only about getting hit. Obviously, the times in between getting hit are also fraught with difficulty. Women describe a life of "walking on eggshells." In this setting, women present symptoms of an intratraumatic stress disorder not unlike that of soldiers who come home from war to experience post-traumatic stress disorder (PTSD). Headaches, abdominal pains, atypical chest pains, and other kinds of symptoms form the bulk of presentations to medical care. Primary care providers recognize that some patients present repeatedly with somatic complaints. With a little bit of questioning, the clinician may find that these patients are likely to be victims of domestic violence. Complications of previous, recurrent trauma are a second source of medical illness among battered women and include, for instance, recurrent sinus infections among those who have suffered fractured facial bones and hearing deficits following repeated blows to the ears.

*Isolation.* Lacking outside intervention, women try strategies to end or control the level of violence. If a woman is beaten because she goes to school, she quits school. If she gets beaten because the cost of the long-distance call to her mother is too much, she may stop calling. If she gets beaten because she visits her girlfriends, she stops visiting. But without outside intervention, her strategies to control the violence tend to enhance her isolation within the violent relationship.

Isolation is what we need to break for the woman to reach safety, yet look at traditional interventions: In response to the pain, headaches, multiple injuries, and somatic complaints, we are likely to give the battered woman pain medications, sleeping medications, and anxiolytics. Look closely at the meaning of these prescriptions. If a woman goes to the doctor and the doctor gives her medicines, she is sick. Who else says she is sick? Her batterer. Now the doctor and the batterer appear to say the same thing. Similarly, if the doctor sends her to see a psychiatrist, she is crazy. Who else says that? The batterer. Medical interventions unwittingly echo the message of the batterer.

Finally, the woman who comes back not 4 times but 12 or 15 times to the emergency department is a frequent visitor to the emergency room. She is one whom we think is likely to use too many resources, and so we abandon diagnosis altogether and resort to various labels, such as "frequent ER visitor," "hypochondriac," "hysteric," to validate a lack of intervention. All these relatively common medical practices contribute to and enhance the battered woman's isolation.

*Complex Psychosocial Problems.* As injury continues, as illness accumulates, as the battered woman becomes more isolated from health care providers and other significant resources, we begin to see the development of significant problems of alcohol and substance abuse. We estimate that 45% of all female alcoholics start out as battered women (Stark & Flitcraft, 1992). Yet women go into treatment accompanied too often by their abusive partner, with the result that treatment of alcoholism is attained through an escalation in coercive control.

Similarly, for women who abuse illicit substances, we estimate about half started out as battered women. Those involved in addiction programs for women know that the overlap between intimate violence and illegal drug use among women approximates 100%. To go forward with drug treatment programs for women without simultaneous advocacy to protect them from the domestic violence of pimps, boyfriends, and partners is to doom women to fail. About 60% of women hospitalized in psychiatric facilities are victims of childhood or adult abuse (Carmen et al., 1984; Post et al., 1980). About 25% of all female suicide attempts can be traced to domestic violence (see Chapter 4, this volume). We can no longer afford to overlook the relationship of women's mental health to their experience of violence among intimates.

## Clinical Violence Intervention

It is not surprising to find that many children are abused in households where there is domestic violence. Studies estimate that 45% to 60% of the mothers of battered children are themselves battered (see Chapter 3, this volume; Stark & Flitcraft, 1992). We used to think this was because dad hit mom, and mom hit son, and son hit daughter, and daughter chased the dog, and the SPCA came in and unraveled the whole thing; a sort of "hi-ho the derry-o" theory of family violence. But if we go back to the dynamics of coercive control, it appears that hurting the child is an effective way to hurt or coerce the mother. Child abuse in this setting is *tangential spouse abuse.* By linking the child's abuse to the mother's, a pattern frequently emerges: Violence against mom escalates and the child is hurt as yet another escalation of violence against mom. As clinicians, we see domestic violence and a little bit of child abuse. But when we put the child's and mother's abuse together, we see that the little bit of child abuse is a marked escalation in the level of domestic violence, in the same way that the introduction of a gun into the household is a marked escalation of domestic violence.

Domestic violence can be seen from a clinical perspective as a staged experience that involves injury, illness, isolation, and complex psychosocial problems. The complexity of interventions varies depending on the stage at which a woman presents. The needs and resources of the woman who comes into primary care or the emergency room with her first episode of violence contrast markedly with the needs and resources of a 45-year-old mother who is abusing alcohol and is seriously depressed. Relatively straightforward patient education may help the first woman use appropriate family and community supports, whereas the second woman will need very complex case management strategies to find safety and address her substantial mental health problems.

We can, however, identify a general framework for clinical violence intervention. The first step is to identify and acknowledge domestic violence. Direct questions in a confidential environment have been demonstrated to be an effective way to elicit a history of domestic violence. Such questions include "When there are fights at home, have you ever been hurt or afraid?" This is a question we routinely include in new patient assessments and in periodic reevaluations of clients. Obviously, when a new patient walks into the doctor's office with a black eye, something a bit more direct is useful: "It looks like someone has hurt you. Tell me about it." Acknowledge domestic violence when you see it. Explicit questions demonstrate that the provider is aware of domestic violence, and concern about abuse validates the patient's sense that violence is a threat to her physical and mental health.

Incorporating domestic violence awareness into clinical practice means that we provide medical care in the context of the ongoing risk of violence and coercive control. We may send the woman over for X rays but explain "Let's get the X rays, and while we are waiting for the results, we can talk more about the violence at home." This trick of providing medical care in the context of the violence is good for the patient and the provider because such an approach reinforces an understanding for both that the major issue at hand is violence. This helps prevent us from feeling overwhelmed by a list of seemingly unrelated issues and focuses care, a strategy that is particularly helpful for residents and medical students.

The next step in clinical violence intervention is safety assessment. Once the danger in domestic violence is recognized as coercive control, it becomes obvious that the severity of the injury does not predict immediate danger. This leads to some confusing situations. One patient, after requiring two dozen sutures to close a leg wound, assured us, "No, I'm really fine. After he finally does me good, it's all right for about a month." She claims she is not in danger, that the danger for her has passed. This is in contrast to the woman in the next cubicle who cries quietly. She has a minor soft tissue injury to the shoulder; the X rays have been negative. But she's crying and says, "I'm scared. He's got the kids and a gun and he says 'This is it.' "

Safety assessment depends on talking directly to the client about the level of violence she faces. To assess safety, we are looking for a history of change in various aspects of the relationship to identify escalating patterns of violence. In listening to a woman talk about her partner, we listen for three voices that communicate danger:

1. Injuries: How have they changed over time; are they becoming more frequent, more severe; are guns involved; are children involved when they were not before? Listen and ask about changes in this injury vector.
2. Constraints: Is she free to come and go? Is she in school? What did she used to do that she wishes she could do now? If her freedoms are diminishing, then she is becoming increasingly trapped within this relationship; listen and ask if delay will make escape even more difficult.
3. Fear: If fear is increasing, then danger is increasing. This was illustrated by a client who said, "He doesn't beat me anymore but he sleeps with a gun under the pillow." The injury vector was not escalating, the entrapment vector was not escalating, but the fear vector was escalating quickly. As we discussed her fears, it became obvious that she needed to make important decisions right away.

Documentation of domestic violence is terribly important and can be very simple, very straightforward. Helpers should stick with what they do best, that is, reporting nonjudgmentally what patients say, for example, "Mary says John beat her up with a hammer tonight," and go on with a description of the physical findings. One does not need to say that Mary alleges that John hit her tonight anymore than one says that John alleges that he has chest pain.

greater challenge, however, lies in institutional documentation.
eed to look at things like diagnostic categories, clinical indicators,
and quality assurance measures. Increasingly, these are the ways that
health care organizations measure problems and allocate resources. If
we have no diagnostic categories, clinical indicators, or quality assurance measures to recognize domestic violence, we will not be able to
garner the resources that we and our clients need.

Follow-up plans involve educating the patient about resources within
the community and facilitating her access to those resources. In doing
so, we all become involved in community resources. Here, once again,
patients lead us into new ways of seeing and new ways of being. Follow-up
plans involve changes for her and changes for us.

One can learn four lessons from battered women, some of which we
share from our history in health care (Whitman, 1988):

The first is do no harm. This means therapists must change, because
the kind of judgmental, blaming attitudes that battered women sometimes face in health care do real harm. Also, pretending not to see does
real harm. It is one thing to say "I don't know"; it is another thing to
say "I don't see."

The second is to seek strategies that empower the woman and promote long-term social change while meeting her immediate needs.
Meeting her immediate needs without strategies that empower her or
promote long-term social change is the equivalent of providing protective services.

Third, whatever you do, do with her, not to her. If you remember
this, then you will find that you are building an arena in which the
woman can build control, build her own sense of accomplishment, and
recover her self-esteem; all these features are necessary not only to the
woman's safety but to her recovery.

Finally, to determine "Was this a success?" ask yourself if changes in
your clinical practice have diminished the woman's isolation, contributed to an arena of safety and freedom, and enhanced the understanding of domestic violence in organizations within your community.
Ultimately this is the goal, not shelters for women and prisons for men,
but the development of safe and free communities.

# Discharge Planning
# With Battered Women

The purpose of this chapter is to provide a framework for discharge planning with female patients at risk for woman battering.

## The Background of Medical Concern

In the early 1970s, emergency service nurses in many hospitals working in conjunction with rape crisis groups established programs for victims of sexual assault. Building on this initiative and responding to an emerging movement to provide community-based shelter for battered women, the Ambulatory Nursing Department of the Brigham and Women's Hospital in Boston formed a multidisciplinary committee in 1977 to develop a therapeutic intervention for victims of domestic violence. The intervention at Brigham—like a parallel program developed at Harborview Hospital in Seattle—relied on a Social Service Trauma

AUTHORS' NOTE: This chapter is adapted from Stark (1994). Reprinted with permission of the American Hospital Association, copyright 1994.

Team initially comprising volunteer social workers who met weekly with nursing staff.

Equally important in stimulating medical interest in domestic violence was the development of a database indicating the significance of battering for women's health. A review of medical records at Yale-New Haven Hospital indicated that battering was the single most common cause of injury for which women sought medical attention. Research also showed that battered women whose problems went unattended suffered disproportionate rates of alcohol and drug abuse, rape, depression, and unwanted or aborted pregnancies. Conversely, battering emerged as a major factor in child abuse, female suicide attempts, rape, mental illness, addiction, AIDS, and homelessness. Despite the importance of battering, medical personnel rarely identified the problem, failed to link it to its multiple sequelae, and almost never identified violence as the focus of intervention.

Today, the medical response to domestic violence extends from the Office of the U.S. Surgeon General and the Centers for Disease Control to state health departments, professional medical and public health organizations, a federally funded center for information on health and domestic violence housed at the San Francisco-based Domestic Violence Prevention Fund, and state-funded health training organizations such as the Domestic Violence Training Project in Connecticut. Since January 1992, the Joint Commission on Accreditation of Healthcare Organizations has recommended that all accredited hospitals implement policies and procedures in their emergency departments and ambulatory care facilities for identifying, treating, and referring victims of abuse.

## The Challenge to Discharge Planning

Despite these initiatives and the well-documented significance of battering for the health of women and children, many hospitals lack standards of practice for managing domestic violence cases. Whatever the reason for a hospital stay, battered women's ensured safety is an important facet of health management on discharge. Standard hospital policy should include questions on family violence in all intake and screening procedures in emergency, ambulatory care, in-patient, and mental health settings. Where family violence is suspected, all patients should be asked about violence and control in a confidential setting, security during the hospital stay should be ensured, and discussion of future needs for safety and support should be initiated. Despite this ideal, formulating an appropriate discharge plan for hospitalized battered women requires the planner to take initiatives to revise intake sheets and screening mechanisms, provide for patient safety during hospitalization, and help implement quality assurance measures. The discharge planner is a crucial member of any hospitalwide effort to plan for domestic violence intervention.

## DEFINING THE PROBLEM

*Battering* describes the most devastating context of social partner assault, in which repeated episodes of physical abuse, usually by a spouse, ex-spouse, lover, or dating partner, are accompanied by sexual assault, threats, verbal abuse, the destruction of property, child abuse, stalking, degradation, isolation from friends and family, and a pattern of coercive control over key aspects of the victim's life, including money, food, sexuality, physical appearance, social life, transportation, work, religion, and access to help.

Most people think of battered women only in terms of physical trauma and the emergency service. Yet although women's physical abuse extends from occasional pushing or restraint to hair pulling, choking, punching, kicking, or assault with weapons or objects, most battered women are in the hospital for reasons other than trauma. Indeed, assaults associated with battering are typified less by severity than by the fact that they are frequent—often occurring more than once a week over many years; that they are often sexual in nature—involving forced intercourse or injuries to the breast, abdomen, or face; and that their aim is to instill fear and obedience in the victim.

Another misconception is that there is a specific risk profile for battering. In fact, the demographic profile of battered women is identical to the population at large. Neither race, income, age, religion, nor marital status differentiates women who are battered from other medical patients. Adolescent girls are at high risk for battering; so are women over 60. Between 50% and 75% of battered women in the hospital are single, separated, or divorced. Pregnancy is a high-risk period during which violence may begin or escalate, harming the fetus as well as the mother. Approximately 23% of obstetrical patients are in abusive relationships (Helton & Snodgrass, 1987).

## IDENTIFICATION

What distinguishes battering and frames its health consequences is the experience of coercive control. The greatest proportion of medical visits by battered women involves general medical, behavioral, and psychiatric problems that follow from the isolation, fear, and stress of a violent relationship, evidence that coercion and control are the most salient features. Thus, in reviewing a woman's medical history, in addition to a history of adult trauma, suspicion that battering has occurred is raised by headache or nonspecific pain, the abuse of licit or illicit substances, sleep disorders, anxiety, dysphagia, hyperventilation, and other signs of living in a stressful environment. A careful history of substance abuse, for instance, often reveals that use became addictive through efforts to self-medicate. Self-induced or attempted abortions, multiple therapeutic abortions, miscarriages, and divorce or separation during pregnancy are important presentations of abuse, particularly in obstetrical or gynecological admissions. Persistent gynecological complaints, particularly abdominal pain and dyspareunia in the context of normal physical examinations, are frequently overlooked manifestations of domestic violence. Again, however, the strongest clues of abuse are the clustering and repetition of presentations and complaints rather than isolated events.

The batterer's threats and intimidation frequently extend to the medical setting, in which coercion may be manifest as intrusive control over medical decisions. The batterer may prevent the woman from using the hospital until she is quite ill, remain with her constantly during her stay, or insist that she be released prematurely. In a recent case, a woman who was admitted with septicemia and a fever of 105 degrees turned out to have an abusive husband. Himself a physician, the assailant had intimidated medical staff into releasing her 2 days earlier, 24 hours after cancer surgery. The woman had complied with the medical decision because she feared the consequences if she displeased her spouse. The problem emerged in response to questioning by social work staff; the woman decided she could not successfully fight her illness and her husband as well, and filed for divorce.

## DYNAMICS

Many battered women stay in the relationship for a period of time after their partners become abusive. The reasons for this include economics, fear, the degree of control the batterer has over the woman's life, a desire to make the relationship work, pressure from family or peers, religious prescriptions against divorce, concern for the children, and naiveté about what will happen if the woman stays. Before the relationship is finally ended, however, women try a variety of means to stop, minimize, or escape from the violence and they change their strategies as their options change.

In general, battering relationships pass through phases marked by increasing fear, isolation, and control, often accompanied by increasingly complex psychological and psychosocial adaptations. During this period, the victim's response to her situation alternates between hope (that things will improve, he will change, the violence will end, she will escape) and mounting fear that she or the children will be hurt or killed if they leave or she will not be able to survive on her own. Many victims believe, falsely, that if they change their behavior, the violence will stop. Because she feels repeatedly frustrated by the contradictory nature of the batterer's demands, the unpredictability of his impulsive behavior, his refusal to accept responsibility for any part of the problem or to change, and the chronic fear of violence to herself and children, the woman may have little self-confidence as a mother, be suspicious and on guard, and have little sense of control over her environment.

THE HAZARDS OF LABELING

Failure to identify the importance of battering often results when the psychosocial consequences of coercion, such as alcohol or drug use, are mistaken for its cause. Research shows that battered women develop addictive and other psychosocial problems only after the onset of abuse, indicating the etiological importance of violence in women's lives. In addition, because battered women often present with long-standing tranquilizer or analgesic use, chronic symptomatology unresponsive to treatment, vague complaints, and frequent clinic visits, they may accumulate a range of pseudopsychiatric labels that identify them as difficult, demanding, or noncompliant patients who do not deserve serious attention. This pattern of labeling also highlights the importance of properly identifying domestic violence as the major issue.

Whatever the circumstances of the hospital admission, the inpatient stay is a window of opportunity to uncover a history of battering and design a plan for help.

## The Patient-Centered Interview

Regardless of why a woman has stayed in an abusive relationship or whether she has tried to leave, most battered women talk frankly about their predicament in the context of a supportive and confidential interview. Assessment begins with a patient-centered interview conducted in a place that affords privacy. It may be necessary to use security staff to ensure confidentiality for a patient if a batterer poses a threat of assault during the hospital stay or accompanies the patient and tries to stay with her to prevent disclosure.

To survive in battering relationships, victims often deny, minimize, or "forget" details of control or violence. We have found that repeat, shorter interviews, the use of other significant events in a woman's life as "markers" for violent episodes, and asking the woman to provide a written chronology of her experience help elicit complete information as well as trust.

## Assessment

Although family members are often enlisted in the discharge planning process to determine what resources are available at home or in the community, a major objective in assessment with battered women is to determine jointly immediate danger and future risks if the client is discharged home.

A full assessment of battering includes a careful history of adult trauma, an overview of the dynamics in the relationship (patterns of control, strategies for resistance), a review of health and mental health problems that may be associated with abuse, and consideration of risk to any children involved.

The possibility of life-threatening violence must always be considered, particularly if violence has resulted in hospitalization. The risk of life-threatening violence is significantly increased if the woman believes her life is in danger; if violence has resulted in previous hospital visits; if the batterer has used a gun or knife, stalked her, or threatened to kill her or himself; or if the couple is in the throes of divorce, separation, or conflict over children.

Assessment should differentiate long-standing personality disorders or psychiatric disease from adaptations to the situational stress of a battering relationship. The newly developed diagnosis of posttraumatic stress disorder (PTSD) is used to describe an adaptive pattern whose most prominent characteristics are paralyzing terror, agitation and anxiety bordering on panic, numbing alternating with flooding of emotion, hypersensitivity to any sudden noise or event even remotely connected with violence (such as a door slamming), and hypervigilence and nightmares in which past and future violence are constant themes (Herman, 1992). However, if a psychiatric diagnosis is required to elicit resources but no frank symptomatology of disease is present, the *DSM-IV* (V61.1) designation of "Physical abuse of adult" offers a nonstigmatizing alternative.

Suicidality is also a risk that must be weighed, particularly if there have been previous suicide attempts or the woman is severely depressed, is anxious about the fate of her children, is isolated from friends or family, or feels trapped or hopeless. The use of tranquilizers, antidepressants, antianxiety agents, and pain medication in some circumstances may genuinely facilitate a woman's ability to function effectively, but are too often prescribed indiscriminately, leading to misuse, addiction, or reinforcing the batterer's claim that the woman is crazy.

## ENTRAPMENT

A useful way to frame the client's safety concerns is to help her identify her degree of entrapment by specifying elements of control that might prevent her from defending herself, escaping, or using helping resources when she is threatened or hurt again. In the most difficult cases, the victim presents a hostagelike profile characterized by almost complete material and psychological dependence on the batterer: the Stockholm syndrome. Like full-blown PTSD, this pattern represents a normal adaptation to extraordinary stress, though it is more likely than PTSD to respond to short-term supportive counseling and reestablishing safety for the woman and her children.

Taking the patient's assessment as the basis for evaluating the situation helps her realize she is in no way responsible for the violence and that her emotional needs cannot be met by maintaining contact with someone who hurts her.

## CHILDREN'S SAFETY

Cross-assessment for woman battering and child abuse is an essential component of any domestic violence procedure. Children in homes in which there is battering are likely to suffer physical and psychological consequences both as witnesses and as covictims of the man's violence. These run the gamut from low self-esteem in girls and aggression and behavior problems in boys and girls to reduced social competence, helplessness, fragmentation, sleep disorders, depression and anxiety, failure to thrive, clinging, constant vigilance, and a range of somatic disorders in preschool children. In addition, the coercive control elements of battering may so disable the mother that neglect of basic child needs is a distinct risk. The risk to the child is best determined by considering the absolute level of violence and coercion in the relationship and not only by whether there has been prior child abuse. In these cases, the mother's trust can be gained and accurate information secured only if the mother is assured that revealing that there are dual victims will not jeopardize her parental rights. On the other hand, because domestic violence is increasingly being identified as a risk factor for child abuse by child protective service (CPS) systems, issues of mandated reporting should be sensitively discussed with the mother, particularly if a report is indicated or temporary placement seems advisable.

## Safety Planning

The objectives with battered women at discharge are to review the woman's priorities in relation to available options and resources, facilitate the implementation of a safety plan for the woman and her children, and plan for ongoing support.

The presumption underlying safety planning is that a woman's current vulnerability to battering can be reduced by reinforcing strategies she is already using to prevent, minimize, or avoid violence and by increasing her autonomy whether she decides to stay or to leave the relationship. Questioning proceeds from how she has managed so far to what has worked to what she sees as the next step. Confidentiality in all aspects of working with a battered woman is a precondition to implementing a safety plan. Although domestic violence is a crime, hospital authorities in most states are not mandated to report cases to legal authorities and should do so only at the patient's request. Independent safety planning for children in abusive homes is also suggested when possible.

If a life-threatening risk is suspected, *enhanced advocacy* should include informing the client about the therapist's perspective on her risk and exploring the client's options in great detail. Even in today's fiscal climate, an extended hospital stay may be justified by the absence of a safe option for discharge. Although leaving the area or going into hiding may be the most protective option available, there may be many reasons why a woman will not choose it.

Discharge staff are not expected to have in-depth legal knowledge regarding domestic violence. They should communicate the criminal nature of battering to the client, however, as well as the options state law affords in criminal and civil court to initiate formal separation or have the offender arrested, removed from the home, or ordered into counseling for his violence. A working relationship with local police and court agencies will facilitate appropriate handling of domestic cases within the legal system as well as linking the client with agencies that can provide legal advocacy.

Designed for short-term crisis intervention, the battered woman's shelter meets the need for safe, emergency housing and can usually offer counseling around violence, housing, nonviolent parent education, child care, and advocacy with the legal, social service, and welfare systems. To ensure that referrals are appropriate, the planner should explore other formal and informal options for emergency shelter, including friends and family, and acquaint the patient with the strengths—and limitations—of the local shelter.

When serious psychiatric conditions are present, an appropriate discharge plan includes psychiatric evaluation and referral. Because mental health professionals are often unfamiliar with the special issues posed by domestic violence, continued advocacy may be needed to ensure the client's safety in the mental health setting, particularly if family treatment modalities will be recommended.

## DOCUMENTATION

Careful documentation, using direct quotes from the client or photographs of injuries where appropriate, can sensitize subsequent health care providers to the importance of domestic violence in a patient's life and provide an ongoing record for the client of resources and survival strategies she has explored and used. Because the medical chart may also support the woman in criminal or civil proceedings, descriptions of domestic violence should clearly include evidence of injury, illness, and distress; identify the perpetrator (e.g., injured in assault by boyfriend); and summarize safety assessment. Euphemisms such as "stormy relationship" or "marital discord" should be avoided.

A secondary role of documentation is to provide data needed to demonstrate hospital resources necessary for comprehensive care of this client population and monitor improvements in clinical practice.

## EMPOWERMENT

The empowerment strategies appropriate for battered women differ markedly from the protective service orientation that characterizes intervention with vulnerable populations of children or the elderly. Interventions around woman battering should not be confused with strategies used to resolve family conflicts such as couple counseling or parenting education—interventions that may be appropriate only after safety and empowerment strategies have been fully used.

In addition to shelter and other emergency housing, legal services, and treatment for substance abuse, planning for safety with battered women often includes women's groups; ongoing physical therapy; changing jobs; continuing education; applying for Aid to Families With Dependent Children (AFDC) or emergency assistance; links to Alcoholics Anonymous, Narcotics Anonymous, or Alanon; counseling for children; work with child or adult protective services; and programs for the disabled.

The success of each stage of the process—identification, assessment, the formulation of a safety plan, and referral—depends on accountability achieved through monitoring and feedback, including follow-up to determine what has actually changed in relation to what a woman hopes to gain through each step in her plan. Even if things go badly after discharge, as they may, the sense of control a woman gains from having identified her problem and developed a plan to manage it is a significant step toward her recovery.

# 9

☐

# Physicians and Domestic Violence

*Challenges for Prevention*

In 1985, Surgeon General C. Everett Koop convened an unprecedented workshop on violence and public health. This conference, which focused on the use of traditional public health tools to understand violence in epidemiological terms, marked a turning point in the involvement of public health officials with domestic violence. Shelters for battered women had sprung up around the country during the 1970s, focusing the awareness of lawmakers, service providers, and researchers on the problems of women victimized by domestic violence. Not until this historic meeting, however, did an articulated strategy emerge to address violence as a public health problem. This strategy encompassed prevention and intervention tools, which then were disseminated to the public health community through regional conferences. A newly created National Center for Injury Prevention and Control within the Centers for Disease Control and Prevention (CDC) quickly expanded its emphasis

AUTHORS' NOTE: This chapter is adapted from Flitcraft (1993). Reprinted by permission of Project HOPE, The People-to-People Health Foundation, *Health Affairs,* 7500 Old Georgetown Road, Suite 600, Bethesda, MD 20814, (301) 656-7401.

on deliberate interpersonal injury to provide leadership and support for research on a wide range of issues, including domestic violence (U.S. Commission on Civil Rights, 1982).

Starting with support for model shelter programs and court-based services supported by the Law Enforcement Assistance Administration in the early 1970s, federal involvement in domestic violence has emphasized an improved criminal justice response as well as direct services to victims. Hearings on domestic violence by the U.S. Commission on Civil Rights in 1978 were followed by a short-lived Office of Domestic Violence under President Jimmy Carter, then by an Attorney General's Task Force, whose report focused attention on the need for a uniform policy of sanctions, including mandatory arrest. The Domestic Violence Assistance Act of 1984 affirmed the federal commitment to domestic violence services. Federal initiatives since have included the 1990 House Concurrent Resolution 172 (the so-called Morella resolution) urging courts to give presumptive child custody to victims of domestic violence, to establish national and regional centers on domestic violence, to incorporate domestic violence into the medical school curriculum, and to increase funding to the CDC's National Center for Injury Prevention and Control for research and demonstration projects on violence against women (U.S. Commission on Civil Rights, 1982). In 1994, after several years of negotiation, Congress approved the Violence Against Women Act (VAWA) as Title IV of the Violent Crime Control and Law Enforcement Act of 1994. VAWA provides $1.6 billion over 6 years to fund state grants to strengthen law enforcement, prosecution, and victim services; established education and prevention grants to reduce sexual assaults against women and a national domestic violence hotline; and included new penalties under federal law for sex crimes. Important too is the appointment of Bonnie Cambell, former attorney general of Iowa, as director of the Justice Department's Violence Against Women Office. In response to the VAWA, various interagency task forces have convened to develop research, planning, and program initiatives between the Departments of Justice and Health and Human Services and other branches of government. Although the VAWA strongly encourages local coordination in planning and service delivery between health, justice, and community-based services, no federal funds have been explicitly targeted for this purpose.

Passage of the VAWA was the culmination of a growing consensus between the largely community-based shelter movement and state and federal policymakers that (a) family violence is as serious a crime as other crimes against persons, (b) the safety of domestic violence victims and their children should be a top priority, and (c) meeting victims' needs requires significant changes to be made to a range of traditional services. Reflecting this consensus, virtually all states have greatly expanded civil and criminal remedies to victims and changed their policies on arrest and judicial sanctions to be more supportive of the victims of domestic assault. Recent state initiatives have extended training in domestic violence to include police, court personnel, prosecutors and judges, parole and probation officers, substance abuse counselors, and child protective services (CPS) workers. The interface of law enforcement and domestic violence services has expanded consistently over the past decade (Buzawa & Buzawa, 1990; Lerman, 1981).

In marked contrast, the response of the health care community to domestic violence has been slow and inconsistent. By the late 1970s, researchers funded by the National Institute of Mental Health had demonstrated the importance of domestic violence as a determinant of women's health problems and had documented widespread failure to identify the problem in health care settings. But efforts to expand hospital-based rape crisis teams to include domestic violence were sporadic and proved difficult to sustain. Koop's (1991) message helped guide the response of health professionals by targeting violence as a priority for the public health and medical care systems:

> Identifying violence as a public health issue is a relatively new idea. Traditionally, when confronted by the circumstances of violence, the health professions have deferred to the criminal justice system. . . . Today the professions of medicine, nursing, and the health related social services must come forward and recognize violence as their issue. (p. v)

Defining what it means for clinicians to "recognize violence as their issue" has proved to be difficult, particularly because it has implications that reach beyond the physician's office. Various rationales have evolved to explain physicians' consistent distance from domestic violence. One early theory suggested that identification in medical settings was difficult because battered women were reluctant to discuss the real cause of their injuries. Yet researchers have used simple interview techniques and questionnaires to uncover substantial rates of domestic violence in various medical settings, suggesting that identification is not so difficult after all. Next was concern that some patients would be offended by questions about violence at home; in deference, physicians were reluctant to discuss the issue. Again, high rates of patient participation in domestic violence research have belied this concern. More recent explanations explore physicians' projected helplessness and their belief that domestic violence is a Pandora's box without solution (Friedman, Samet, Roberts, Hudlin, & Hans, 1992; Kurz & Stark, 1988; Sugg & Inui, 1992; Warshaw, 1989). This rationale is inconsistent with physicians' usual determination when faced with near-certain failure in other areas. Obviously, other factors are at work.

However much it is idealized, only a small portion of what happens in the physician-patient encounter is determined by individual physicians. The encounter is shaped by its social and cultural context; the policies and resources of health care institutions; and the beliefs, values, and professional norms of the medical community. It is naive to expect substantial changes in how victims of domestic violence are treated by individual physicians unless there are concurrent changes in these latter areas.

This chapter suggests a framework for the change required at each of these levels—clinical practice, institutional resources, and professional norms—to link the prevention of domestic violence with appropriate care for its victims. Adapting this framework, we believe, provides a way for physicians to recognize domestic violence as the issue.

## Definition and Classification

Domestic violence is defined as the threat or infliction of physical harm among past or present social partners irrespective of the legal or domiciliary status of the relationship in which domestic violence occurs. Physical and sexual assault may be accompanied by verbal intimidation and abuse; destruction of property; isolation from friends, family, and other potential sources of support; threats to significant others, including children; stalking; and control over access to money, personal items, food, transportation, the telephone, and sources of care and protection. Battering is rarely an isolated event. One episode builds on past episodes and sets the stage for future episodes.

There is some debate about which groups to include in a clinical consideration of domestic violence. The term *spouse abuse* reflects an awareness that both men and women can be abused in intimate relationships, but research to date has focused on women who have been abused by male partners. We do not know to what extent current findings about battered women can be applied to the experience of men who may be abused, to violence within homosexual relationships, or to abuse among the disabled or elderly. Within these groups, however, it is likely that gender-specific patterns help shape the dynamics of an abusive relationship.

Our current awareness of the violence women face within domestic relationships can be traced to the movement of battered wives in Britain in the 1970s, closely followed by the battered women's movement in the United States. One of the first federal initiatives in this area was the U.S. Civil Rights Commission Hearings titled, "Battered Women: Issues for Public Policy." Ironically, with expanded funding in shelter services and the expansion of legal options to afford battered women greater safety in their communities, the term *domestic violence* was introduced to comply with civil rights prohibitions against gender discrimination. The emerging shelters for *battered women* and the state coalitions for battered women in the early 1980s became the domestic violence services we know today.

The reported clinical problems linked to domestic violence include homicide and repeated episodes of trauma, rape, substance abuse, attempted suicide, depression, child abuse, perinatal morbidity, chronic pain, and somatic complaints (Stark & Flitcraft, 1991). Psychologically, the combination of ongoing assault and coercive control may evoke symptoms of posttraumatic stress disorder, characterized by flashbacks, nightmares, hypervigilance, loss of boundaries, numbing, and chronic fear and anxiety (Herman, 1992; Koss & Heslet, 1992; Koss, Koss, & Woodnuff, 1991).

## PREVALENCE

Each year, more than 1.5 million women nationwide seek medical treatment for injuries related to abuse (American Medical Association Council on Scientific Affairs, 1992). The incidence of new cases among injury victims is relatively low, only about 27 of every 1,000 female victims (Stark, 1984). But because so many cases remain unresolved, the prevalence of domestic violence is quite high. For instance, domestic violence is a factor for at least 20% of the female patients who use emergency services for injury (McLeer & Anwar, 1989; Stark, 1984; Stark & Flitcraft, 1991; see Chapter 1, this volume). An even more significant proportion of other populations requiring medical care is abused women: rape victims, suicide attempts, alcoholics and drug users, mothers of abused children, psychiatric patients, pregnant women, and those seeking care for stress-related complaints (see Chapters 1, 3, 4, 7, and 8, this volume; Gelles, 1988; McKibben, Devos, & Newberger, 1989; Stark & Flitcraft, 1991).

 **Clinical Violence Intervention**

The traditional public health division of primary, secondary, and tertiary prevention offers a useful way to conceptualize the merger of a preventive health perspective and a clinical perspective on domestic violence. Effective clinical violence intervention requires medical involvement at all three levels.

## PRIMARY PREVENTION: PROFESSIONAL CHANGE

In traditional public health terms, primary prevention entails lowering the number of new cases by changing behavior or environmental factors. One way for physicians to address environmental factors is to recognize ways in which the medical profession may be helping perpetuate a harmful environment.

Following the U.S. surgeon general's workshop in 1985 and the revelation that battering was a problem for a significant number of pregnant women, the American College of Obstetricians and Gynecologists led the way in recognizing domestic violence as a threat to women's health and mounted a campaign to educate its members. In 1991, the American Medical Association (AMA) followed suit with a campaign to address family violence as a major health problem. The development of diagnostic and treatment guidelines on child abuse and neglect, child sexual abuse, domestic violence, and elder abuse and neglect formed the backdrop for the AMA's organizational efforts. The AMA also played a key role in the formation of the National Coalition of Physicians against Family Violence, with institutional membership from more than 75 major medical organizations. The American Medical Women's Association, the American Academy of Family Practice, and the American College of Emergency Physicians also have participated in the creation of a comprehensive medical response to family violence. The success of these and other professional organizations in bringing these issues to the attention of their membership is significant.

Further changes to the structure of medical practice are needed if the environment surrounding domestic violence is to be altered successfully. The status structure of medicine, its traditional male bias, and the strict hierarchical organization of medical training all have been identified as barriers to physicians' participation in domestic violence intervention efforts. To move medicine into the mainstream of political and community life, in which domestic violence is unacceptable, primary prevention efforts must address both the substance of physician norms and their organizational context. At present, such efforts are rare (Warshaw, 1989).

## SECONDARY PREVENTION:
## THE DOCTOR-PATIENT ENCOUNTER

Routine assessment for domestic violence is a form of health education. A physician's acknowledgment of the problem validates the fact that battering is a threat to health. Just as routine questions regarding a patient's smoking habits identify smoking-related problems and reinforce a patient's decision not to smoke, routine questions about violence identify the problems of abused women, assess the current safety of women who were battered in the past, and heighten the awareness of women who have not been in an abusive relationship.

Secondary prevention extends beyond identification to include appropriate early intervention. To date, specific elements of intervention generally include identification, validation, treatment of medical needs, assessment of mental health needs, clear documentation, safety assessment, and referral to law enforcement and/or community-based domestic violence services. Limited by the relative paucity of clinical experience with victims of domestic violence, current secondary prevention protocols need to be updated based on ongoing evaluation in clinical settings (AMA Council on Ethical and Judicial Affairs, 1992; Bowker & Maurer, 1987; Burge, 1989; McFarlane, Parker, Stoeken, & Bullock, 1992; Mehta & Dandrea, 1988).

At first glance, it seems intuitively obvious that physicians' intervention in domestic violence must be modeled after their involvement in other abuse situations or other criminal investigations such as homicide or rape. In fact, numerous issues in clinical practice overlap with law enforcement and criminal justice concerns. For instance, current approach to alcohol and drug use, human immunodeficiency virus (HIV) disease, tuberculosis and syphilis treatment, birth control, prenatal testing, and pregnancy termination, as well as the assessment and confinement of persons who are a danger to themselves or others, all provide experience relevant to the development of models for secondary intervention strategies in domestic violence. Meanwhile, because of its emphasis on patient empowerment, domestic violence intervention converges with many contemporary challenges in medical practice—including smoking cessation, cancer screening, HIV prevention, occupational and environmental health, and the care of terminally ill patients—where new models of physician-patient relationships are emphasized.

Developing appropriate intervention strategies will involve the skills of many medical disciplines, including nursing and social work, and will call on the expertise of a broad range of clinicians. Emphasis on evaluation and research in this area is vital.

## TERTIARY PREVENTION:
## HEALTH CARE ORGANIZATIONS

The role of health care organizations in a comprehensive response to domestic violence is the least developed. In 1992, the Joint Commission on the Accreditation of Healthcare Organizations (JCAHO) expanded its guidelines on emergency departments and hospital-sponsored ambulatory care centers to encourage the development of staff education and protocols on domestic violence. Such protocols outline the responsibilities of clinical staff to identify abuse with referral to police, domestic violence services, CPS, social services, and mental health treatment programs.

The JCAHO guidelines were part of a strategy to expand the identification of victims of domestic violence seen predominantly in emergency departments. To this extent, the current guidelines are based on an extremely limited notion of the essential components of medicine's response to domestic violence. Protocols based on the identification of victims of domestic violence and referral to community organizations use the medical encounter largely for case finding and evidence gathering for subsequent criminal proceedings. Current protocols generally do not commit additional health care resources to victims of domestic violence, nor do they contribute to shifting resources (in alcohol treatment, intensive care unit trauma admissions, or adverse birth outcomes) to include specific domestic violence interventions.

Blue Cross/Blue Shield of Pennsylvania estimates that at least $32 million a year is spent in Pennsylvania to treat domestic violence injuries.

Given the cost of health care related to violence and its associated problems, health care organizations must begin to shift resources directly into intervention services to augment the efforts of community-based services. Research suggests that prenatal care programs, alcohol and drug treatment programs, and mental health centers routinely treat victims of domestic violence; in fact, victims of violence may consume a disproportionate amount of resources devoted to these services (Berenson, Stiglich, Wilinson, & Anderson, 1991; Koss et al., 1991; McFarlane et al., 1992). Tertiary prevention of domestic violence will require health care organizations to incorporate and invest in crisis intervention, emergency hospitalization for shelter, counseling, support groups, and advocacy, rather than simple identification and referral. Such a comprehensive approach will require changes in medical practice that rival those seen in law and law enforcement practice.

## The Message to Physicians

Communitywide efforts to address domestic violence have grown over the past 20 years. Comprehensive community-based domestic violence services as well as expanded legal protection and enhanced law enforcement interventions thus far have provided the mainstay of interventions. Health care professionals, physicians in particular, have joined in efforts to address domestic violence only recently. To date, physicians have concentrated on changing professional awareness and implementing changes in clinical practice, based predominantly, although not exclusively, on case finding and documentation. In an era of rising costs and shrinking budgets, concerns about efficiency and cost-effectiveness sometimes have impeded changes in institutional policies and shifts in resource allocation to areas that meet the needs of persons victimized by domestic violence. Without such investment, the medical profession will have little to offer to victims or perpetrators of domestic violence. Ironically, if physicians' role is essentially that of case finder or mandated reporter, women will be reluctant to tell their physician about the real cause of their injuries and clinicians will engender the offense of patients while reaffirming their suspicion that domestic violence is indeed a Pandora's box. Clearly, another role for physicians is needed.

A comprehensive medical response to domestic violence requires primary, secondary, and tertiary prevention efforts and consequent changes in the actions and programs of professional societies, physicians, and health care organizations. Only such a concerted response can fulfill Koop's (1991) vision of a medical profession that is devoted to improving the lives of patients through its members' efforts to combat domestic violence.

# References

Abbott, J., Johnson, R., Koziol-McLain, J., & Lowenstein, S. R. (1995). Domestic violence against women: Incidence and prevalence in an emergency department population. *Journal of the American Medical Association, 273,* 1763-1767.

Ackerknecht, E. G. (1953). *Rudolf Virchow.* Madison: University of Wisconsin Press.

Alessi, J. J., & Hearn, K. (1978). Group treatment for children in shelters for battered women. In A. R. Roberts (Ed.), *Battered women and their families: Intervention strategies and treatment programs* (pp. 49-61). New York: Springer.

American Humane Society. (1978). *National analysis of official child neglect and abuse reporting.* Denver, CO: Author.

American Medical Association Council on Ethical and Judicial Affairs. (1992). Physicians and domestic violence: Ethical considerations. *Journal of the American Medical Association, 267,* 3190-3193.

American Medical Association Council on Scientific Affairs. (1992). Violence against women: Relevance for medical practitioners. *Journal of the American Medical Association, 267,* 3184-3189.

Appleton, W. (1980). The battered woman syndrome. *Annals of Emergency Medicine, 9*(2), 84-91.

Arcel, L. T., Mantonakis, J., Petersson, B., Jemos, J., & Kaliteraki, E. (1992). Suicide attempts among Greek and Danish women and the quality of their relationships with husbands and boyfriends. *Acta Psychiatrica Scandinavica, 85*(3), 189-195.

Aronowitz, S. (1973). *False promises.* New York: McGraw-Hill.

221

Baher, E. et al. (1976). *At risk: An account of the work of the battered child research department*. Boston: Routledge Kegan Paul.

Baker-Miller, J. (1976). *Toward a new psychology of women*. Boston: Beacon.

Bancroft, J., Skrimshire, A., Casson, J., Harvard-Watts, O., & Reynolds, F. (1977). People who deliberately poison or injure themselves: Their problems and contacts with helping agencies. *Psychological Medicine, 7*, 289-303.

Barnard, G. W., Vera, H., Vera, M. I., & Newman, G. (1982). 'Til death do us part: A study of spouse murder. *Bulletin of the American Academy of Psychiatry and Law, 10*(1), 271-280.

Bayatpour, M., Wells, R. D., & Holford, S. (1992). Physical and sexual abuse as predictors of substance use and suicide among pregnant teenagers. *Journal of Adolescent Health, 13*(2), 128-132.

Bell, C. A. (1991). Female homicides in United States workplaces, 1980-1985. *American Journal of Public Health, 81*(6), 729-732.

Benjamin, J. (1978). Authority and the family revisited: Or a world without father? *New German Critique, 13*, 35-57.

Berenson, A., Stiglich, N. J., Wilinson, G. S., & Anderson, G. D. (1991). Drug abuse and other risk factors for physical abuse among white, non-Hispanic, black, and Hispanic women. *American Journal of Obstetrics and Gynecology, 164*, 491-499.

Bergman, A., Larsen, R. M., & Mueller, B. (1986). Changing spectrum of serious child abuse. *Pediatrics, 77*(1), 113-116.

Bergman, B., & Brismar, B. (1991). Suicide attempts by battered wives. *Acta Psychiatrica Scandinavica, 83*, 380-384.

Berk, R. (1993). What the scientific evidence shows: On the average we can do no better than arrest. In R. Gelles & D. R. Loseke (Eds.), *Current controversies on family violence* (pp. 323-337). Newbury Park, CA: Sage.

Berliner, H. (1975). A larger perspective on the Flexner Report. *International Journal of Health Services, 5*(4), 573-592.

Bernardez, T. (1987, April). *Women and anger: Cultural prohibitions and the feminine ideal*. Paper presented at Learning From Women: Theory and Practice, Boston.

Bersherov, D. (1978, February 14). Testimony before the Committee on Science and Technology (DISPAC Subcommittee), U.S. House of Representatives.

Blau, J. R., & Blau, P. M. (1982). The cost of inequality: Metropolitan structure and violent crime. *American Sociological Review, 47*, 114-129.

Blum, B. W., Harmon, B., Harris, L., Bergeisen, L., & Resnick, M. D. (1992). American Indian—Alaska Native youth health. *Journal of the American Medical Association, 267*(12), 1637-1644.

Blum, J. (1978). On changes in psychiatric diagnosis over time. *American Psychologist, 33*(11), 1017-1103.

Bograd, M. (1986). A feminist examination of family systems models of violence against women in the family. In M. Ault-Richie (Ed.), *Women and family therapy* (pp. 84-107). Rockville, MD: Aspen.

Bowker, L. H., Arbitell, M., & McFerron, J. R. (1988). On the relationship between wife beating and child abuse. In K. Yllö & M. Bograd (Eds.), *Feminist perspectives on wife abuse* (pp. 158-176). Newbury Park, CA: Sage.

Bowker, L. H., & Maurer, L. (1987). The medical treatment of battered wives. *Women's Health, 12*, 25-45.

Breines, W., & Gordon, L. (1983). The new scholarship on family violence. *Signs: Journal of Women and Culture in Society, 8*(3), 490-531.

Brown, G. W., & Harris, T. (1978). *Social origins of depression—A study of psychiatric disorder in women.* London: Tavistock.

Brown, L. J., Powell, J., & Earls, F. (1984). Stressful life events and psychiatric symptoms in black females. *Journal of Adolescent Research, 4,* 140-151.

Browne, A. (1987). *Women who kill.* New York: Free Press.

Brownmiller, S. (1975). *Against our will.* New York: Simon & Schuster.

Bryer, J. B., Nelson, B. A., Miller, J. B., & Krol, P. A. (1987). Childhood sexual and physical abuse as a factor in adult psychiatric illness. *American Journal of Psychiatry, 144,* 1426-1430.

Burge, S. K. (1989). Violence against women as a health care issue. *Family Medicine, 21,* 368-373.

Bush, G. (1992). *State of the union address.* Washington, DC: Government Printing Office.

Buzawa, E., & Buzawa, C. G. (1990). *Domestic violence: The criminal justice response.* Newbury Park, CA: Sage.

Cambell, A., & Gibbs, J. (1986). *Violent transactions.* London: Basil Blackwell.

Campbell, J. C. (1989). A rest of two explanatory models of women's response to battering. *Nursing Research, 38,* 18-24.

Canetto, S. S., Feldman, L. B., & Lupei, R. L. (1989). Suicidal persons and their partners: Individual and interpersonal dynamics. *Suicide and Life-Threatening Behavior, 19*(3), 237-248.

Caplan, P., & Hall-McCorguodale, I. (1985). The scapegoating of mothers: A call for change. *American Journal of Orthopsychiatry, 55*(4), 344-353.

Carmen, E., Rieker, P., & Mills, T. (1984). Victims of violence and psychiatric illness. *American Journal of Psychiatry, 141,* 378-383.

Carter, J. (1995). Introduction. In S. Schechter & A. Ganley (Eds.), *Domestic violence: A national curriculum for family preservation practitioners* (pp. vii-xi). San Francisco: Family Violence Prevention Fund.

Caulfield, M. D. (1974). Imperialism, the family and cultures of resistance. *Socialist Revolution, 5,* 20.

Centers for Disease Control. (1983). *Homicide surveillance.* Atlanta, GA: U.S. Department of Health and Human Services.

Centers for Disease Control. (1988). Premature mortality due to homicide—United States, 1968-1985. *Morbidity and Mortality Weekly Review, 37,* 543-545.

Centerwall, B. S. (1984). Race, socioeconomic status and domestic homicide, Atlanta, 1971-72. *American Journal of Public Health, 74,* 813-815.

Chessler, P. (1971). Women as psychiatric and psychotherapeutic patients. *Journal of Marriage and the Family, 33*(4), 746-759.

Chester, R., & Streather, J. (1972). Cruelty in English divorce: Some empirical findings. *Journal of Marriage and the Family, 34*(4), 706-712.

Chodorow, N. J. (1985). Gender relation and difference in psychoanalytic perspective. In H. Eisenstein & A. Jardine (Eds.), *The future of difference* (pp. 3-20). New Brunswick, NJ: Rutgers University Press.

Cicourel, A. (1964). *Method and measurement in sociology.* New York: Free Press.

Cicourel, A. (1967). *The social organization of juvenile justice.* New York: John Wiley.

Cloward, R., & Ohlin, L. (1960). *Delinquency and opportunity.* Glencoe, IL: Free Press.

Cobbe, F. P. (1878). Wife torture in England. *Contemporary Review, 32,* 55-87.

Committee on Cultural Psychiatry. (1989). Suicide and ethnicity in the United States. In *Report of the Group for the Advancement of Psychiatry* (pp. 1-131; No. 128). Washington, DC: U.S. Public Health Service.

Committee on Trauma Research. (1985). *Injury in America: A continuing health problem.* Washington, DC: National Academy of Medicine.

Commonwealth Fund. (1993). *The Commonwealth Fund survey of women's health.* New York: Louis B. Harris Associates.

Connecticut Task Force on Abused Women. (1978). *Household violence study, north central and capital regions.* Hartford: Connecticut Coalition Against Domestic Violence.

Contoni, L. (1981). Clinical issues in domestic violence. *Social Casework, 62*(1), 3-12.

Cooper, D. (1971). *The death of the family.* London: Penguin.

Cott, N. (1977). *The bonds of womanhood: "Women's sphere" in New England 1780-1835.* New Haven, CT: Yale University Press.

Crawford, R. (1977). You are dangerous to your health: The ideology and politics of victim blaming. *International Journal of Health Services, 7*(4), 663-680.

Currens, J. (1991). Homicide followed by suicide—Kentucky, 1985-1990. *Mortality Morbidity Weekly Review, 40*(38), 652-653.

Curtis, L. (1975). *Violence, race and culture.* Lexington, MA: Lexington Books.

Davis, A. F. (1967). *Spearheads for reform: The social settlement and the progressive movement, 1890-1914.* New York: Oxford University Press.

Dawson, J. M., & Langany, P. A. (1994). *Murder in families.* Washington, DC: U.S. Department of Justice.

DiLalla, L. F., & Gottesman, I. (1991). Biological and genetic contributors to violence: Widom's untold tale. *Psychological Bulletin, 109,* 125-129.

Dinnerstein, D. (1977). *The mermaid and the minotaur.* New York: Harper & Row.

Dobash, R. E., & Dobash, R. (1977, August). *Violence between men and women within the family setting.* Paper presented at the VIII World Congress of Sociology, Toronto, Canada.

Dobash, R. E., & Dobash, R. (1977-1978). Wives: The appropriate victims of marital violence. *Victimology: An International Journal, 2*(3-4), 426-442.

Dobash, R. E., & Dobash, R. (1979). *Violence against wives.* New York: Free Press.

Dobash, R. E., & Dobash, R. P. (1992). *Women, violence and social change.* London: Routledge Kegan Paul.

Donzelot, J. (1977). *La police des families.* Paris: Editions de Minuit.

Dubos, R. (1968). *Man, medicine and environment.* New York: Praeger.

Durkheim, E. (1951). *Suicide: A study in sociology.* Glencoe, IL: Free Press.

Dutton, D. G., & Painter, S. (1993). Emotional attachments in abusive relationships: A test of traumatic bonding theory. *Violence and Victims, 105*(8), 139-155.

Dutton, M. A. (1992). Understanding women's response to domestic violence: A redefinition of battered woman's syndrome. *Hofstra Law Review, 21,* 1191.

Earls, F., Escobar, J. I., & Spero, M. M. (1991). Suicide in minority groups: Epidemiologic and cultural perspectives. In S. J. Blumenthal & D. J. Kupfer (Eds.), *Suicide over the life cycle: Risk factors, assessment and treatment of suicidal patients* (pp. 571-598). Washington, DC: American Psychiatric Press.

Ehrenreich, B., & English, D. (1979). *For her own good: 150 years of expert advice*. New York: Anchor.

Esterson, A., & Laing, R. D. (1970). *Sanity, madness and the family*. Middlesex, UK: Penguin.

Ewen, S. (1976). *Captains of consciousness*. New York: Vintage.

Family Violence Reporting Program. (1993). *Family violence arrests—Annual report, 1993*. Meriden: Connecticut Department of Public Safety.

Fanon, F. (1978). *The wretched of the earth*. New York: Grove.

Farrager, J., & Stansell, C. C. (1975). Women and their families on the overland trail, 1842-1867. *Feminist Studies, 2,* 150-166.

Figley, C. (1992). Post-traumatic stress disorder: Relationship with various traumatic events. *Violence Update, 2*(9), 1, 8-12.

Finkelhor, D., & Browne, A. (1985). The traumatic impact of child sexual abuse: A conceptualization. *American Journal of Orthopsychiatry, 55,* 530-541.

Finkelhor, D., & Yllö, K. (1985). *License to rape*. New York: Holt, Rinehart & Winston.

Finn, J. (1985). The stresses and coping behavior of battered women. *Social Casework, 66,* 341-349.

Flax, J. (1985). Mother-daughter relationships: Psychodynamics, politics and philosophy. In H. Eisenstein & A. Jardine (Eds.), *The future of difference* (pp. 20-41). New Brunswick, NJ: Rutgers University Press.

Flitcraft, A. H. (1977). *Battered women: An emergency room epidemiology with a description of a clinical syndrome and critique of present therapeutics*. Unpublished doctoral dissertation, Yale University School of Medicine.

Flitcraft, A. (1993). Physicians and domestic violence: Challenges for prevention. *Health Affairs, 12*(4), 154-161.

Flitcraft, A. (1995). Clinical violence intervention: Lessons from battered women. *Journal of Health Care for the Poor and Underserved, 6*(2), 187-197.

Flynn, J. (1977). Recent findings related to wife abuse. *Social Casework, 58,* 13-20.

Foucault, M. (1973). *The birth of the clinic: A technology of medical perception* (A. M. Sheridan Smith, Trans.). New York: Pantheon.

Freidan, B. (1963). *The feminine mystique*. New York: Dell.

Freud, S. (1963). Mourning and melancholia. In S. Freud, *General psychological theory: Papers on metapsychology* (pp. 164-180). New York: Collier.

Friedman, L. (1983). Biological explanations. In L. Friedman (Ed.), *Crimes of violence* (Vol. 13, pp. 7-20). New York: Chelsea.

Friedman, L. C., Samet, J. D., Roberts, M. S., Hudlin, M., & Hans, P. (1992). Inquiry about victimization. *Archives of Internal Medicine, 152,* 1186-1190.

Garbarino, J., & Sherman, D. (1980). High risk neighborhoods and high risk families: The human ecology of child maltreatment. *Child Development, 51*(1), 188-198.

Garrison, C. Z., McKeown, R. E., Valois, R. F., & Vincent, M. L. (1993). Aggression, substance use and suicidal behaviors in high school students. *American Journal of Public Health, 83*(2), 179-184.

Gayford, J. J. (1975a). Battered wives. *Medicine, Science and the Law, 15*(4), 237.

Gayford, J. J. (1975b). Wife battering: A preliminary survey of 100 cases. *British Medical Journal, 25*(1), 194-197.

Gayford, J. J. (1976). Ten types of battered wives. *Welfare Officer, 1,* 5-9.

Gelles, R. J. (1974). *The violent home*. Beverly Hills, CA: Sage.

Gelles, R. J. (1975). Violence and pregnancy: A note on the extent of the problem and needed services. *The Family Co-ordinator, 24*(1), 81-86.

Gelles, R. J. (1988). Violence and pregnancy: Are pregnant women at greater risk of abuse? *Journal of Marriage and the Family, 50*(3), 841-847.

Gelles, R., & Straus, M. (1988). *Intimate violence: The causes and consequences of abuse in the American family.* New York: Simon & Schuster.

Gibbs, J. J. (1986). Alcohol consumption, cognition and context: Examining tavern violence. In A. Cambell & J. Gibbs (Eds.), *Violent transactions* (pp. 133-152). London: Basil Blackwell.

Gibbs, J. T. (1988). The new morbidity: Homicide, suicide, accidents, and life-threatening behaviors. In J. T. Gibbs (Ed.), *Young, black and male in America: An endangered species* (pp. 258-288). Dover, MA: Auburn.

Gil, D. (1973). *Violence against children: Physical abuse in the United States.* Cambridge, MA: Harvard University Press.

Gilligan, C. (1985). In a different voice: Women's conceptions of self and morality. In H. Eisenstein & A. Jardine (Eds.), *The future of difference* (pp. 274-317). New Brunswick, NJ: Rutgers University Press.

Gilman, C. P. (1935). *The living of Charlotte Perkins Gilman: An autobiography.* New York: D. Appleton-Century.

Gin, N., Rucker, L., Frayne, S., Cygan, R., & Hubbell, A. (1991). Prevalence of domestic violence among patients in three ambulatory care internal medicine clinics. *Journal of General Internal Medicine, 6,* 317-322.

Glick, P. (1975). Some recent changes in American families. *Current population reports* (Series P-23, No. 52). Washington, DC: U.S. Bureau of the Census.

Gondolf, E. W. (1990). *Psychiatric response to family violence: Identifying and confronting neglected danger.* Lexington, MA: Lexington Books.

Goode, W. (1971). Force and violence in the family. *Journal of Marriage and the Family, 33*(4), 624-636.

Goodman, L. A., Koss, M. P., & Russo, N. F. (1993). Violence against women: Mental health effects: 2. Conceptualizations of posttraumatic stress. *Applied and Preventive Psychology, 2,* 123-130.

Gordon, L. (1988). *Heroes of their own lives: The politics and history of family violence.* New York: Viking.

Gordon, M., & Riger, S. (1991). *The female fear.* Chicago: University of Illinois Press.

Gove, W. (1972). Sex, marital status and suicide. *Journal of Health and Social Behavior, 13,* 204-213.

Gove, W., & Grimm, H. W. (1973). The family life cycle: Internal dynamics and social consequences. *Sociology and Social Research, 57,* 182-195.

Graff, T. T. (1980). Personality characteristics of battered women. *Dissertation Abstracts International, 40*(7-B), 3395.

Haddon, W. J. (1980). Advances in the epidemiology of injury as a basis for public policy. *Public Health Report, 95,* 411-421.

Hall, S., Critcher, C., Jefferson, T., Clarke, J., & Roberts, B. (1979). *Policing the crisis: Mugging, the state, and law and order.* London: Macmillan.

Hamberger, L. K., Saunders, D., & Harvey, M. (1986). Prevalence of domestic violence in community practice and rate of physician inquiry. *Family Medicine, 24,* 283-287.

Hamdi, E., Amin, Y., & Mattar, T. (1991). Clinical correlates of intent in attempted suicide. *Acta Psychiatrica Scandinavica, 83*(5), 406-411.

Hampton, R. L. (1987). Family violence and homicide in the black community—Are they linked? In R. L. Hampton (Ed.), *Violence in the black family* (pp. 133-156). Lexington, MA: Lexington Books.

Hanks, S. E., & Rosenbaum, P. (1977). Battered women: A study of women who live with violent alcohol-abusing men. *American Journal of Orthopsychiatry, 47*(2), 291-306.

Hare-Mustin, R. T., & Marecek, J. (1986). Autonomy and gender: Some questions for therapists. *Psychotherapy, 25*(2), 205-212.

Hartmann, H. (1976). Capitalism, patriarchy, and job segregation by sex. *Signs: Journal of Women in Culture and Society, 1*(3), 137-169.

Hawkins, D. (1986). Longitudinal-situational approaches to understanding black on black homicide. *Report of the Secretary's Task Force on Black and Minority Health* (Vol. 5). Washington, DC: U.S. Department of Health and Human Services.

Hawkins, D. (1987). Devalued lives and racial stereotypes: Ideological barriers to the prevention of family violence among blacks. In R. L. Hampton (Ed.), *Violence in the black family* (pp. 189-207). Lexington, MA: Lexington Books.

Health Policy Advisory Center. (1970). *The American health empire.* New York: Random House.

Helfer, R. E. (1976). Basic issues concerning prediction. In R. E. Helfer & C. H. Kempe (Eds.), *Child abuse and neglect: The family and the community* (pp. 362-373). Cambridge, MA: Ballinger.

Helton, A. S., & Snodgrass, F. G. (1987). Battering during pregnancy: Intervention strategies. *Birth, 14,* 142-147.

Hendrix, M. H., LaGodna, G., & Bohen, C. A. (1978). The battered wife. *American Journal of Nursing, 78*(4), 650-653.

Henriques, J., Holloway, W., Urwin, C., Venn, C., & Walkerdine, V. (1984). *Changing the subject: Psychology, social regulation and subjectivity.* London: Methuen.

Henry, A. F., & Short, J. F., Jr. (1964). *Suicide and homicide.* New York: Free Press.

Herman, J. L. (1986). Histories of violence in an outpatient population: An exploratory study. *American Journal of Orthopsychiatry, 56*(1), 137-141.

Herman, J. L. (1987, April). *Sexual violence.* Paper presented at Learning From Women: Theory and Practice, Boston.

Herman, J. L. (1992). *Trauma and recovery.* New York: Basic Books.

Hilberman, E. (1980). Overview: The "wife-beater's wife" reconsidered. *American Journal of Psychiatry, 137,* 1336-1347.

Hilberman, E., & Munson, K. (1977-1978). Sixty battered women. *Victimology: An International Journal, 2*(3-4), 460-470.

Horkheimer, M. (1972). *Authority and the family in critical theory* (M. J. O'Connell, Trans.). New York: Herder & Herder.

Hornung, C. A., McCullough, B. C., & Sugimoto, T. (1981). Status relationships in marriage: Risk factors in spouse abuse. *Journal of Marriage and the Family, 43,* 675-692.

Howell, M. C. (1978). Pediatricians and mothers. In J. Ehrenreich (Ed.), *The cultural crisis of modern medicine* (pp. 201-211). New York: Monthly Review Press.

Imber-Black, E. (1986). Women, families and larger systems. In M. Ault-Richie (Ed.), *Women and family therapy* (pp. 25-33). Rockville, MD: Aspen.

Irigaray, L. (1977). *Ce sexe wui n'en est pas un*. Paris: Minuit.

Jacobson, A., & Richardson, B. (1987). Assault experiences of 100 psychiatric inpatients: Evidence of the need for routine inquiry. *American Journal of Psychiatry, 144,* 908-913.

Jacoby, R. (1975). *Social amnesia*. Boston: Beacon.

Jaffe, P. G., Wolfe, D. A., & Wilson, S. K. (1990). *Children of battered women*. Newbury Park, CA: Sage.

Janeway, E. (1971). *Man's world, women's place: A study in social mythology*. New York: Dell.

Jankowski, M. S. (1991). *Island in the street*. Berkeley: University of California Press.

Jarrar, L. (1985). The impact of battering and sheltering on select psychological states of battered women. *Dissertation Abstracts International, 47,* 376B.

Jason, J., Strauss, L. T., & Tyler, C. W., Jr. (1983). A comparison of primary and secondary homicides in the U.S. *American Journal of Epidemiology, 117*(3), 309-319.

Johnson, K. (1979). Durkheim revisited: Why do women kill themselves? *Suicide and Life-Threatening Behavior, 9*(3), 145-153.

Jones, A. (1994). *Next time she'll be dead*. Boston: Beacon.

Jones, A., & Schechter, S. (1992). *When love goes wrong*. New York: HarperCollins.

Jones, E. D. (1981). The District of Columbia's Firearms Control Regulation Act of 1975: The toughest handgun control act in the U.S.—Or is it? *Annuals of the American Academy of Political Science, 455,* 138-149.

Kate, K. (1994). *The beast in the boudoir: Petkeeping in nineteenth century Paris*. Berkeley: University of California Press.

Kaufman, J., & Zigler, E. (1987). Do abused children become abusive parents? *American Journal of Orthopsychiatry, 57*(2), 186-193.

Kellerman, A. (1992). Gun ownership as a risk factor for homicide in the home. *New England Journal of Medicine, 329,* 1084-1091.

Kellerman, A., & Mercy, J. (1992). Men, women and murder: Gender-specific differences in rates of fatal violence and victimization. *Journal of Trauma, 33*(1), 1-5.

Kelly, G. (1926). *Craig's wife*. New York: Samuel French.

Kelly, L. (1988). *Surviving sexual violence*. Cambridge, UK: Polity Press.

Kelman, S. (1975). The social nature of the definition problem in health. *International Journal of Health Services, 5*(4), 625-642.

Kempe, C. H., Silverman, F. N., Steele, B. F., Droegemueller, W., & Silver, H. K. (1962). The battered child syndrome. *Journal of the American Medical Association, 181,* 17-24.

Kempe, R., & Kempe, C. H. (1976). Assessing family pathology. In R. E. Helfer & C. H. Kempe (Eds.), *Child abuse and neglect: The family and the community* (pp. 115-127). Cambridge, MA: Ballinger.

Klaus, P. A., & Rand, M. R. (1984). *Family violence*. Washington, DC: Bureau of Justice Statistics.

Klein, A. R. (1993). *Spousal/partner assault: A protocol for the sentencing and supervision of offenders*. Swampscott, MA: Production Specialties.

Klugman, D., Litman, R. E., & Wold, C. I. (1984). Suicide: Answering the cry for help. In F. J. Turner (Ed.), *Differential diagnosis and treatment in social work* (3rd ed., pp. 840-851). New York: Free Press.

Koop, C. E. (1991). Foreword. In M. L. Rosenberg & M. A. Fenley (Eds.), *Violence in America: A public health approach* (pp. v-vi). New York: Oxford University Press.

Koss, M. P., & Heslet, L. (1992). Somatic consequences of violence against women. *Archives of Family Medicine, 1,* 53-59.

Koss, M. P., Koss, P. K., & Woodnuff, W. J. (1991). Deleterious effects of criminal victimization on women's health and medical utilization. *Archives of Internal Medicine, 151,* 342-347.

Kott-Washburne, C. (1984). A feminist analysis of child abuse and neglect. In D. Finkelhor, R. Gelles, H. Hotaling, & M. Straus (Eds.), *The dark side of families* (pp. 289-293). Beverly Hills, CA: Sage.

Krishnan, P., & Kavani, A. (1974). Estimates of age specific divorce rates for females in the U.S., 1960-1969. *Journal of Marriage and the Family, 36*(2), 72-76.

Kurz, D., & Stark, E. (1988). Not so benign neglect: The medical response to battering. In K. Yllö & M. Bograd (Eds.), *Feminist perspectives on wife abuse* (pp. 249-266). Newbury Park, CA: Sage.

Lachman, J. A. (1978). *A theory of interpersonal conflict with application to industrial disputes.* Unpublished discussion paper, Institute of Public Policy Studies, Ann Arbor, MI.

Laing, R. D. (1959). *The divided self.* London: Tavistock.

Laing, R. D., & Esterson, A. (1980). *Sanity, madness and the family* (Vol. 1). New York: Penguin.

Lardner, G. (1993, June 3). *Keynote address.* Preventing Violence to Women: Integrating the Health and Legal Communities, Association of Trial Lawyers of America, Washington, DC.

Lasch, C. (1977). *Haven in a heartless world.* New York: Basic Books.

Leary, D. K. (1988). Physical aggression between spouses: A social learning theory perspective. In R. L. Van Hasselt, A. S. Morrison, M. Bellack, & V. N. Hersen (Eds.), *Handbook of family violence* (pp. 31-57). New York: Plenum.

Lerman, L. (1981). *Prosecution of spouse abuse: Innovations in criminal justice response.* Washington, DC: Center for Women's Policy Studies.

Lerner, H. (1984). Female dependency in context: Some theoretical and technical considerations. In P. Reiker & E. Carmen (Eds.), *The gender gap in psychotherapy: Social realities and psychological processes* (pp. 125-139). New York: Plenum.

Letchner, A. (1993). *Invisible violence: Adolescent African American girls and street violence.* Unpublished paper, University of Pennsylvania School of Medicine.

Levine, M. (1975). Interparental violence and its effect on the children: A study of 50 families in general practice. *Medicine, Science and the Law, 15*(3), 172.

Levinger, G. (1965). Sources of marital dissatisfaction among applicants for divorce. *American Journal of Orthopsychiatry, 36*(5), 803-807.

Lewin, T. (1994, October 21). What penalty for killing in passion? *New York Times,* p. A18.

Lewis, O. (1965). *La vida.* New York: Vintage.

Loseke, D. R. (1992). *The battered woman and shelters.* Albany: State University of New York Press.

Loftin, C., & McDowell, D. (1981). One with a gun gets you two: Mandatory sentencing and firearms violence in Detroit. *Annals of the American Academy of Political Science, 455,* 50-67.

Luckenbill, D. F. (1977). Criminal homicide as a situational transaction. *Social Problems, 25,* 176-186.

Lundsgaarde, H. P. (1977). *Murder in space city: A cultural analysis of Houston homicide patterns.* New York: Oxford University Press.

Lynd, R., & Lynd, H. (1929). *Middletown: A study in contemporary American culture.* New York: Harcourt Brace.

Lystad, M. (1975). Violence at home: A review of the literature. *American Journal of Orthopsychiatry, 45*(3), 328-345.

Mann, C. R. (1987). Black women who kill. In R. L. Hampton (Ed.), *Violence in the black family* (pp. 157-186). Lexington, MA: Lexington Books.

Marcus, S. (1992). Fighting bodies, fighting words: A theory and politics of rape prevention. In J. Butler & J. W. Scott (Eds.), *Feminists theorize the political* (pp. 385-403). New York: Routledge Kegan Paul.

Marcuse, H. (1958). *Eros and civilization.* New York: Vintage.

Maris, R. W. (1971). Deviance as therapy: The paradox of the self-destructive female. *Journal of Health and Social Behavior, 12,* 113-123.

Marsden, D. (1978). Sociological perspectives on family violence. In J. M. Martin (Ed.), *Violence and the family* (pp. 103-135). London: Wiley.

Martin, D. (1977). *Battered wives.* New York: Pocket Books.

Martin, J. (1983). Maternal and paternal abuse of children: Theoretical and research perspectives. In D. Finkelhor, R. Gelles, G. Hotaling, & M. Straus (Eds.), *The dark side of families* (pp. 293-305). Beverly Hills, CA: Sage.

Martin, W. T. (1968). Theories of variation in the suicide rate. In J. Gibbs (Ed.), *Suicide* (pp. 74-95). New York: Harper & Row.

Marx, K. (1967). *Capital: A critique of political economy.* New York: International Publishers.

McClain, P. D. (1982). Cause of death-homicide: A research note on black females as homicide victims. *Victimology: An International Journal, 7,* 204-212.

McFarlane, J., Parker, B., Stoeken, K., & Bullock, L. (1992). Assessing for abuse during pregnancy: Severity and frequency of injuries and associated entry into prenatal care. *Journal of the American Medical Association, 267,* 3176-3178.

McKeown, T. (1977). *The modern rise in population.* New York: Academic Press.

McKibben, L., Devos, E., & Newberger, E. (1989). Victimization of mothers of abused children: A controlled study. *Pediatrics, 84,* 531-535.

McLeer, S. V., & Anwar, R. (1989). A study of women presenting in an emergency department. *American Journal of Public Health, 79,* 65-67.

Mead, M. (1953). Social change and cultural surrogates. In C. Kluckhohn & H. Murray (Eds.), *Personality in nature, society and culture* (pp. 651-662). New York: Knopf.

Mednick, S. A., Pollack, V., Volavka, J., & Gabrielli, J. (1982). Biology and violence. In M. E. Wolfgang & N. A. Weiner (Eds.), *Criminal violence* (pp. 21-80). Beverly Hills, CA: Sage.

Megargee, E. L. (1982). Psychological determinants and correlates of criminal violence. In M. E. Wolfgang & N. A. Weiner (Eds.), *Criminal violence* (pp. 81-170). Beverly Hills, CA: Sage.

Mehta, P., & Dandrea, A. (1988). The battered woman. *American Family Physician, 37*(1), 193-199.

Mercy, J., & Saltzman, L. (1989). Fatal violence among spouses in the U.S., 1976-1985. *American Journal of Public Health, 79*(5), 595-599.

Messner, S. F. (1982). Poverty, inequality and the urban homicide rate. *Criminology, 20,* 103-142.

Mills, C. W. (1959). *The sociological imagination.* New York: Oxford University Press.

Mollica, R., & Redlich, F. (1978). *Equity and changing patient characteristics in south central Connecticut, 1950-1975.* Unpublished paper, Yale University, Department of Psychiatry.

Mooney, J. (1993). *Domestic violence in north London.* Middlesex: Middlesex University, Centre for Criminology.

More, J., & Day, B. (1979). Family interaction associated with abuse of children over five years of age. *Child Abuse & Neglect, 3,* 857-861.

Morgenthau, R. M. (1995, July 25). Letter to the editor. *New York Times,* A14.

Morris, T., & Blum-Cooper, L. (1967). Homicide in England. In M. E. Wolfgang (Ed.), *Studies in homicide* (pp. 29-36). New York: Harper & Row.

Moynihan, D. P. (1973). *The politics of a guaranteed income.* New York: Vintage.

Mullen, P. E., Romans-Clarkson, S. E., Walton, V. A., & Herbison, G. P. (1988). Impact of sexual and physical abuse on women's mental health. *Lancet, 1,* 841-845.

Muller, V. (1977). The formation of the state and the oppression of women. *Review of Radical Political Economics, 9*(3), 7-22.

Muscat, J. E. (1988). Characteristics of childhood homicide in Ohio, 1974-1984. *American Journal of Public Health, 78,* 822-844.

Neighbors, H. W. (1984). The distribution of psychiatric morbidity in black Americans: Review and suggestions for research. *Community Mental Health Journal, 20,* 169-181.

Nelson, B. J. (1984). *Making an issue of child abuse.* Chicago: University of Chicago Press.

Newberger, C. M., & Cook, S. (1983). Parental awareness and child abuse: A cognitive-developmental analysis of urban and rural samples. *American Journal of Orthopsychiatry, 53*(2), 512-524.

Newberger, E., & Bourne, R. E. (1978). The medicalization and legalization of child abuse. *American Journal of Orthopsychiatry, 48*(4), 593-606.

New Jersey Network (Producer). (1985). *Battered wives, shattered lives* [Video]. Trenton, NJ: Public Broadcasting Service.

Nichols, N. (1976). The abused wife problem. *Social Casework, 57*(1), 27-32.

Nisonoff, L., & Bitman, I. (1979). Spouse abuse, incidence and relationship to selected demographic variables. *Victimology: An International Journal, 4,* 131-140.

O'Brien, J. (1971). Violence in divorce prone families. *Journal of Marriage and the Family,* 692-698.

O'Carroll, P. (1991). Suicide. In J. M. Last (Ed.), *Maxcy-Rosenau: Public health and preventive medicine* (13th ed., pp. 1054-1062). New York: Appleton-Century-Crofts.

Okun, L. (1986). *Woman abuse: Facts replacing myths.* Albany: State University of New York Press.

Owens, D. J., & Straus, M. A. (1975). The social structure of violence in childhood and approval of violence as an adult. *Aggressive Behavior, 1*(3), 193-211.

Palley, H. A., & Robinson, D. A. (1988). Black on black crime. *Society, 25*(5), 59-62.

Parliament. (1974-1975). Report from the Select Committee on Violence in Marriage. In *Proceedings of the Committee: Report, Minutes of Evidence and Appendices* (Vol. 2, H.C. 553-II). London: HMSO.

Parnas, R. (1967). The police response to the domestic disturbance. *Wisconsin Law Review, 2,* 914-960.

Pfouts, J. J. (1978). Violent families: Coping responses of abused wives. *Child Welfare, 57*(2), 101-111.

Pillay, A. L., & Vawda, N. B. M. (1989). Alcohol-related parasuicide among married people. *South African Medical Journal, 75,* 120-121.

Pizzey, E. (1974). *Scream quietly or the neighbors will hear.* London: Penguin.

Pizzey, E., & Shapiro, J. (1981). Choosing a violent relationship. *New Society, 56*(962), 23.

Platt, A. (1969). *The childsavers: The invention of delinquency.* Chicago: University of Chicago Press.

Pleck, E. (1977). *Wife-beating in nineteenth century America.* Unpublished paper, University of Michigan.

Pleck, E. (1987). *Domestic tyranny: The making of American social policy against family violence from colonial times to the present.* New York: Oxford University Press.

Post, R. D., Willet, A. B., Frank, R. D., House, R. M., Back, S. M., & Weisberg, M. P. (1980). A preliminary report on the prevalence of domestic violence among psychiatric inpatients. *American Journal of Psychiatry, 137,* 974-975.

Poussaint, A. F. (1972). *Why blacks kill blacks.* New York: Emerson Hall.

Rapp, C., & Wintersteen, R. (1989). The strengths model of case management: Results from twelve demonstrations. *Psychosocial Rehabilitation Journal, 13*(1), 23-32.

Rath, G. D., Jarratt, L. G., & Leonardson, G. (1989). Rates of domestic violence against adult women by male partners. *Journal of the American Board of Family Practice, 2,* 227-233.

Reiker, P. P., & Carmen, E. H. (Eds.). (1984). *The gender gap in psychotherapy.* New York: Plenum.

Reisman, D. (1953). *The lonely crowd.* New York: Doubleday.

Renvoize, J. (1978). *Web of violence.* London: Routledge Kegan Paul.

Rhodes, R. M., & Zelman, A. B. (1986). An ongoing multifamily group in a woman's shelter. *American Journal of Orthopsychiatry, 56*(1), 120-131.

Richardson, D. C., & Campbell, J. C. (1980). Alcohol and wife abuse: The effect of alcohol on attributions of blame for wife abuse. *Personality and Social Psychology Bulletin, 6,* 51-56.

Rico-Velasco, J., & Mynko, L. (1973). Suicide and marital status: A changing relationship? *Journal of Marriage and the Family, 35*(2), 239-244.

Roberts, A. R. (1976). Police social workers: A history. *Social Work, 21*(4), 294-299.

Robertson, B. A., & Juritz, J. M. (1979). Characteristics of the families of abused children. *Child Abuse & Neglect, 3,* 861.

Roper, M., Flitcraft, A., & Frazier, W. (1979). *Rape and battering: An assessment of 100 cases.* Unpublished paper, Department of Surgery, Yale Medical School.

Rose, S. M., Pebody, C. G., & Stratigeas, B. (1991). Responding to hidden abuse: A role for social work in reforming mental health systems. *Social Work, 36*(6), 408-413.

Rosen, B. (1978). Self-concept disturbances among mothers who abuse their children. *Psychological Reports, 43,* 323-326.

Rosenbaum, A., & O'Leary, D. (1981). Children: The unintended victims of marital violence. *American Journal of Orthopsychiatry, 51*(4), 692-699.

Rosenberg, M., & Mercy, J. (1991). Assaultive violence. In M. Rosenberg & M. A. Fenley (Eds.), *Violence in America: A public health approach* (pp. 14-50). New York: Oxford University Press.

Rosenberg, M., Stark, E., & Zahn, M. (1986). Interpersonal violence: Homicide and spouse abuse. In J. M. Last (Ed.), *Maxcy-Rosenau: Public health and preventive medicine* (12th ed., pp. 1399-1426). New York: Appleton-Century-Crofts.

Ross, E. (1993). *Love & toil: Motherhood in outcast London 1870-1918.* New York: Oxford University Press.

Rounsaville, B. J. (1977). *Very common but difficult to reach.* Unpublished paper, Connecticut Mental Health Center.

Rounsaville, B. J., & Weissman, M. (1977-1978). Battered women: A medical problem requiring detection. *International Journal of Psychiatry in Medicine, 8*(2), 191-202.

Rubin, G. (1975). The traffic in women. In R. Reiter (Ed.), *Toward an anthropology of women* (pp. 157-211). New York: Monthly Review Press.

Safilios-Rothschild, C. (1970). The study of family power structure: A review, 1960-1969. *Journal of Marriage and the Family, 33,* 539-552.

Schechter, S. (1978, October). *Psychic battering: The institutional response to battered women.* Paper presented at Midwest Conference on Abuse of Women, St. Louis.

Schechter, S. (1982). *Women and male violence.* Boston: South End.

Schmid, C., & Van Arsdol, M., Jr. (1955). Completed and attempted suicide: A comparative analysis. *American Sociological Review, 20,* 273-283.

Schmidt, J. D., & Sherman, L. (1993). Does arrest deter domestic violence? *American Behavioral Scientist, 36*(5), 601-610.

Schulman, M. A. (1979). *Survey of spousal violence against women in Kentucky* (Harris Study No. 7092701). Washington, DC: Government Printing Office.

Scott, P. D. (1974). Battered wives. *British Journal of Psychiatry, 125,* 433-441.

Selye, H. (1956). *The stress of life.* New York: McGraw-Hill.

Sennett, R., & Cobb, J. (1973). *Hidden injuries of class.* New York: Vintage.

Silberman, C. (1978). *Criminal violence, criminal justice.* New York: Random House.

Skinner, E., & German, P. S. (1978). Use of ambulatory health services by the near poor. *American Journal of Public Health, 68*(12), 1195-1202.

Sklar, K. K. (1976). *Catherine Beecher: A study in American domesticity.* New York: Norton.

Sklar, M. (1969). On the proletarian revolution and the end of political-economic society. *Radical America, 3,* 23-66.

Sloan, J. H., Rivera, F. P., Reay, D. T., Ferris, J. A. J., & Kellerman, A. L. (1988). Handgun regulations, crime, assaults and homicide: A tale of two cities. *New England Journal of Medicine, 319*(19), 1256-1262.

Smith-Rosenberg, C. (1975). The female world of love and ritual: Relations between women in 19th century America. *Signs: Journal of Women and Culture in Society, 1*(1), 1-31.

Snell, J. E., Rosenwald, R. J., & Roby, A. (1964). The wifebeater's wife: A study of family interaction. *Archives of General Psychiatry, 11,* 107-113.

Sommers, C. H. (1994). *Who stole feminism?* New York: Simon & Schuster.

Spatz-Widom, C. (1989). Child abuse, neglect and adult behavior: Research design and findings on criminality, violence and child abuse. *American Journal of Orthopsychiatry, 59,* 355-367.

Star, B. (1978). Comparing battered and nonbattered women. *Victimology: An International Journal, 3*(1-2), 32-44.

Star, B., Clark, C., Goetz, K., & O'Malia, L. (1979). Psychosocial aspects of wife battering. *Social Casework, 6,* 479-487.

Stark, E. (1977). The epidemic as a social event. *International Journal of Health Services, 7*(4), 681-705.

Stark, E. (1984). *The battering syndrome: Social knowledge, social therapy and the abuse of women.* Unpublished doctoral dissertation, State University of New York, Binghamton.

Stark, E. (1990). Rethinking homicide: Violence, race and the politics of gender. *International Journal of Health Services, 20*(1), 3-27.

Stark, E. (1992). Framing and reframing battered women. In E. Buzawa (Ed.), *Domestic violence: The criminal justice response* (pp. 271-292). Westport, CT: Auburn.

Stark, E. (1993). The myth of black violence. *Social Work, 38*(4), 485-491.

Stark, E. (1994). Discharge planning with victims of domestic violence. *Discharge Planning Update, 14*(2), 1, 3-7.

Stark, E. (1995). Killing the beast within: Woman battering and female suicidality. *International Journal of Health Services, 25,* 43-64.

Stark, E., & Flitcraft, A. (1983). Social knowledge, social therapy, and the abuse of women: The case against patriarchal benevolence. In D. Finkelhor, R. Gelles, G. Hotaling, & M. Straus (Eds.), *The dark side of families* (pp. 330-349). Beverly Hills, CA: Sage.

Stark, E., & Flitcraft, A. (1988a). Personal power and institutional victimization: Treating the dual trauma of woman battering. In F. Ochberg (Ed.), *Post-traumatic therapy and victims of violence* (pp. 115-152). New York: Brunner/Mazel.

Stark, E., & Flitcraft, A. (1988b). Violence among intimates: An epidemiological review. In V. N. Hasselt, A. S. Morrison, M. Bellack, & V. N. Hersen (Eds.), *Handbook of family violence* (pp. 293-319). New York: Plenum.

Stark, E., & Flitcraft, A. (1988c). Women and children at risk: A feminist perspective on child abuse. *International Journal of Health Services, 18*(1), 97-118.

Stark, E., & Flitcraft, A. (1991). Spouse abuse. In J. M. Last (Ed.), *Maxcy-Rosenau: Public health and preventive medicine* (13th ed., pp. 1040-1043). New York: Appleton-Century-Crofts.

Stark, E., & Flitcraft, A. (1992). Spouse abuse. In M. Zahn & M. Rosenberg (Eds.), *Violence in America: A public health approach* (pp. 123-158). New York: Oxford University Press.

Stark, E., Flitcraft, A., & Frazier, W. (1979). Medicine and patriarchal violence: The social construction of a private event. *International Journal of Health Services, 9*(3), 461-493.

Stark, E., Flitcraft, A., Zuckerman, D., Grey, A., Robison, J., & Frazier, W. (1981). *Domestic violence: Wife abuse in the medical setting* (Monograph No. 7). Washington, DC: Office of Domestic Violence.

Steele, B. F. (1976). Violence within the family. In R. E. Helfer & C. H. Kempe (Eds.), *Child abuse and neglect: The family and the community* (pp. 3-25). Cambridge, MA: Ballinger.

Steele, B. F., & Pollock, C. B. (1974). A psychiatric study of parents who abuse infants and small children. In R. E. Helfer & C. H. Kempe (Eds.), *The battered child* (pp. 103-147). Chicago: University of Chicago Press.

Steinmetz, S. K. (1974). Occupational environment in relation to physical punishment and dogmatism. In M. Straus & S. Steinmetz (Eds.), *Violence in the family* (pp. 116-172). New York: Harper & Row.

Steinmetz, S. K. (1977-1978). The battered husband syndrome. *Victimology: An International Journal, 2*(3-4), 499-509.

Steinmetz, S., & Straus, M. (1973). The family as a cradle of violence. *Society, 10*(6), 50-58.

Steinmetz, S., & Straus, M. (1974). General introduction. In S. Steinmetz & M. Straus (Eds.), *Violence in the family* (pp. 3-25). New York: Dodd, Mead.

Stone, A. M. (1980). Presidential address: Conceptual ambiguity and morality in modern psychiatry. In P. P. Reiker & E. H. Carmen (Eds.), *The gender gap in psychotherapy* (pp. 5-14). New York: Plenum.

Straus, M. (1971). Some social antecedents of physical punishment: A linkage theory interpretation. *Journal of Marriage and the Family, 33,* 658-663.

Straus, M. A. (1976). Sexual inequality, cultural norms, and wife-beating. *Victimology: An International Journal, 1*(1), 54-70.

Straus, M. A. (1977-1978). Wife beating: How common and why. *Victimology: An International Journal, 2*(3-4), 443-459.

Straus, M. A. (1986). Domestic violence and homicide antecedents. *Bulletin of the New York Academy of Medicine, 62,* 446-465.

Straus, M. A., & Gelles, R. (1986). Societal change and change in family violence from 1975 to 1985 as revealed by two national surveys. *Journal of Marriage and the Family, 48,* 465-470.

Straus, M. A., Gelles, R., & Steinmetz, S. (1980). *Behind closed doors: A survey of family violence in America.* New York: Doubleday.

Straus, M. A., & Kantor, G. K. (1994, July). *Change in spouse assault rates from 1975-1992: A comparison of three national surveys in the United States.* Unpublished paper presented at the Thirteenth World Congress of Sociology, Bielefeld, Germany.

Sugg, N. K., & Inui, T. (1992). Primary care physicians' response to domestic violence: Opening Pandora's box. *Journal of the American Medical Association, 267,* 3157-3160.

Suval, E. N., & Brisson, R. C. (1974). Neither beauty nor beast: Female homicide offenders. *International Journal of Criminology and Penology, 2,* 23-34.

Sweet, J. A. (1974). Differentials in the rate of fertility decline: 1960-1970. *Family Planning Perspectives, 6,* 103-107.

Szinovacz, M. E. (1983). Using couple data as a methodological tool: The case of marital violence. *Journal of Marriage and the Family, 45,* 633-644.

Teske, R. H. C., & Parker, M. L. (1983). *Spouse abuse in Texas: A study of women's attitudes and experiences.* Huntsville, TX: Sam Houston State University, Criminal Justice Center.

Thompson, M. S., & Peebles-Wilkins, W. (1992). The impact of formal, informal and societal support networks on the psychological well-being of black adolescent mothers, *Social Work, 37*(4), 322-328.

Townsend, P. (1975). *The cycle of deprivation: The history of a confused thesis.* Unpublished paper, University of Essex, UK.

Turner, F. (1984). Suicide. In F. Turner (Ed.), *Adult psychopathology: A social work perspective* (pp. 181-199). Glencoe, IL: Free Press.

Turshen, M. (1977). The political ecology of disease. *Review of Radical Political Economics, 9*(1), 45-60.

U.S. Commission on Civil Rights. (1982). *The federal response to domestic violence.* Washington, DC: U.S. Department of Justice.

Verkko, V. (1967). Static and dynamic "laws" of sex and homicide. In M. E. Wolfgang (Ed.), *Studies in homicide* (pp. 36-44). New York: Harper & Row.

Vinoda, K. S. (1966). Personality characteristics of attempted suicide. *American Journal of Psychiatry, 112,* 1143-1150.

Waitzkin, H. B., & Waterman, B. (1974). *The exploitation of illness in capitalist society.* New York: Bobbs-Merrill.

Walker, G. A. (1990). *Family violence and the women's movement.* Toronto: University of Toronto Press.

Walker, L. (1977-1978). Battered women and learned helplessness. *Victimology: An International Journal, 2*(3-4), 525-534.

Walker, L. (1979). *The battered woman.* New York: Harper & Row.

Walker, L. (1983). The battered woman syndrome study. In D. Finkelhor, R. Gelles, G. Hotaling, & M. Straus (Eds.), *The dark side of families* (pp. 31-49). Beverly Hills, CA: Sage.

Walker, L. (1984). *The battered woman syndrome.* New York: Springer.

Warshaw, C. (1989). Limitations of the medical model in the care of battered women. *Gender and Society, 3,* 506-517.

Weber, M. (1968). Patriarchalism and patrimonialism. In G. Roth & C. Wittich (Eds.), *Economy and society* (pp. 1006-1070). New York: Bedminister.

Weissman, M. (1983). The depressed mother and her rebellious adolescent. In H. Morrison (Ed.), *Children of depressed parents: Risk, identification and intervention* (pp. 99-113). New York: Grune & Stratton.

Weissman, M., Fox, K., & Klarman, G. L. (1973). Hostility and depression associated with suicide attempts. *American Journal of Psychiatry, 130*(4), 450-455.

West, C. (1994). *Race matters.* New York: Vintage.

Whitehurst, R. (1971). Violence potential in extramarital sexual responses. *Journal of Marriage and the Family, 33*(4), 683-691.

Whitman, S. (1988). Ideology and violence prevention. *Journal of the National Medical Association, 80*(7), 737-743.

Whyte, W. (1956). *Organization man.* New York: Doubleday.

Williams, G. (1980). Toward the eradication of child abuse and neglect at home. In G. Williams & J. Money (Eds.), *Traumatic abuse and the neglect of children at home* (pp. 588-605). Baltimore, MD: Johns Hopkins University Press.

Wilson, E. (1976). *Research into battered women: Why we need research and why what exists is potentially dangerous—A reply to Dr. Jasper Gayford.* London: National Women's Aid Federation.

Wilson, E. (1983). *What is to be done about violence against women?* Harmondsworth, Middlesex: Penguin.

Wilson, J. Q. (1985). *Crime and human nature.* New York: Simon & Schuster.

Wilson, W. J. (1987). *The truly disadvantaged.* Chicago: University of Chicago Press.

Wolfgang, M. E. (1956). Husband and wife homicides. *Journal of Social Therapy, 2,* 263-271.

Wolfgang, M. E. (1958). *Patterns in criminal homicide.* Philadelphia: University of Pennsylvania Press.

Wolfgang, M. E., & Ferracuti, F. (1967). *The subculture of violence.* London: Tavistock.

Woods, S. J., & Campbell, J. C. (1993). Posttraumatic stress in battered women: Does the diagnosis fit? *Issues in Mental Health Nursing, 14,* 173-186.

Zaretsky, E. (1973). Capitalism, the family and personal life. *Socialist Revolution, 3*(1-2), 69-127.

Zonana, H., & Henisz, J. (1973). Psychiatric emergency services a decade later. *Psychiatry in Medicine, 4*(3), 273-290.

# Name Index

# Subject Index

# About the Authors

**Evan Stark** and **Anne Flitcraft** are nationally recognized authorities on interpersonal violence, including woman battering, child abuse, and homicide. Since 1976 when they helped found one of the first shelters for battered women in the United States, they have worked as researchers, in direct service, and as advocates for the rights and needs of battered women and their children in policy debates and in the courts.

With a Ph.D. from the State University of New York and an M.S.W. from Fordham University, Evan Stark is Associate Professor of Public Administration and Social Work at Rutgers University. A graduate of the Yale School of Medicine, Anne Flitcraft is an Associate Professor of Medicine at the University of Connecticut Health Center, where she teaches Primary Care Internal Medicine and maintains a clinical practice at the Burgorf Health Center in the North End Community of Hartford. Dr. Stark and Dr. Flitcraft codirect the Domestic Violence Training Project, an award-winning program dedicated to enhancing the health care system's response to domestic violence.

Twenty years ago, Dr. Stark and Dr. Flitcraft directed the first major federal research program on domestic violence in health care settings and identified domestic violence as a leading cause of female injury and the context for multiple medical and mental health problems. Former cochairs of the U.S. Surgeon General's Working Group on Domestic Violence and Public Health, the couple has served as consultants on domestic violence to the U.S. Civil Rights Commission, the Centers for Disease Control, the U.S. House and Senate, the National Institutes of Justice and the National Research Council.

For their efforts in bringing this issue to the attention of contemporary medicine and their leadership in the developing health care programs on domestic violence, Dr. Stark and Dr. Flitcraft received the National Health Council's Trendsetter Award and Connecticut's Governor's Victim Services Award. In addition, Dr. Flitcraft received the Elizabeth Blackwell Award, the highest honor bestowed by the American Medical Women's Association, and Dr. Stark received the Sanctity of Life Award from Brandeis University.

Dr. Flitcraft works with numerous state and national medical organizations to enhance access to care for battered women. Dr. Stark frequently testifies on behalf of battered women in criminal and civil cases.